research methods

RULES FOR SURVEY DESIGN AND ANALYSIS

WINSTON JACKSON

St. Francis Xavier University

Prentice-Hall Canada Inc., Scarborough, Ontario

For Marlies

Canadian Cataloguing in Publication Data

Jackson, Winston
Research methods
Includes index.
ISBN 0-13-774225-8

1. Social sciences – Research – Methodology.
2. Social sciences – Research – Methodology –
Problems, exercises, etc. 3. Social surveys.
4. Social surveys – Problems, exercises, etc.
I. Title.
H62.J32 1988   300'.1'8   C87-095098-3

Prentice-Hall, Inc., Englewood Cliffs, New Jersey
Prentice-Hall International, Inc., London
Prentice-Hall of Australia, Pty., Ltd., Sydney
Prentice-Hall of India Pvt., Ltd., New Delhi
Prentice-Hall of Japan, Inc., Tokyo
Prentice-Hall of Southeast Asia (Pte.) Ltd., Singapore
Editora Prentice-Hall do Brasil Ltda., Rio de Janeiro
Prentice-Hall Hispanoamericana, S.A., Mexico

ISBN 0-13-774225-8

Production Editors: Heather Scott McClune/Chelsea Donaldson
Design: Bruce Farquhar
Production Coordinator: Matt Lumsdon
Typesetting: PrimeType Inc.

1 2 3 4 5 WC 92 91 90 89 88

Printed and bound in Canada by Webcom Ltd.

TABLE OF CONTENTS

PREFACE

The assumption of this book is that the best way to learn methods is to apply them, not just talk about them. Written for the beginning survey researcher, the book presents practical tips, rules, and guidelines for constructing questionnaires, determining sample size, and linking research to theory. The basic steps in analyzing data are also discussed. A review of basic statistical procedures is included, and integrated with computer analysis. The beginning researcher is shown how to perform tests of simple causal models and is given rules for the interpretation and the presentation of results.

Among the special features of the book:

a. the listing of rules, steps, and tips to guide the first-time researcher through questionnaire design, sample size determination, bias avoidance, statistical analysis, and data interpretation;

b. a minimum of computational formulae; any notations are kept simple;

c. the introduction of visual estimation techniques to help students understand the fundamentals of correlational analysis;

d. a chapter devoted to sources of bias and ethical issues that sensitizes students to the many sources of error (Chapter 4);

e. an emphasis on the appropriate use of tests of significance (Chapter 8);

f. a discussion of the importance of diagramming causal relationships to ensure precision (Chapter 5);

g. coverage of the steps in error checking data, and the analysis of data using SPSS^x (Chapters 10 and 11);

h. the introduction of a *rule of thirds* to assist in interpreting causal models; this rule may be used in interpreting CROSSTABS, BREAKDOWN, and PARTIAL CORR approaches to simple causal model analysis (Chapter 12).

Supplementary items include: (1) an Instructor's Manual providing sample examination questions and a series of laboratory assignments to introduce the student to social science data analysis using SPSS^x; (2) a floppy disk which includes the laboratory assignments, three data cleaning utilities, a sample raw data set, and a procedure file for creating an SPSS^x system file for use in the laboratory assignments. These assignments will provide training in the use of the computer and SPSS^x while students are designing their surveys and collecting data. By the time the data are collected, the student should be well prepared to do the analysis.

Virtually all instructors presenting a "methods course" to undergraduates find that many students are intimidated by it, being wary of statistics and mystified by computers. As much as possible, this book attempts to gently walk students through the steps in doing a survey, limiting itself to the fundamentals, and paying attention to the practical problems students will face while completing a project.

Since this is the first edition of this text, I would welcome suggestions for additional rules and tips which other researchers and instructors have found helpful. Any suggestions for improving the usefulness of this text are most welcome and should be addressed to: Dr. Winston Jackson, Department of Sociology and Anthropology, St. Francis Xavier University, Antigonish, Nova Scotia, Canada B0K 1A0.

Acknowledgements. The author wishes to thank the reviewers of the manuscript: Taylor Buckner, Harvey Krahn, and Harry Rosenbaum. I trust that I have improved the text along the lines suggested. Don Clairmont read through an early draft and encouraged me to continue. I wish to thank you, the major and honours students in sociology and the nursing students at St. F. X., for the freshness and enthusiasm you bring to your projects. You invariably challenge me and my discipline.

I am grateful to the literary executor of the late Sir Ronald Fisher, F.R.S., to Dr. Frank Yates, F.R.S. and to the Longman Group Ltd., London for permission to reprint Tables IV and V (Appendixes B and C) from their book *Statistical Tables for Biological, Agricultural and Medical Research* (6th Edition, 1974).

I am also particularly indebted to SPSS Inc. for permission to present the commands for various SPSS^x procedures. As always, they have been most helpful and cooperative.

Finally, I wish to acknowledge the support and professional help of the staff at Prentice-Hall Canada Inc. In particular, I would like to thank Patrick Ferrier, Monica Schwalbe, Heather Scott McClune, Chelsea Donaldson and Marta Tomins.

PART ONE

PRELIMINARIES

CHAPTER ONE

CONCEPTS
SURVEY RESEARCHERS USE

In *The Rules of Sociological Method*, the French sociologist, Emile Durkheim, attempted to establish methodological principles to guide the new discipline of Sociology.[1] In his book, published in 1895, he argued that Sociology should model itself on the physical sciences, treating *social facts* as objects. It is Durkheim's view that knowledge is to be based on systematic observations of the social world.

A. SCIENCE AND SOCIAL SCIENCE

Indeed, the social and physical sciences have much in common at the core though many differences on the surface. They have similar orientations to knowledge, have a shared view of what science is, and largely share the fundamental postulates of science. But as one might expect, they differ substantially in technique. Let us begin by examining what science is and what the scientific approach is all about.

1. What is Science?

In attempting to state a consensus on the essential attributes of science, Carlo L. Lastrucci defines science as:

> "...an objective, logical, and systematic method of analysis of phenomena, devised to permit the accumulation of reliable knowledge."[2]

Objective means an approach which is without bias, is impersonal, and seeks its authority in fact, not opinion. *Logical* refers to the use of those rules of derivation and of statistical analysis that are regarded as appropriate for the problem at hand. The phrase *systematic method of analysis* refers to a carefully organized approach to analysis. Finally, *reliable knowledge* means knowledge you can count on, knowledge which allows you to predict outcomes.

2. Some Postulates of Science

There are a number of basic postulates, or working assumptions, scientists make when approaching their research. Again, following Lastrucci, some of the major ones are as follows:[3]

a. All Behavior is Naturally Determined. The view in this case is that to understand behavior one must look for causes in the natural world. This postulate emphasizes a mechanistic view of the world, arguing that each outcome is produced by the impact of one or more causes.

b. Humans are Part of the Natural World. Human behavior is to be understood as the behavior of one of the species of this world. The study of human behavior can follow the methods used to study other living organisms, although the study of humans involves enormous possibilities given the presence of language.

c. Nature is Orderly and Regular. The natural world is orderly and predictable and therefore knowable. The patterns of nature may be identified and observed. Those events which appear to be random may simply reflect our inability to fully comprehend the natural forces at work.

d. All Objective Phenomena are Eventually Knowable. This postulate suggests that there are no intellectual limits on what we may eventually know about nature or about human behavior.

e. Nothing is Self-Evident. Our knowledge of behavior should be demonstrated objectively. And while we may wish to use folk wisdom as a starting point, we ultimately must test ideas systematically.

f. Truth is Relative. What is regarded as a scientific truth today may not be so regarded tomorrow. There is a dynamic element to what we know to be true; this means that our knowledge is always on the road to some ultimate truth, but never quite reaches it.

g. Knowledge Comes from Experience. A fundamental principle of science is that knowing is based on systematically testing our understandings of the world with knowledge gained through our senses; "reliable knowledge is that which is both objectively and empirically verifiable".[4]

3. On the Role of Folk Wisdom

In the social sciences, there is a special problem concerning the search for knowledge and that is the role of folk wisdom. Many findings by social scientists are dismissed as "obvious." However, it turns out that many of our observations are only obvious once they have been made. All too often, folk wisdom accounts for all outcomes. The following anecdote may help to illustrate the problem:

> Charlie McMullin was in love. He had been dating Sally for seven months when she decided to take a trip to Europe. After two weeks, and four letters home to Charlie, the letters stopped. Charlie was in agony. It was then that his dear aunt, Aunt Betsy, explained the whole thing by saying, "Well that just proves once again, 'out of sight, out of mind.'" But, after six weeks Sally wrote, full of apologies, and suggested that they get married on her return. Good old Aunt Betsy understood that too. "Oh," she exclaimed, "that's easy, 'absence makes the heart grow fonder!'" For a while Charlie thought that his aunt was a first-rate observer of the human scene until he realized that she had an answer for all outcomes.

Folk wisdom is an important source of ideas for the social researcher. But one must always be careful to distinguish between wisdom which has been scientifically tested and that which has not been scrutinized. The most compelling predictions the social scientist can make will be those which run counter to "common sense."

In the ninety years since Durkheim's book on methods was published, a good deal has been written and we have certainly documented many *social facts*. There has been an impressive increase in the number of social scientists, and we have developed relatively sophisticated techniques for gathering data and delightful machines to help us analyze the data. But, it is not clear whether, with all our numbers, techniques and machines, we have developed a commensurate number of well-confirmed theories about how societies or individuals work. Progress is slow, but perhaps we should not be impatient.

4. The Survey

Surveys have been around for a long time — there are biblical references to counts of the children of Israel; Napoleon did surveys; and, in 19th century England, Charles Booth did a series of important descriptive surveys. Indeed, his work laid the foundations for the contemporary survey researcher. Booth was largely concerned with providing an accurate count of the number of poor people living in London, and reporting the characteristics they exhibited. Later, he attempted to show how variables were related to one another. Booth had a major impact on North American sociology through his influence on the Chicago School.[5]

Today, survey research — which includes mail questionnaires, personal interviews, phone interviews, opinion polls, and group administered questionnaires — has become a major approach to the description and analysis of human behavior used by academic social scientists, and is also central to the work of market researchers and public opinion pollsters. There are important descriptive and explanatory aspects to contemporary survey research which need to be understood.

B. DESCRIPTIVE AND EXPLANATORY RESEARCH

All explanatory studies will have descriptive dimensions, and some descriptive studies will have explanatory dimensions. A study which is primarily *descriptive* has as its major concern the accurate description of some aspect of society. A researcher may wish, for example, to assess the popularity of a political party or leader. The aim is to gauge the general sentiments in a society toward each political party, describing as precisely as possible the proportion of the population which supports each party. Similarly, a census of the population is largely a descriptive enterprise. The intention is to count a variety of attributes of the society, whether the count is of people, dogs, or sheep. A census is a stocktaking of the objects, people, and resources available within a society.

Fundamentally, the descriptive study is about *what and how many of what*. Since the concern is to describe, survey researchers will frequently select a sample in order to make estimations about some larger population. As used by the survey researcher, the term *population* refers to that collection of individuals, communities, or nations about which one wishes to make a general statement. In order to save money and time, the researcher draws a *sample* from the population which will be interpreted as representing that population. While including the whole population would prove to be more accurate (as in a census), the costs may be prohibitive. In simple terms, public opinion pollsters, market researchers, and census takers are largely involved in descriptive research, although academic researchers also include descriptive elements in their research.

If a survey researcher wished to explore the differences between female students who select non-traditional programs in university and those who select traditional ones, he/she would be interested in describing the characteristics of the two sets of students. Are rural students more likely to opt for traditional programs, such as education, nursing, or home economics; are females from higher socio-economic levels more likely to choose non-traditional programs such as engineering, business, or chemistry?

An *explanatory* study, while certainly being concerned with descriptive issues, nonetheless is primarily concerned with attempting to understand, or to explain, relationships. Why is it that girls who pursue non-traditional occupations are more likely to be from more elite backgrounds than those who enrol in traditional programs of study? Here the issue is two fold: first, what *is* the relation between background and type of program selected? Second, if there is a relationship, *why* does it exist? Explanatory studies ask *why* questions.

Explanatory studies sometimes relax strict sampling procedures to reduce costs. The idea is that if there is a relationship occuring regularly in society, then the mechanism producing the relationship will manifest itself in most samples, even badly selected ones.

Given that explanatory studies try to answer why questions; theory is important to the researcher. It is theory — and only theory — which provides explanations for relationships. Let us now explore the various levels of the research enterprise, identifying the basic components of research.

C. LEVELS IN THE RESEARCH PROCESS

The research enterprise can be conceived of as having three levels: the theoretical, the conceptual, and the operational.

1. Theoretical Level

Theories propose explanations for phenomena. Theories try to tell us how things work, how parts are interconnected, how things influence each other. General theories propose explanations that can be applied to many phenomena; a measure of a theory's power is the number of predictions which can be derived from it. Theories may be conceived of as being on a continuum varying from highly detailed explicit statements of relations between concepts (with underlying assumptions specified), through to those at the other end of the continuum which offer an explanation of one particular relation. A theory may be viewed as an explanation accounting for social patterns or for relationships.

Social scientists use theories to predict behavior and continually refine them, to see if they hold true under all conditions. It is through efforts to disconfirm theories that we extend our general knowledge of human behavior. One way to test a theory is to derive a prediction, or hypothesis, from it, and then to test the hypothesis. Chapter 3 will explore the nature of theory and approaches to testing hypotheses.

2. Conceptual Level

The conceptual level involves the definition of the variables to be used in the research. *A conceptual variable is an idea with a dimension which varies.* A prediction made at the theoretical level may be formed into a conceptual hypothesis. *A conceptual hypothesis is a statement of relationship between two or more conceptual variables.* Ordinarily, a hypothesis will take the form of *the greater X, the greater Y.* (For example, "the higher one's socioeconomic status, the higher one's educational aspirations.") Conceptual definitions for variables are important because they provide clear statements of what each variable means and also provide guidelines for how each should be measured. For example, socio-economic status might be defined as "differences in access to scarce resources." Given such a definition, a researcher would then measure the variable with indicators reflecting the conceptual definition as precisely as possible — in this case, reflecting differences in access to scarce resources.

3. Operational Level

The operational level of research involves the implementation of a project, including the precise procedures used. *Operationalization is a process referring to both the selection of indicators to reflect conceptual variables, and to the implementation of a research project.* If socio-economic status is defined as "differences in access to scarce resources," any measurement should attempt to reflect this definition. In this case, a measure of annual income might nicely reflect the conceptual variable. In the study of program choice, the classification of programs into traditional and non-traditional would constitute a measure of the concept. The operational level includes not just the measurement of variables, but also the procedures to collect data and to analyze them. Chapters 5 and 6 provide a number of suggestions for the measurement of variables, while Chapters 7 through 13 discuss aspects of data analysis.

4. Linkages Between Levels

It should be understood that there are linkages between the three levels of research. The beginning researcher should strive to document these carefully. It is only possible to claim to have "tested" a theory to the extent that the connections between the theoretical and the conceptual levels and between the conceptual and the operational levels have been documented explicitly.

Social researchers use two terms, validity and reliability, to refer to the connection between the conceptual and the operational levels. *The validity of a measurement refers to the extent to which a measure reflects the concept, reflecting nothing more or less than that implied by the conceptual definition.* Validity, then, refers to the connection between the conceptual and the operational levels of research. It is not unusual for researchers to use markedly different "indicators" for similar conceptual variables. The validity issue concerns the adequacy with which these indicators reflect the concepts.

Reliability refers to the extent to which, on repeated measures, an indicator will yield similar readings. One can think of reliability as the extent to which a measurement will produce similar readings for similar phenomena. A tire gauge that indicates 26 pounds of pressure, but a moment earlier had indicated 29 pounds, suggests an unreliable gauge – either that or a bad leak in the tire. In survey research we sometimes repeat a question to test for reliability. Both responses to the question should be the same if the item is generating reliable responses.

5. Deduction and Induction

Moving from the theoretical level to the conceptual stage involves *deduction*. Conceptual hypotheses may be deduced from a set of theoretical propositions. There is a similar process involved in moving to the operational level – the researcher determines what indicators will represent the concepts. After selecting measures, collecting data and analyzing them, the researcher's reasoning must become *inductive*. When the relationship between the operational variables is consistent with the conceptual hypothesis, the researcher has one inductive piece of evidence supporting the validity of the measurements and the validity of the deductive steps taken to derive the hypothesis. Figure 1.1 illustrates the components of reasoning and their relationships to one another.

Figure 1.1 Deductive and Inductive Reasoning in Research Design

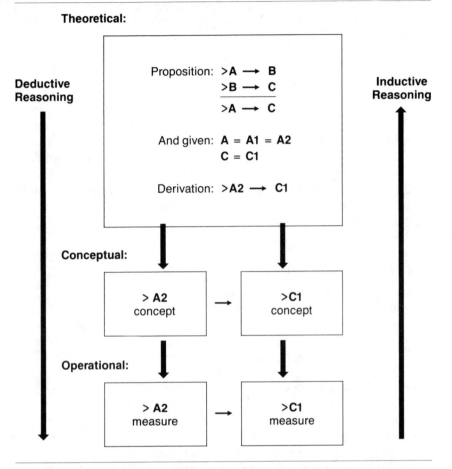

Theoretical:

Deductive Reasoning

Proposition:
$$>A \longrightarrow B$$
$$>B \longrightarrow C$$
$$>A \longrightarrow C$$

And given: $A = A1 = A2$
$C = C1$

Derivation: $>A2 \longrightarrow C1$

Inductive Reasoning

Conceptual:

> A2 concept → >C1 concept

Operational:

> A2 measure → >C1 measure

Note that the process of deriving testable hypotheses from theory involves deductive reasoning. Each link within the set of theoretical propositions, between the theoretical and conceptual, and between the conceptual and operational levels, involves deductive reasoning. Having collected the data and analyzed them, if the results are consistent with the derived operational hypothesis, one can then make a validity claim for all derivations and measures. If the predicted result is not supported then one is unable to locate whether the problem is in the theory, the derivations, the measures, or if one simply has a sample that is not representative of the patterns in the social world.

D. KEY ELEMENTS

Besides the distinction between conceptual and operational variables as discussed above, there are a number of different types of variables researchers use.

1. Dependent Variable

A dependent variable is one which is viewed as being influenced by other variables. It is the "effect" in a cause-effect relationship; it is "dependent" for its variation on other variables. If a researcher is examining those factors which influence the traditionality of students' program choices, then "program choice" would be treated as the dependent variable. However, this would not preclude exploring whether variations in program choice have an impact on a variable such as income. In the latter case, income would be treated as the dependent variable.

2. Independent Variable

An independent variable is a "cause" in a cause-effect relationship. It is a variable which has been selected as a possible influence on variations in a dependent variable. Typically, one finds a number of independent variables in any survey. Once again, it is how the variable is treated – how it is thought of – that determines whether it is an independent or a dependent variable. The nature of the variable does not determine whether it is dependent or independent – it is how the researcher thinks about and uses the variable that matters.

In the program choice illustration, among the independent variables would certainly include such factors as rural/urban home community, subject preference and performance in high school, types of games and activities preferred in childhood, parental socio-economic status, measures of mother's participation in the labour force, and the presence of role models who have opted for non-traditional female occupations.

3. Control Variable

A control variable is one which is held constant when the relation between an independent and dependent variable is being explored. There are three basic types of control variables: source of spuriousness, intervening, and conditional variables.

a. Source of Spuriousness Variable. This kind of variable is viewed as possibly influencing both the independent (X) and the dependent (Y) variables, rendering the relationship between them spurious – simply produced because they are mutually influenced by the source of spuriousness variable (S/S). If a researcher was exploring the relationship between socio-economic background and choice of a non-traditional program, a possible source of spuriousness might include rural/urban background. Here the idea is that it may be the type of home community that influences both the socio-economic achievement of parents and the program preferences of children. The relationship between socio-economic status and program choice might therefore be spurious. A source of spuriousness variable can be represented in the following manner:

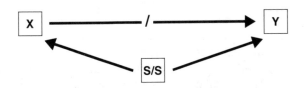

b. Intervening Variable. An intervening variable (I) is a variable that links an independent variable (X) to a dependent one (Y). An intervening variable represents an explanation of how the independent variable influences the dependent variable. For example, suppose a researcher is investigating the relationship between socio-economic status and preference for a non-traditional program. A possible explanation for how SES influences type of program preferred would be that high SES students are more likely to be exposed to people in non-traditional occupations and this is why there is a relationship between SES and type of program preferred. An intervening variable can be illustrated as:

c. Conditional Variable. A conditional variable (C) is used when one wishes to find out if a relationship between an independent variable (X) and a dependent variable (Y) is altered under different conditions. Suppose a researcher was investigating the relationship between socio-economic status and attitudes toward capital punishment and wanted to see if that relationship is fundamentally altered, or is entirely different, for each sex. In this case the researcher might consider the relationship between SES and attitude separately for males and then for females. A conditional variable may be diagrammed by representing each condition with a separate box:

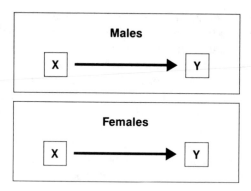

4. Units of Analysis

Social scientists study nations, communities, groups, institutions, and individuals. Moreover, an institution such as the family may be studied across cultures or may be studied within a culture. It is important for the beginning researcher to realize that it is difficult to deal simultaneously with more than one level of analysis. The question to ask is: "Am I studying individuals or aggregations?"

a. The Individual as the Unit of Analysis. If the unit about which you are collecting information is individual-level, then only those questions reflecting individual properties are asked. All the data collected will measure variations between individuals on a variety of subjects. Any analyses of the data will have individuals as the basic unit. Most surveys will use the individual as the unit of analysis, although it is possible that knowledgeable persons (known as key informants) could be used to report on data for other levels of analysis such as communities, companies, or groups. Furthermore, categories of individuals may be aggregated and then summarized to produce measures beyond the individual level. (Proportion non-white, for example.)

b. An Aggregation as the Unit of Analysis. Alternatively, if the researcher is interested in comparing communities (average levels of crime, for example, might be the dependent variable), then all the information would represent properties of communities. Individual characteristics, such as income or race, would have to be expressed as average income in the community, or the proportion non-white. The point is that all measures must reflect properties of communities.

If a study has started out using an individual level of analysis, then it is difficult to switch to a higher level, such as the community level. To do so would require computing average scores for members from various communities and almost certainly this would prove difficult, not from a computational point of view – computers can do that sort of calculation in a flash – but because many communities would have too few cases upon which a meaningful average could be calculated.

It is important, therefore, when one starts designing a project to be absolutely clear about the level of analysis to be used in the study. And, if different levels are to be used, the researcher must carefully think through how the analysis is to be done, making certain there will be a sufficient number of cases to perform the analysis.

5. Independent and Independence

Researchers use the terms *independent* and *independence* in a number of ways and some familiarity with these usages is necessary. We have already referred to independent variables when discussing causal variables. But these variables are also to be measured independently of one another, and should reflect different concepts. For example, if we measured the lengths of the rooms in a building in inches and then repeated the measures, but this time using centimeters, our two sets of measures would lack independence. These measures would be powerfully associated with each other but would be meaningless because they simply represent different measures of the same variable. The survey researcher must be careful not to fall into the trap of thinking that a powerful causal connection between variables exists when the measures lack independence and simply represent alternate measures of the same thing.

In analyzing data, researchers frequently assume that the groups being compared have been selected using independent random sampling procedures. The assumption here is that the selection of any unit is not influenced by the selection of any other one. It would not be appropriate to use a sampling procedure to select a person and then interview the spouse as well.

E. ORGANIZATION OF THE BOOK

Surveys involve distinct stages. We will briefly introduce each of them now; later chapters will provide guidelines for getting through each one.

1. Stages of a Survey Project

a. Problem Selection. Here the researcher decides what the subject of the research is to be. Is a theory being tested, some known relationship being explored in detail, or is the researcher attempting to solve some applied problem?

b. Design. What kind of design is appropriate for the problem being researched? The scientific literature is reviewed to find out what has been discovered by other researchers working in the selected area. If the design is of the survey form, which particular type of survey will it be? What variables are to be measured? What hypotheses are to be tested?

c. Development of a Questionnaire. The questionnaire is designed and pre-tested; a final version is agreed upon by the research team.

d. Sampling. Type of sampling procedure and size of sample are determined. Any necessary permissions (such as a school system, parents, etc.) are sought.

e. Data Collection. The data are collected using the procedures that have been developed.

f. Data Coding. The questionnaires have any codes entered onto them as required; questionnaires are numbered, sorted.

g. Data Entry. The information from the questionnaires is entered into the computer.

h. Data Cleaning. Data is checked for errors, final corrections are made.

i. SPSS File Creation. Instructions are entered into the computer, defining the variables and data. This information will be saved in an SPSS system file.

j. Data Analysis. Using SPSS, the data are now analyzed with the appropriate procedures needed to describe the data and to test the various hypotheses under investigation.

k. Final Report. A final report is written on the project.

2. Data Analysis With SPSS[x]

Survey researchers, and those engaged in secondary data analysis, are particularly dependent on computers. There are two major reasons for this. First, survey research usually involves collecting information from a large number of individuals on many variables. Since computers work quickly, it is possible to deal with large numbers easily. Second, survey researchers frequently build models involving many variables and only with computer technology is it possible to do the kinds of multivariate (many variable) analysis necessary to test such models.

SPSS (Statistical Package for the Social Sciences) is a collection of procedures for processing social science data.[6] The most recent version of the package, first introduced in 1984, is known as SPSS^x. Earlier versions of SPSS date back to the 1960s. Some version of SPSS is available at most universities and many research organizations. While there are many statistical packages available, few can match the scope of SPSS. This book will use SPSS^x commands throughout. Readers who have access to earlier versions of SPSS will find that, with a few modifications, the commands presented in this book will work. In addition, those working on micros with SPSS PC + will find that the commands are identical in most cases. Any differences will be minor ones.

3. The Ordering and Content of the Chapters

The order of the chapters follows the stages of the research process. Chapters 1 through 4 establish the basic perspective of the book and locate the survey as but one approach to how social scientists come to an understanding of human behavior. The problems of bias and other ethical concerns are discussed in this first section so that the reader will encounter these before starting to design a study.

Chapters 5 and 6 deal with how to get a survey started and include a discussion of measurement and of principles for the development of a questionnaire.

Chapters 7 and 8 present a review of elementary statistical procedures used by the survey researcher. The reader should note that this is not a statistics text and hence it does not provide a comprehensive view of statistical matters. Chapter 9, which assumes knowledge of some basic statistics, reviews sampling procedures and sample size determination, and discusses the administration of surveys.

Chapters 10 through 12 deal with data analysis and integrate the use of SPSS^x into the discussion. Chapter 13 discusses the use of secondary data; and Chapter 14 the writing of a final report.

The chapters may be treated in any order. If the book is being used as a text, it is recommended that the review of statistical matters should be started early, along with any computer labs, so that by the time students have their studies designed and their data collected, they will be ready to commence analysis. Some instructors find that it is best to do every other lecture on statistical material.

This book is meant to assist in executing a competent survey. It will confine itself to the basics and introduce as little complexity as possible, often presenting fundamental rules and steps. No research experience, statistics background, or computer familiarity is assumed. For the student new to computers, some instruction about the kind of terminal and computer operating system to be used will be necessary.

NOTES

[1] Emile Durkheim, *The Rules of Sociological Method*. New York: The Free Press, 1938. (Originally published in 1895.)

[2] Carlo L. Lastrucci, *The Scientific Approach*. Cambridge, Massachusetts: Schenkman Publishing Company, Inc., 1967, p. 6.

[3] *Ibid.*, pp. 37-46.

[4] *Ibid.*, pp. 37-46.

[5] See Gary Easthope, *History of Social Research Methods*. London: Longman Group Limited, 1974.

[6] SPSSˣ is a trademark of SPSS Inc., of Chicago, Illinois, for its proprietary computer software.

CHAPTER TWO

ALTERNATE RESEARCH DESIGNS

A wide variety of designs is available to the social researcher. This chapter introduces the main types of research designs and provides a sense of where the survey, which is the main focus of this book, fits into the overall context of social research.

To appreciate the variety of research designs available is to appreciate the range of *realities* which can be explored. To illustrate, let us consider how birth-related variables might be examined.

For the demographer, economist, or sociologist, birth rates are important, along with other demographic patterns, because of their impact on society. These researchers would be interested, for example, in whether birth rates are depressed by structural constraints (few inexpensive apartment units have more than two bedrooms; unemployment produces insufficient income) or encouraged through family allowance programs as in France, Canada, and the Soviet Union. Researchers who wish to monitor shifts in birth rates normally rely on the analysis of existing government statistics, that is, the research design in this case would be based on secondary data.

Another reality that could be examined is the change in *attitudes toward what constitutes an appropriate family size*. The sociologist, for example, may wish to explore why the province of Québec went from having the second highest birth rate in Canada to the lowest within one generation. What factors influenced such a dramatic shift and, if this shift is related to changing attitudes, what brought about the change? Here the sociologist would probably conduct a survey on a representative sample concerning respondent's "desired family size" along with measures of factors the researcher identifies as probable causes of variability in the dependent variable, desired family size.

A researcher might also be interested in examining the *impact of a film about birth control on attitudes toward family size*. In this case, an experimental design would probably be used: two groups would be established on the basis of random assignment; both would be measured on desired family size; one group would then be shown the film about family planning, while the other would be shown a film not related to the issue at hand; and finally both groups would be re-measured on desired family size.

A nursing researcher might be interested in developing a program to help increase the *parenting confidence* of new mothers. In such a case, the researcher might wish to design a panel study to monitor new mothers over a period of time, attempting to understand the importance of different support systems, education, and other factors in developing confidence. Such an investigation attempts a quasi-experimental design in order to measure the impact of a training program on new mothers.

Yet another reality might concern how we have organized the *birthing process* in our society. How do we organize the obstetrics ward? What are the rules of behavior and rituals surrounding the birth of a child? If this is the reality to be explored, the researcher might possibly do a participant observation study, working perhaps as a ward assistant, attempting to describe the various behaviors. Here the ward would be viewed as a total social system where the needs of a mother and her new child are met within the ward. How are crises, such as the death of a child, managed? What are the unwritten tactics used by nurses to manage patients, newborns, doctors, hospital administrators, and visitors?

Social scientists do not have the luxury of a mechanistic subject matter. The complexity of the questions we ask about human behavior is truly humbling. In attempting to understand them, many theoretical perspectives have been developed along with a diversity of methodologies.

Let us now examine the main research designs in more detail. For purposes of discussion, designs will be divided into four categories: (1) natural setting studies, (2) experiments, (3) secondary data studies, and (4) surveys. Each of the approaches is legitimate in its own way; the selection of a design should be guided by what is most appropriate for the problem under investigation. No one design covers all problems. Each approach has a unique combination of strengths and weaknesses. The approach which is both feasible and optimizes the ability to solve the research problem should be chosen.

A. NATURAL SETTING STUDIES

In natural setting studies the researcher observes and records the behavior of individuals or groups which occurs in natural settings. Such studies can be further subdivided into: (i) participant observation studies, (ii) natural setting experiments, and (iii) covert observational studies.

1. Participant Observation Studies

Participant observation studies ordinarily involve an intensive examination of some culture, community, organization, or group. Normally, such studies are based on a careful and complete study of one case and the researcher often joins the group being investigated for an extended period. The anthropologist studying a pre-literate society, for example, is attempting, by living with the group, to learn its customs and beliefs and to understand the world of the primitive from inside the community. The researcher is a participant in the daily lives of the group, sharing their joys and their pain. Such studies frequently take much time to complete. This is not surprising given the need to learn the native language and to absorb the intricacies of the culture.

Studies of a mental institution (Erving Goffman's *Asylums*,[1] for example) or a street gang (William F. Whyte's *Street Corner Society*[2]) are classic participant observation studies in Sociology. Researchers have gained admission to prisons, become skid-row bums, worked on assembly lines, or joined religious groups all in an effort to "get inside" the organization or group being studied.

The rationale behind such studies is that only through sharing in the daily lives of the group can one really understand the behavior that is manifested. Ordinarily, researchers try to avoid taking any preconceived ideas into these situations. Instead, they try to understand the group, and how its members organize their daily activities by using the group's organizational logic rather than that imported from the researcher's culture. The fundamental point is that the conclusions of a participant observation study should be *grounded* in the data — that is, based on direct and careful observations of everyday life within some group. Indeed, Glaser and Strauss have referred to such research as *grounded theory*.[3]

The advantages of participant observation studies are many. Such studies usually attempt to understand the total social system involved in a case. Since observations are made over time, social processes can be observed (the formation, crystallization, and dissolution of friendships, for example). The interrelationship between individuals and between parts of a system are of concern to the researcher. Emphasis is placed on careful, in-depth descriptions leading to the development of hypotheses worthy of testing using alternate design strategies. Furthermore, since observations of actual, real-life activities are made, there is increased validity in the measures: we do not rely on artificial settings (as in an experiment) or on respondents' ability to report on their behavior (as in a survey) but, instead, record actual behavior. The researcher may also probe deeply into the whole culture in order to fully understand how the various parts fit together. For the anthropologist, the advantages of this kind of study are the opportunity to understand the world from the natives' point of view, and the chance to describe a culture that may be quickly disappearing. Such descriptions are of historic significance since if they are not recorded, they may be lost forever.

One of the weaknesses of participant observation studies is that when patterns in an organization emerge, the researcher is in no position to tell whether these represent general patterns or patterns peculiar to the institution being studied. Nonetheless, such studies can provide important insights into how institutions work. An additional problem is that such studies are hard to replicate, given that any participant observation study involves examining a unique combination of individuals, involved in one institution, at a particular time. While it would be possible for another observer to go into the same institution at a later time, a number of conditions probably would have changed. Moreover, the observers themselves may have rather different impacts on the organization. Thus, there are many factors which would confound an interpretation of any changes observed by different researchers. Making verifiable causal inferences is difficult since only one case is being examined.

Despite these drawbacks and the fact that they are time-consuming, participant observation studies have an important role in answering many research questions.

2. Natural Setting Experiments

There are some natural setting studies, however, which are simple and do not involve enormous amounts of time and energy. Suppose, for example, a researcher greets a stranger while walking along a street and then records the resulting type of response (if any). In this case, the researcher is intervening in a natural environment and is interested in recording the response to a mild form of non-conformity (greeting a stranger). The kinds of observations which can be made in such studies are quite limited. However, like most observational studies, fairly accurate measures may be recorded concerning the subject's age, sex, dress, and type of response. But the key point is that the observation is being made in a natural environment.

Another illustration of such studies would be those investigating proxemics. Proxemics is the study of norms concerning personal space and conditions when such space is or is not violated. For example, a researcher might position two confederates (people working with the researcher) facing one another, apparently discussing some issue, in a narrow corridor.[4] Perhaps an 18″ space is left between the back of one confederate and the wall, while the other confederate stands against the opposite wall. As people pass through the corridor, an observer will record information about the "subjects" (perhaps their age, sex, whether alone or with others, and whether they "cut through" between the confederates, or squeeze through the 18″ space. If the "subjects" cut through, do they acknowledge their cutting through by saying "excuse me" or slightly bowing their heads as a non-verbal apology? Following a number of observations of this sort, the distance between the confederates could be increased or decreased, or, for a control condition, the confederates could be replaced by large ash cans, keeping the same spacing as had been present when the confederates were there. The above example illustrates a natural setting experiment: an environment is set up where conditions are controlled, and systematic observations are made of the people who pass through the space.

Natural setting experiments may also involve the violation of personal space. For example, a confederate student might sit right next to a student of the opposite sex working in the library, when many other spaces are available. Responses vary, but frequently take the form of the subject erecting a barrier with books to mark off territory; rarely do the subjects flee. Similar studies involve a female student joining a group of male students, unknown to the female, who are standing in a public area discussing some issue. (Typically such violations produce a moment of silence, and then the members of the group flee!)

One major advantage of such studies is that the observations are made of behavior occurring in natural settings, and therefore are not subject to the artificiality of laboratory experiments. Also, studies can be relatively inexpensive to do, and since conditions can be altered systematically by the researcher, some control can be maintained over the experimental conditions.

The disadvantages include a limitation on the number of variables that can be measured and the fact that the samples are not typically representative and the findings cannot, therefore, be generalized.

3. Covert Observational Studies

Covert observational studies are done in naturally occurring settings and can be useful in accurately describing everyday behavior. For example, one might be interested in studying mild forms of deviance (perhaps jaywalking, or failure to come to a complete stop at a stop sign). In such instances, one can simply observe and record behavior according to strict rules. The researcher would not want to count someone as a "stopper" at a stop sign if the person had to stop to avoid a collision; similarly one couldn't record a pedestrian as a non-jaywalker if, when that person approaches a traffic light, it turns green. Such cases would have to be recorded as "indeterminable." These studies are covert in the sense that the subjects are not aware they are being observed.

In the area of proxemics, systematic records might be kept of the face-to-face interaction distances between pairs of individuals. Usually the independent variables have to do with whether those observed are both male, both female, or of mixed sexes; age differences can be recorded, as well as status differences (as in teacher/student, parent/child, employer/employee combinations).

The major disadvantage of such studies is the limit on what can be observed. The advantage is that "real" behavior is being observed and it is not subject to the kinds of artificiality that may occur in experimental studies or in surveys.[5] However, such studies can act as the basis for theory testing providing that any predictions made about behaviour can be connected to theoretical propositions.

B. EXPERIMENTAL DESIGNS

Experimental designs provide the best method for making causal inferences. Unfortunately, not all questions can be answered with experiments. Nonetheless, all researchers need to understand experimental designs to heighten their awareness of factors which need to be controlled, in order to design better studies. Experimental designs attempt to produce results which will enable clear interpretations of the impact one variable has on another. In order to understand the factors which can confound a clear causal interpretation, we will begin with two pre-experimental designs and then present an experimental design.

1. Same Group Pre-test/Post-test: A Pre-experimental Design

Suppose we want to measure the impact a film promoting a local university has on high school students. And suppose, further, we had decided that we would need some measure of the students' predispositions toward the university to start with. We could then show the film, and measure the change in the percent wishing to attend the university using the difference between the pre-test and post-test scores. This difference would be taken to represent the impact of the film on the students.

We could diagram the proposed design in the following way:

Time 1		Time 2
O_1	film	O_2

O_1 refers to observations made on the group at Time 1; O_2 refers to those made at Time 2. Could we correctly conclude that any change in attitude was as a result of seeing the film?

Suppose at Time 1, 57.0 percent indicate that they wish to attend the university while at Time 2, the percent increases to 73.0. Could we argue that the film produced a 16.0 percentage point increase in those wishing to attend the university? (73 - 57 = 16) The answer is no. There are a number of factors which may render such an interpretation incorrect. Donald T. Campbell and Julian C. Stanley identify these factors in their book, *Experimental and Quasi-Experimental Design for Research*. The confounding factors are:[6]

Factor 1. History. Any number of events may have happened in addition to the film being shown: the university's basketball team may have won a championship, the university may have announced a new program, a professor may have just won the Nobel prize. Many things, other than the film, may have intervened and influenced the desire to attend the university.

Factor 2. Maturation. People change over time, perhaps become bored with school, and when second measures are taken, some systematic changes may have occurred which influence the difference in response between the two measurement points.

Factor 3. Testing. If identical questions are asked both times then this in itself may influence the responses. Some respondents may want to appear consistent and therefore try to give the same responses as they did the first time; others might want to help the researchers (they may suspect that the study is to demonstrate how good the film is) and respond much more positively the second time.

Factor 4. Instrument Decay. Suppose students indicated their preference by how hard they could squeeze a hand dynometer. The spring in the device may have weakened and therefore the second set of readings would be slightly higher.

Factor 5. Statistical Regression. To explain this idea, we will need to alter the example slightly. Suppose after our pre-test scores had been taken we decide to show the film just to those with the most negative attitudes. Could we legitimately say that any gain in the scores of these students is a result of the film? The answer is no. The reason for this is that when a sample is selected on the basis of extreme scores, retesting will tend to show a regression toward less extreme scores. Even without seeing a film, the students would, on average, be slightly more positive on the second testing. The explanation is that measurement error at the time of the first measurement has tended to negatively distort the data.

Since this idea is a complex one which should be understood, let us use another example. Suppose a reading specialist wants to try out a new reading program. The specialist tests the reading ability of all students in a school and then selects the lowest scoring ten percent of students for the program. When the students are put through the program and then retested, almost certainly the scores will increase. However, the amount attributable to the program and the amount attributable to regression effects would remain uncertain. In short, the scores would increase but the amount attributable to the new program would be unclear.

2. Exposed/Comparison Group: A Pre-experimental Design

After considering the flaws in the previous design, suppose we alter it so that we have a comparison group, as in the following diagram:

Exposed Group   **film** O_1

Comparison Group O_2

In the above design, one group is shown the film, and another is not. Can we legitimately conclude that the difference between the exposed group and the unexposed group represents the impact of the film? (If the percent expressing a desire to attend the university after seeing the film is 75.0 percent; while the figure was only 55.0 percent for those who did not see the film, could we conclude that the film produced this 20 percentage point difference?) Again there are problems. The major difficulty is that we do not know if the groups were the same to start with. Hence, any difference may simply reflect initial differences, or differences which emerge during the study but are unrelated to the impact of the film.

Factor 6. Selection. It is possible, for example, that the students most favorable to the university choose to go to see the film; thus if they score higher in their preference for attending that university it may simply be that they were initially more positively predisposed to the university.

Factor 7. Mortality. Just as people select themselves into a group, so may people choose to select themselves out. Some of those who see the film may withdraw from the study before they have been measured on their attitude toward attending the university.

3. Pre-test/Post-test Control Group: An Experimental Design

There are many variants in experimental design intended to deal with some of the above problems. Only the simplest one will be presented here:

	Time 1		**Time 2**
Experimental	O_1	film	O_2
Control	O_3		O_4

The key point is that the experimental and control groups are to be equivalent before the experimental group is exposed to the film. There are three ways of achieving equivalence: (i) through precision matching (matching on sex, socio-economic status, and grades, possibly); (ii) through randomization (where individuals are randomly assigned to either the experimental or control groups; or (iii) through a combination of the previous two techniques. Randomization (if the numbers are large enough) will tend to control for differences on all factors. Hence, control through randomization yields control over both known and unknown factors.

In the above design, to estimate the impact of the film we could do the following computation on the percent wanting to attend the university before and after seeing the film:

Table 2.1   Percent Wanting to Attend University by Exposure and Non-exposure to Film

Group	Time 1	Time 2	Difference
	Percent Wanting to Attend University		
Experimental Group	57%	73%	73 − 57 = 16
Control Group	55%	61%	61 − 55 = 6
		Estimated Impact of Film:	10

The seven confounding factors discussed above are thus dealt with in experimental designs through: (1) attempting to make certain that the groups are similar to begin with; and, (2) by noting that the various confounding factors should equally influence the experimental and the control groups.

Experimental designs produce the clearest view of causation. This is accomplished through control of the independent variable(s) and of the influence of extraneous variables (through randomization, for example). However, there are three special cautions to be taken in evaluating experimental results.

The first is that few experiments are done on representative samples and therefore the researcher cannot make extrapolations to the general population.

Second, the higher explained variances typically achieved in experimental studies, in contrast to surveys or in secondary data analyses, should not be misinterpreted. To illustrate: if in reality an independent variable X controls ten percent of the variability in the dependent variable Y, then when an experiment is performed, and all external factors are perfectly controlled, one would anticipate that all of the variance should now be explained, except for that accounted for by measurement error, or the application of inappropriate models (linear when the particular relationship is curvilinear, for example). In principle, experiments should produce higher explained variances than those achieved by the survey researcher studying the same variables. The researcher must realize that an experimentally robust variable may be relatively impotent outside the laboratory setting.

The third major caution is that there is an artificiality in laboratory experiments that is difficult to interpret or to control.

Despite some inherent weaknesses, experimental designs allow for the greatest control and precision in causal model testing and deal with many of the worrying sources of bias that plague other approaches. Moreover, through the use of *double blind* designs, where neither subjects nor researchers know which subjects are under what condition, there is a major control over bias on the part of subjects and researchers. However it is neither practically, nor ethically, possible to experiment on all aspects of social behavior and therefore other designs remain important tools for the social science researcher. The beginning researcher must have some understanding of experimental designs to be able to recognize some of the confounding factors which may influence the outcomes of research. When a survey researcher confronts difficult problems it is often necessary to develop quasi-experimental designs in order to produce cleaner inferences about relationships.

C. SECONDARY DATA STUDIES

A major research approach used by economists, historians, and to a lesser degree, sociologists, is to conduct research based on available material. These sources might include virtually any data — ranging from published statistical, census, or business data to the unpublished diaries of important historical figures. A further use of secondary material would involve a content analysis of media such as radio, television, film, or the various written materials such as plays, poetry, songs, novels, newspapers, or textbooks.

1. Analysis of Existing Material

The major limitation in research based on secondary data has to do with the availability and completeness of the data. The researcher is often severely constrained by the kinds of information available. Economists are impressively adept, however, at pulling "indicators" out of available data. Since such data are frequently reported at different points in time, the economist is able to build, and test, elaborate causal models. So whether they are attempting to understand the linkage between interest rates and unemployment or between housing starts and the wage level of plumbers, economists make efforts to understand the world using secondary data. With the exception of those who record oral histories, historians also rely on secondary data sources. Political scientists, sociologists, and psychologists, on the other hand, rely heavily on generating data to answer their research questions.

Secondary data analysis is cost effective and, providing the data are relatively complete, can lead to sound general statements about the social world. Along with survey research, however, there are serious problems with demonstrating the validity of its indicators, and in making convincing causal inferences.

2. Content Analysis

Social scientists frequently wish to examine a medium in terms of what message it communicates. A researcher might wish to understand the level of "sexist" messages communicated on television, or the extent to which traditional sex roles are portrayed in children's school books; or the proportion of negative editorials being written about political officials now, as compared to 50 years ago. The chances are that if these are the kinds of research questions being asked, some form of content analysis will be used. Content analysis may involve going through a sample of films, books, newspapers, or television programs and attempting to categorize the messages being conveyed in them. One might count, for example, the number of times mothers are portrayed playing "traditional" roles in children's readers. Or one might categorize editorial comment as being pro- or anti-government in the newspapers of various decades. In all cases, the researcher is attempting to assess the "content" of the message being communicated.

Content analyses are appropriate for many questions, can be done relatively inexpensively, and, if the material is sampled appropriately, may be taken to represent the available material. Furthermore, the validity of the measures may be fairly high since direct observations and classifications are being made. However, validity is limited if material presented is selected for its dramatic impact and not for its representativeness of the individuals described. A story about a bigot cannot be presumed to represent the views of the author or of the larger culture. It is also often difficult to assess the essential meaning and impact of the messages and to draw clear causal inferences from them.

D. SURVEY DESIGNS

It is important for the beginning survey researcher to understand that the use of surveys is but one approach to social research. Surveys have their strong and weak points. Let us first examine some of the general characteristics of surveys.

Surveys are a relatively inexpensive method of collecting information from a large number of people. If the researcher wants to make extrapolations from a sample to a larger population, then a fairly large sample will be required and hence it is likely that a survey design will be used. The extent to which social behavior is viewed as highly complex — subject to the simultaneous impact of many variables — suggests that a research strategy which measures many variables may be an appropriate one.

With both experimental and survey designs there can be difficulty in establishing the validity of the measures being considered. In the case of surveys, respondents are asked to report their own attitudes, behavior, and backgrounds. Some of the questions asked may require the respondent to remember things from the past. ("How happy were you when you were first married?") Since questionnaires probe into sensitive areas, respondents often try to manage their responses to create an image they feel they ought to have. When researchers attempt to measure attitudes toward minorities, for example, they must be aware that some people will try to appear tolerant — perhaps more tolerant than they actually are. What people say they believe does not always correspond with how they actually behave in real-life situations.[7]

Nonetheless, on matters of fact, surveys can produce reliable and valid responses. If the idea is to measure attitudes, there is little other alternative than to ask people about those they hold. The researcher simply has to live with the problems of measurement, if the variables are to be measured at all. Conventional wisdom frequently has it that surveys are point-in-time studies and that, therefore, they are not good for measuring changes over time. While there is no doubt some difficulty in asking people to reliably recall their past, most surveys in fact do ask questions about a variety of points in time: year of birth, type of community you grew up in, how old were you when you got your first full-time job, etc. Once again, while there are problems with recall data, sometimes there is no practical alternative to the survey for studying some types of variables.

Questionnaires are also restrictive since they can only be used with a literate population. Wordings used in questions must be straightforward so that all — or at least most — of the respondents will be able to handle the language. Also, the requirement that all respondents be able to understand the questions prevents certain areas from being probed in depth. Everyone is given the same set of questions, and while it is advantageous to have all respondents reply to the same question, it does mean that interesting responses cannot be pursued. For in-depth probes a personal interview approach is necessary.

There are many variants of the survey and we will only explore the major approaches here. The main differences have to do with how the data are collected. Each approach has a distinctive set of advantages and disadvantages. Let us begin with the questionnaire that is to be completed by an indvidual.

1. The Self-Administered Questionnaire

There are many ways in which questionnaires can be administered. The first type, the individually completed questionnaire, is one which is handed to an individual who is asked to fill it out. Normally, such questionnaires are also returned directly to the researcher.

Questionnaires which have been explained to respondents and handed to them in person, are likely to generate high response rates. Moreover, since the researcher is present, any questions the respondent has can be answered. The greater the personal contact, the greater the response rate.

2. Group-Administered Questionnaires

There are a few different aspects to questionnaires administered in a group setting. For example, there is considerable informal pressure on individuals to cooperate with the researcher and it is not uncommon to get all of the people present to complete the form. Researchers should recognize this pressure and take steps to inform potential respondents of their complete freedom to refuse to answer any or all questions (see Chapter 4, ethics section). An advantage to having the researcher present is that any respondent's questions may be answered.

One hazard to watch out for, however, is that a few members of the group may decide to make a joke out of the process and provide silly responses. This happens rarely but the group should be carefully monitored and the researcher should discard any questionnaires that appear not to have been taken seriously.

Typically, when questionnaires are administered to groups, probability sampling (see Chapter 9) is not employed and therefore the data collected cannot be used to extrapolate to some larger population.

3. Mailed Questionnaires

The mailed questionnaire shares most of the same advantages and disadvantages with the individually administered one. The major difference between the two is that invariably the mailed questionnaire will have lower response rates. Some questionnaires will never reach potential respondents.

Often, however, there is no choice but to use the mail system: long distance phone interviews would be prohibitively expensive and travel costs would quickly eat up the research budget if the researcher attempted to hand deliver the questionnaires.

4. Panel Studies

Panel studies monitor specific organizations or individuals over time. Perhaps the easiest way to think about panels is to consider them as a survey of a particular group where at least one follow-up interview is conducted. Such studies can be done in natural settings and are particularly useful for examining processes.

Why would a researcher choose to do a panel study rather than an experiment or a survey? The answer is that experimentation is frequently not possible, or judged not to be relevant, for the examination of some relationships. Surveys, on the other hand, might not provide a sufficient basis for making causal inferences.

Suppose, for example, the researcher was interested in studying the impact on individuals of working for large companies in contrast to small ones. In this case, the researcher needs to establish what the individuals in both groups are like at Time 1; next, the changes these individuals undergo over time must be monitored. The individuals in the groups being compared should be as similar as possible at the beginning. A carefully designed panel study provides a naturalistic experiment and may lead to a better understanding of the impact of the work place on workers.[8]

5. Phone Survey

Phone surveys are widely used, particularly by polling organizations, and represent a technique of data collection that will increase in years to come.

Like all surveys, the phone survey relies on self-reported information and is susceptible to image management on the part of the respondent.

The advantages to this method are that it is relatively cheap, produces high response rates, and can be used to generate a representative sample. The representativeness issue, however, has to be monitored carefully because phones are not evenly distributed among the population; moreover, unless interviewers are well-disciplined, there will be a tendency to interview the person who answers the phone and this may not provide everyone in the population with an equal chance of being included in the sample.

Questions and response categories must be kept simple since they are presented verbally. In-depth probes are difficult and, like other surveys, there is always a difficulty in making causal inferences. Given that the phone interviewer has to write down the responses, there is some additional opportunity for bias in noting responses. The interviewer's expectations may inadvertently influence the responses that are recorded. Care must be taken, therefore, to monitor response variations between interviewers.

6. Interviews

The final data collection procedure we will consider is the interview. Generally there are two kinds of interviews: (i) the structured interview during which a questionnaire is read to the respondent; and (ii) the interview schedule which outlines the areas to be probed by the interviewer.

Structured Interview. Structured interviews involve face-to-face interviews where questions are read to the respondents. Such interviews ordinarily will provide for in-depth probes on some of the questions. Interviews also allow the respondents to ask any questions and therefore any ambiguities can be clarified.

Interview Schedule. Interview schedules outline the major questions to be raised. The interviewer has greater freedom to explore questions in detail. Interviews require much skill on the part of the interviewer and care must be taken not to "lead" the respondent. Furthermore, since the responses are filtered through an interviewer, and there may be a number of interviewers, some of the variability in responses will be due to differences between interviewers and not solely to differences between the respondents.

Since conducting interviews is expensive, they are normally done when few interviews are required and in-depth information is needed. One major advantage is that a good rapport is often built up so that if repeated interviews are required, as in a panel study, high response rates can be maintained.

CONCLUSION

In summary, surveys are the major tool in studies attempting to represent large populations. They often attempt to deal simultaneously with many variables and to describe the complexity of human behavior. Surveys also permit the researcher to construct new variables by combining a number of characteristics — status integration (a measure of similarities across status characteristics) is an example of a constructed variable.[9]

Despite the many advantages of survey research, there are problems with making clear causal inferences based on the kind of data obtained. Survey data are normally based on self-reported information and frequently involve

Figure 2.1   Advantages and Disadvantages of Alternate Data Collection Techniques

Data Collection Technique	Cost[1]	Generality[2]	Validity[3]	Causal Inference[4]	Probing[5]
A. NATURAL SETTING STUDIES					
Participant Observation	−	−	+	−	+
Field Experiments	+	−	+	+	−
Covert Observational	+	−	+	−	−
B. EXPERIMENTAL STUDIES					
Pre-experimental	+	−	−	−	−
Experimental Designs	+	−	−	+	−
C. SECONDARY DATA STUDIES					
Existing Material	+	+	−	−	−
Content Analysis	+	+	−	−	−
D. SURVEY STUDIES					
Questionnaire	+	+	−	−	−
Group Administered	+	−	−	−	−
Mailed Questionnaire	+	+	−	−	−
Panel Study	−	+	−	+	−
Phone Survey	+	+	−	−	−
Interview	−	+	−	−	+

[1]*Cost* is the time and expense involved in collecting data for each of the data collection procedures. A + means that this is an advantage of the technique; a − means this is a disadvantage.

[2]*Generality* refers to the extent to which general statements may be extrapolated to larger populations using each of the data collection techniques.

[3]*Validity* is the extent to which indicators clearly measure what they are intended to reflect.

[4]*Causal inference* means the ease with which causal inferences may be made.

[5]*Probing* means the extent to which responses may be probed in depth.

recall data. While it is probably not difficult to recall factual information (such as reporting the community you were born in, or the salary of your first full-time job), there may be serious problems in recalling "how well you got along with your mother when you were six years old."

Another fundamental issue concerns the connection between words (what people say they will do) and deeds (what they actually do). There is therefore some question about the extent to which surveys reflect *ideal* behavior as opposed to *real* behavior. To what extent, then, can we claim to reflect reality with survey data?

Figure 2.1 summarizes the advantages and disadvantages of the various approaches to research design. The greatest validity of measures occurs in natural setting studies; causal inferences are most easily made with experimental data and, to a lesser degree, panel studies; and generalizing to larger populations is the forte of survey design and secondary data analyses. To probe in depth, participant observation studies and interviews appear to be the most useful.

Whatever research design is selected, it is important to understand the strengths and weaknesses of each of the approaches. Such knowledge helps the researcher to select an appropriate design and to try to deal with the weak points of each design.

E. EXERCISES

1. Suppose you wished to investigate the impact of a guaranteed income scheme on the withdrawal of youth from the labour force. What research design(s) would be appropriate to deal with such a question? Outline the rationale for your choice.

2. Suppose you wished to understand what factors influence the grade performance of university students. What kind of design would you recommend for such a study? Outline the rationale for your choice.

3. Suppose you wished to investigate four alternative explanations for the relationship between socio-economic status and attitudes toward minorities. What kind of design would you recommend? Outline the rationale for your choice.

4. Suppose you are interested in exploring gender differences in the conditions when violence is acceptable. What design would you recommend for exploring such a question? Outline the rationale for your choice.

5. Propose four projects not more than a page each in length, to illustrate the various general designs discussed in this chapter.

NOTES

[1] Erving Goffman, *Asylums.* Chicago: Aldine Publishing Company, 1962.

[2] William F. Whyte, *Street Corner Society: The Social Structure of an Italian Slum* (2nd ed.). Chicago: University of Chicago Press, 1955.

[3] Barney G. Glaser and Anselm Strauss, *The Discovery of Grounded Theory.* Chicago: Aldine Publishing Company, 1967.

[4] Efian Cheyn, "The Effect of Spatial and Interpersonal Variables on the Invasion of Group Controlled Territories," *Sociometry*, 1972, pp. 477-88.

[5] Eugene J. Webb, Donald T. Campbell, Richard Schwartz, and Lee Sechrest, *Unobtrusive Measures: Nonreactive Research in the Social Sciences.* Chicago: Rand-McNally & Company, 1966.

[6] Donald T. Campbell and Julian C. Stanley, *Experimental and Quasi-Experimental Designs for Research.* Chicago: Rand-McNally & Company, 1966.

[7] Irwin Deutscher, "Words and Deeds: Social Action and Social Policy," *Social Problems*, (Winter 1966) 13, pp. 235-54.

[8] Donald H. Clairmont and Winston Jackson, "Segmentation and the Low Income Blue Collar Worker: A Canadian Test of Segmentation Theory," Halifax: Institute of Public Affairs, Dalhousie University, 1980.

[9] J.P. Gibbs and W.T. Martin, *Status Integration and Suicide: A Sociological Study.* Eugene, Oregon: University of Oregon Press, 1964.

CHAPTER THREE

THEORY AND THEORY TESTING

As we have noted, social scientists are interested in understanding social behavior. In their quest for understanding, they have devoted energy to carefully describing behavior, and to developing and testing general explanations which try to account for patterns of human behavior. Perhaps because of the devilish complexity of behaviour – or perhaps because of the tough standards we set for what we are prepared to consider an adequate explanation of it – what we are missing are *well-confirmed*, and *widely accepted*, explanations for behavior. This chapter explores the role of theory and provides some simple theory testing techniques that may be applied by the beginning researcher attempting to understand the elusive patterns characterizing the social world.

A. WHAT IS A THEORY?

Perhaps the best way to begin to consider this question is to ask about the *function* of theory – what is theory supposed to do? The major function of theory is to explain, or account for, the behavior of humans or of human institutions. A relationship may be said to be explained once someone has offered a satisfactory explanation for it – offered a satisfactory answer to a "why" question.[1] But what is satisfactory? For some, almost any answer might satisfy. For others, tough rules of evidence will have to be followed in order for the explanation to be considered adequate. The social scientist is more likely than the lay person to insist on considerable evidence before accepting an explanation. A simple opinion will not do. ''What is your evidence?,'' is the question that will be asked. The scientist's skepticism and curiosity is what distinguishes him or her from the lay person.

The job of theory, then, is to explain: to offer satisfactory, testable explanations for relationships. A *testable* explanation is one which can be disconfirmed – one which could turn out to be true or false. The American philosopher, Ernest Nagel, has distinguished four basic types of testable explanations:[2]

Type 1. The Deductive Explanation. In this case, the thing to be explained is a logically necessary consequence of the explanatory premises. As in: if A = B, and B = C, then A = C. Emile Durkheim's analysis, for example, of why the suicide rate in Spain will be low is based on the following set of interrelated propositions:

> **i)** In any social grouping, the suicide rate (SR) varies directly with the degree of individualism (I).
>
> $\rangle$I $\longrightarrow$ $\rangle$SR

> **ii)** The degree of individualism (I) varies with the incidence of Protestantism (P). (Untested assumption)
>
> $\rangle$P $\longrightarrow$ $\rangle$I

> **iii)** Therefore, the suicide rate (SR) varies with the incidence of Protestantism (P).
>
> $\rangle$P $\longrightarrow$ $\rangle$SR (Derivation)

> **iv)** The incidence of Protestantism in Spain is low. (Empirical observation)

> **v)** Therefore, the suicide rate (SR) in Spain is low. (Empirically testable hypothesis)

In the above illustration, by combining an untested but stated assumption (ii above), with a theoretical proposition (i), along with an empirical observation (iv), and a deductive step (iii), we get a testable hypothesis. If, indeed, the data prove to be consistent with the prediction, this would constitute one piece of evidence not inconsistent with the theory. We could not claim to have *proven* the theory to be correct because alternative theories might also make the prediction that suicide rates will be comparatively low in Spain.

Type 2. Probabilistic Explanations. This form of explanation rests on linking a particular case to its general category. If you were asked to explain why Joe College drinks excessively, and you responded by saying, "there's a lot of drinking on campus these days," you would have given a probabilistic explanation. Joe drinks a lot *because* he is a member of a category of individuals who tend to drink a lot. The explanation suggests that an individual tends to be like others in the same category.

Type 3. Functional or Teleological Explanations. Here the explanation is that the presence of a phenomenon is due to the role it plays in maintaining a system. For example, explaining the universal presence of the family unit in all cultures in terms of its role in population maintenance, would be a *teleological* explanation: the family exists to propagate in order to maintain the social system.

Type 4. Genetic or Causal Explanations. This kind of explanation considers an event, or sequence of events, leading to something. The event is explained by making reference to preceding events. The explanation traces the sequence of steps, each influencing the next, which has led to the event. Causal sequence thinking dominates the thinking of most survey researchers.

The function of theory is to explain patterns in the world. Theories may be more or less explicit. A theory may be highly detailed, with its underlying assumptions specified, and with a whole host of predictive statements encompassed in it; or a theory may be entirely lacking in detail – it may be a simple explanatory variable. For example, the variable, "variations in socialization patterns," may be used to explain why there are variations in educational aspirations across the SES (socio-economic status) continuum. This explanation proposes that across the SES continuum, there are differences in socialization patterns, which, in turn, account for variations in aspirations. This theory is a partial one because it fails to specify the underlying assumptions it makes about human behavior; it does not tell us anything about how the explanatory variable (variations in socialization patterns) is connected to any other variables.

Given the broad range of what may be considered a theoretical explanation, it is instructive to explore the properties of both formal and partial theoretical constructs.

1. Formal Theory

What are the components of formal, explicit theory? According to George Homans,[3] a theory consists of three key elements. First, there is a *set of concepts*, or a conceptual scheme. Some of the concepts may be descriptive, serving to identify what the theory is about (in the Durkheim suicide case, the terms "individualism," "suicide," and "Protestantism" are such terms). Other concepts are operatives or properties of nature (such as suicide rate, degree of individualism, incidence of Protestantism). These last concepts are the variables. A conceptual scheme by itself does not constitute a theory. (Labelling types of deviance is not a theory of deviance, rather it is a classification of deviance.)

A theory consists, second, of a *set of propositions*, each stating a relationship (such as "inversely related to") between some of the concepts. Further, the set of propositions must be interrelated so that one can derive new propositions by combining them deductively. When new propositions are derived they are said to be explained by the previous ones.

Third, Homans argues, some of the *propositions must be contingent* – that is, they must be amenable to some form of empirical test. A theory, Homans argues, cannot be made up entirely of non-contingent propositions: some, but not necessarily all, must be testable (e.g., Is the suicide rate in Spain low?).

The *power* of a theory refers to the number of propositions which may be derived from it; that is, the more predictive statements which can be derived from it, the more powerful it is. The most powerful theories are general theories. In the case of Durkheim's analysis of suicide, the theoretical formulation is not as general (and hence not as powerful) as it might be. By using the highly specific variable suicide, he has limited the generalizability of the theory. Had Durkheim used the term deviance, then the theory would have been more powerful. Not only could the suicide hypothesis have been derived from it, but many other predictions worth testing could have been developed as well.

Definitions of formal theory similar to Homans' are to be found in the work of Braithwaite, Zetterberg, and Gibbs. Braithwaite defines theory as a "deductive system in which observable consequences logically follow from the conjunction of observed facts with the set of fundamental hypotheses of the system."[4] For Zetterberg, theory is defined as a set of "systematically organized, law-like propositions about society that can be supported by evidence."[5] Gibbs defines theory as "a set of logically interrelated statements in the form of empirical assertions about properties of infinite classes of events or things."[6]

In summary, then, a formal, explicit theory does not exist "until one has properties, and propositions stating the relations between them, and the propositions form a deductive system – not until one has all three does one have a theory."[7] While Homans' minimum requirements for theory are tough, they nonetheless provide a useful guideline. The essence of formal theories is the precision and explicitness with which they are stated. Assumptions are specified, as are statements of relationship.

However, given that any satisfactory answer to a "why" question constitutes an explanation, there may be some advantage to viewing theory as a continuum, ranging from formal theory (such as that defined above by Homans, Braithwaite, or Zetterberg) through to partial theories, such as single intervening variable explanations (e.g., "variations in socialization patterns" explaining the connection between SES and educational aspirations). While partial theories may not meet the requirements of the more formal constructions, they can sometimes be linked to existing formal theories, or lead to the development of new ones.

2. Partial Theory

A partial theory attempts to explain an assumed or known relationship by specifying a testable causal model. An earlier illustration concerned the connection between socio-economic status and educational aspirations. A number of possible explanations were suggested which might account for the relationship. Each of these explanations represents a possible answer to the "why" question about the connection between the two variables. As such, each is a theory. However, such theoretical formulations remain at an implicit level and are therefore partial. As worded, they fail to specify what assumptions are being made, or to articulate the underlying model of human behavior involved in the explanation. To illustrate, let us explore two of the explanations: (a) that the reason high SES students are more likely to aspire to higher educational levels is to fulfill their parent's expectations of them; and (b) that high SES students have been more exposed to high achievers and are more likely, therefore, to model themselves after such individuals.

a. Fulfilling Parental Expectations. This explanation contains two critical elements: (i) that high SES parents have different educational expectations of their children than do low SES parents; and (ii) that students try to fulfill the expectations of their parents. Theoretically the idea is that people are influenced, or shaped, by the expectations of others. This type of explanation is most consistent with reinforcement theory in Psychology[8] or exchange theory in Sociology.[9] In this particular case, the child is seen as a rather passive object being shaped by parental expectations and by a reward system controlled by parents. Students become what they are rewarded to become.

b. Differential Exposure to Role Models. This second explanation involves at least three assumptions: (i) that there will be differences, by students' SES levels, in the amount of exposure to people in elite occupations; (ii) that students recognize the connection between educational and occupational achievement; and (iii) that students recognize and desire the rewards that come to people who achieve higher occupational levels. The implicit model of behavior here is that the individual aspires to higher educational levels as a vehicle for moving into occupations similar to those people whose life-styles they admire. This view of human behavior suggests that the individual is not so much molded by the expectations of others but rather the individual actively chooses to become what will bring him or her the desired rewards: the mechanism for this "becoming" is through education. *Significant Others* become models to be copied. This view is most compatible with the view expressed by symbolic interactionists.[10]

Other explanations for the connection between SES and educational aspirations could be developed and connected to existing theoretical perspectives. Frequently it is possible for the researcher to generate theoretical connections by carefully exploring the underlying theory of human behavior proposed in the research. In short, it is possible to make a backward connection to theory – starting with a partial theory and moving backward to existing formal theories in the discipline. Carefully thought out, such research can then have more general application to our understanding of human behavior.

But what is the use of theory? What do we gain by connecting research to new or existing theoretical models? The answer has to do with power. Research that limits itself to the particular, to the unique, will not contribute to our general understanding of the human condition. General explanations give research implications for our overall understanding of behavior and increase our knowledge of the particular variables involved in a project.

B. APPROACHING THEORY TESTING

Hypothesis testing is a part of theory testing but, by itself, does not necessarily constitute a test of theory. *The fundamental issue in theoretical research is to demonstrate the linkage between the set of theoretical propositions and the conceptual hypothesis selected for examination.* Only to the extent that this connection has been articulated successfully can we claim our research has bearing on theory. This next section will consider approaches to testing partial theories followed by approaches to testing formal theories.

1. Testing Partial Theories

Previously the argument was made that the testing of alternative explanations is a primitive form of theory testing. This is the case because "theory" and "explanation" function the same way – to answer a "why" question. The reason testing of alternative explanations is called a primitive form of theory testing is because such formulations fail to identify the model of human behavior or the assumptions being considered.

To test partial theories there are no prerequisites save perhaps that there is some relationship which seems to need explanation. All that is required is a statement of a relationship and an explanation, or series of explanations, for it. After that, all we have to do is measure the appropriate variables and do the analysis.

For example, if we were to attempt to test an explanation for the connection between educational aspirations and socio-economic background, we might wish to test whether variations in socialization patterns (and consequent attitudes) explain the relationship or whether it is to be explained in terms of the individual making a realistic assessment of his or her being able to afford an expensive education. To conduct a piece of research which would allow us to evaluate the adequacy of each explanation would be a test of two theories, or two explanations.

Note, however, that, as stated, the explanations are not well documented. One presumably is a value explanation, the other an economic one. Nevertheless, since both are answers to a "why" question, each may be viewed as constituting a theory of human behavior (albeit an implicit one).

The basic requirements for the testing of alternative explanations are that: (1) one has a relationship between two variables which one suspects will be strong (either positive or negative); (2) one has a series of alternative explanations for the relationship; (3) it is possible to get measures for the appropriate variables; and (4) that after data are collected, suitable procedures are used for the analysis of the data, making possible an evaluation of the adequacy of the competing explanations.

2. Testing Formal Theories

Formal theories involve a number of formally stated, interconnected propositions. They contain clearly defined variables and indicate the nature (direct or inverse) and the direction (what is causing what) of the relationships among the variables. The propositions normally take the form of *the greater A, the greater B*. All the concepts in the propositions need not be directly measurable. However at some point, a connection to measurable variables must be made. This link must be specified in order for research to have bearing on a theoretical formulation. We will examine two approaches to the demonstration of such connections: these will be labelled as (a) axiomatic derivations and (b) replacement of terms.

a. Axiomatic Derivations. Axiomatic derivations will be illustrated using five statements from Peter Blau's *Exchange and Power in Social Life*.[11]

The following five statements are contained in Chapter Two of his work:

(1) The greater the group cohesion (a), the greater the consensus on normative standards (b).

(2) The greater the group cohesion (a), the greater the effective enforcement of these shared norms (c).

(3) The greater the cohesion (a), the greater the significance of the informal sanctions of the group (d).

(4) The more the integrative bonds of social cohesion (a), the stronger the group in the pursuit of common goals (e).

(5) The greater the cohesion (a), the fewer the proportion of deviants from group norms (f). (Note that "f" is negative.)

Note that the wordings of the "a" variable vary somewhat from proposition to proposition. In doing a propositional inventory of any theoretical work, the student has to decide whether variations of this sort are intended to convey a different meaning, or are simply stylistic considerations.

Now, suppose that the relationships between "a" and "f" and between "a" and "d" are assumed to be reversible. This means that we are going to assume that there is a mutual causal link such that "a" influences "f", but also that "f" influences "a". This kind of relationship can be represented as:

Causally, the argument is that the greater a group's cohesion (a), the fewer members will deviate from the group's norms (f). The second argument is that the reverse is also assumed to be true; namely, that having fewer deviants in a group (f) will lead to a strengthening of group cohesion.

Since the original propositions indicated a number of variables to which cohesion is related, we can now suggest some new *derived* propositions which should be true if the original propositions are correct, and a reversiblity assumption is correct. They are as follows:

(Derivation 1) The fewer the proportion of deviants from group norms (f), the greater the consensus on normative standards (b);

$< f \longrightarrow > b$

(Derivation 2) The fewer the proportion of deviants from group norms (f), the greater the effective enforcement of shared norms (c);

$< f \longrightarrow > c$

(Derivation 3) The fewer the proportion of deviants from group norms (f), the greater the significance of the informal sanctions of the group (d);

< f ⟶ > d

(Derivation 4) The fewer the proportion of deviants from group norms (f), the stronger the group in the pursuit of common goals (e).

< f ⟶ > e

How are these derivations made? Given that the "a" to "f" relation is assumed to be reversible, we are able to argue that since "f" leads to "a", and we were given the "a" to "b" relation in the original proposition, we can then conclude that "f" leads to "a" and this leads to "b". This may be represented as:

f ⟶ a ⟶ b

The remaining derivations are made in a similar fashion. In each case, the relationship can be simplified by leaving out the linking, or intervening, variable. Any time one has a situation such as the following, derivations may be made:

If, ⟩ X ⟶ ⟩ Y
and, ⟩ Y ⟶ ⟩ Z
therefore, ⟩ X ⟶ ⟩ Y ⟶ ⟩ Z
or simply, ⟩ X ⟶ ⟩ Z

The new derived propositions should be true if the assumptions, derivations, and original theoretical propositions are accurate. Derivations are made to locate testable hypotheses which, when tested, constitute a test of the theory. The reason one makes derivations is to identify a theoretically predicted relationship which is not obvious in common sense terms.

Why would one want to prove a counter-intuitive relationship? Here the answer is psychological rather than scientific. If an unexpected relationship is predicted and if, indeed, the results of the study confirm it, the evidence is much more convincing. On the other hand, if the predicted relationship is common-sensical, even if confirmed, critics will claim that the results only show what everyone already knew and certainly do not demonstrate any theory. Albert Einstein's prediction that a clock moved rapidly should run slower than one that is moved slowly is a simple, but counter-intuitive prediction, that, when demonstrated, is powerfully convincing.

b. Replacement of Terms. A further way of extending the number of predictions is to use a technique which will be called replacement of terms. *Replacement of terms* refers to the replacing of general theoretical concepts with specific instances of these concepts. For example, if the general concept is deviance, such a concept could be replaced by a specific instance of deviance—perhaps shoplifting, or burglary, or drunk driving. To the extent that one is able to derive new statements of relationships through such replacements, one can provide a virtually unlimited number of testable relationships. One can then select the better ones—choosing those that are both counter-intuitive and that permit one to refine and specify conditions under which the theory does, or does not, hold.

The combination of axiomatic derivations and replacement of terms yields a powerful, yet simple, method of deriving interesting testable hypotheses. The student would be well advised, however, to directly test the propositions of a theory and, if that is not possible, to make as few axiomatic steps in locating testable hypotheses as possible. The reason for this is that given the complexity of social relations, and given that few relations are extremely powerful, it is problematic to make a large number of axiomatic steps and expect to retain an iron-clad connection to the original set of propositions.[12]

Having selected the hypothesis, we will now turn our attention to ethical questions and the problem of bias in social research.

C. EXERCISES

1. Choose a major theoretical work. Do a propositional inventory of a section of the work, selecting the major propositions involved. Label the concepts with letters, using the same letter for those you presume are intended to refer to the same variable. Attempt to derive new theoretical statements using axiomatic derivations and replacement of terms approaches. Be certain to specify the assumptions you are making in doing the derivations. Identify testable propositions you think are not obvious on a common sense basis.

2. Choose a relationship that you think would hold true and propose three alternative explanations for the relationship. Connect your proposed explanations to existing social science theory. Could a study be designed which would allow you to reject the various explanations?

NOTES

[1]R.B. Braithwaite, *Scientific Explanation*. New York: Harper Torchbooks, 1960.

[2]Ernest Nagel, *The Stucture of Science: Problems in the Logic of Scientific Explanations*. New York: Harcourt, Brace & World, Inc., 1961.

[3]George C. Homans, "Bringing Men Back In," *American Sociological Review*, Vol. 29 (1964), pp. 809-18.

[4]R.B. Braithwaite, p. 22.

[5]Hans L. Zetterberg, *On Theory and Verification in Sociology*. Totowa, New Jersey: The Bedminster Press, 1965.

[6]Jack P. Gibbs, *Sociological Theory Construction*. Hinsdale, Illinois: The Dryden Press, Inc., 1972, p. 5.

[7]Homans, p. 812.

[8]John W. Thibaut and Harold H. Kelley, *The Social Psychology of Groups*. New York: John Wiley & Sons, Inc., 1959.

[9]George C. Homans, *Social Behavior: Its Elementary Forms*. New York: Harcourt, Brace and World, Inc., 1961.

[10]Herbert Blumer, "Collective Behavior." in A.M. Lee (ed.), *Principles of Sociology*. New York: Barnes and Noble, 1951, pp. 167-222. Also Jerome G. Manis and Bernard N. Meltzer (Eds.), *Symbolic Interaction: A Reader in Social Psychology* (3rd Ed.). Boston: Allyn and Bacon, 1978.

[11]Peter Blau, *Exchange and Power in Social Life*. New York: John Wiley & Sons, Inc., 1964.

[12]For a more sophisticated discussion of theory construction and some of the problems in axiomatic derivations see: H.L. Costner and R.K. Leik, "Deductions from 'axiomatic theory.'" *American Sociological Review*, Vol 29, December, 1964, pp. 819-35; Jack P. Gibbs, *Sociological Theory Construction*. Hinsdale, Illinois: The Dryden Press, 1972; Hubert M. Blalock, Jr., *Theory Construction*. Englewood Cliffs, New Jersey: Prentice-Hall Inc., 1969; Kenneth D. Bailey, "Evaluating Axiomatic Theories," in Edgar F. Borgatta and George W. Bohrnstedt, *Sociological Methodology 1970*. San Francisco: Jossey-Bass, Inc., Publishers, 1970.

CHAPTER FOUR

ON BIAS AND ETHICAL ISSUES

This chapter explains the distinctions between pure and applied research, examines sources of bias, provides suggestions for minimizing bias, and discusses the major ethical issues survey researchers face.

A. PURE AND APPLIED RESEARCH

Some social scientists are interested in understanding social relationships, others are interested in figuring out how to bring about specific changes in society. The former may be characterized as *pure researchers*, the latter as *applied researchers*.

1. Pure Research

The social scientist engaged in pure research tries to understand patterns of social behavior. However, it is usually the case that many explanations can be offered to account for any particular behavior. The challenge of social science is to determine which, if any, of the possible explanations accounts for any given pattern, uniformity, or diversity. Patterns may be understood through a variety of qualitative and quantitative techniques. But whatever the approach, the ultimate goal is to offer better descriptions and better explanations of human behavior.

Frequently the sociologist is confronted with "interesting" findings for which an explanation should be offered. Suppose, once again, that a project is being done which measures high school students' socio-economic backgrounds (SES) and their aspirations for higher education. And suppose, during data analysis, that a robust relationship emerges which indicates that the higher an individual's socio-economic origin, the greater the likelihood that individual will aspire to post-secondary education. At this stage, the researcher may wonder how to explain this emergent pattern. Possibilities such as the following might come to mind: (1) peers of high SES students have high aspirations themselves and influence their friends to plan on attending post-secondary institutions; (2) among high SES students, parental expectations of children's educational achievement are higher; (3) high SES students know that they have the financial backing to attend a post-secondary institution and therefore plan on it; (4) teachers encourage high SES students more; (5) high SES students have been more exposed to high occupational achievers and are more likely to model themselves after such individuals.

Unfortunately, the study may not have been designed to test, and possibly rule out, competing explanations. Hence, little empirical evidence may be brought to bear on the explanation that is finally presented by the researcher.

The problem is that a report may present considerable data documenting a variety of relationships and the reader of such a report may be convinced, inappropriately, that the researcher has evidence for the particular explanation being offered: "after all, look at all the tables that are presented." There may, however, be little or no evidence for the particular explanation presented. The researcher must design studies which systematically test a variety of possible explanations for the relationship under examination.

The goals of pure research include: (1) to test proposed or existing theories of social behavior; (2) to explain patterns of behavior that exist; (3) to develop and to test general theories of behavior; and (4) to document our knowledge of the emergence, modification, and persistence of patterned human behavior.

2. Applied Research

A first-rate applied researcher needs to have many of the same skills as the pure researcher. The two are distinguished, however, because the pure researcher wishes to understand phenomena while the applied researcher wishes to have an impact on some specific social behavior — whether it is maintaining the enrollment in a music school, changing people's attitudes toward wearing seat belts, buying a new toothpaste, eliminating deviance, or assessing the popularity of a government.

It could be argued that the pure researcher attempts to be value-free — not promoting a particular theory, or view of the world — while the applied researcher tries to provide the basis for achieving particular goals which may, or may not, be shared by the researcher. The applied researcher rents his or her skills out. The service may be to monitor public responses to a new government policy, or to measure the impact of an advertising campaign to discourage smoking. The inherent bias of the applied researcher is to facilitate goal achievement by an employer. The applied researcher is not so much concerned with understanding the whole phenomenon but focusses, particularly, on those variables which are causally important and which can be changed so as to better achieve desired goals.

B. BIAS: NOTES ON "RESEARCHER AFFECT"

The previous section presented a simple view of pure and applied research and may have left the mistaken impression that pure research is without bias while applied research involves a built-in bias. Such an impression would be wrong because there are worrying sources of bias in all research, and in all disciplines. It is important for the beginning researcher to be sensitive to potential sources of bias so as to guard against them. While there may be dangers in the researcher becoming overly self-conscious about research procedures, nonetheless he or she should be aware of the many sources of bias that may affect the final conclusions of a scientific report. The danger of becoming overly concerned is that the researcher may spend far too much time contemplating the difficulties of research, and, as a result, not get the job done.

The contention expressed here is that much of what is said about methods in social science represents *ideal* practices and is not always a good description of what *actually* is done. Much is not reported. The term *researcher affect* refers to *a process whereby the researcher, having fallen in love with a particular explanation for some relationship, or view of the world, may inadvertently engage in procedures which maximize the probability of producing evidence supporting the preferred view* . All stages of the research process have potential sources of bias: (1) selection of the problem, (2) research design, (3) data collection, (4) data analysis, (5) reporting of the findings, and (6) use of the findings.

1. Selection of the Problem

The issue in problem selection is that some phenomena are judged to be more important than others — some are judged as worthy of exploration, others not. Because of this, the choice of subject matter provides a clue as to the values held by the researcher. Within North American culture, researchers are more likely to study armed robbery than tree climbing. The former is viewed as a social problem, the latter is not. The researcher is likely to see robbery as a problem having negative consequences, and also as one which should be controlled or eliminated, if possible. On the other hand, a functionalist might argue that robbery is part of the economy of the underclass, a phenomenon which reinforces property norms and creates solidarity both within the underclass and the middle classes. The point is that not only does the choice of subject matter reflect values, but the researcher's theoretical predisposition may also influence the conclusions of the study as much as any data collected. Marxists come to Marxist conclusions, functionalists to functionalist ones.

It could be argued that the identification of the most effective variables for reducing robberies could be done without bias. But there is probably no value-free, culturally independent way of choosing variables for a study. The bias will usually be to choose those variables conventionally seen as important. Thus the bias will be to include the conventional and exclude the unconventional.

Research operates in a social context. The researcher is constrained by peers and granting agencies not to engage in "trivial" research but to tackle issues that are viewed as "important". It is naive to think that research is free of social constraint.

2. Research Design

Whether one opts for a survey, panel study, case study, or experimental design, there are potential sources of bias in the design itself. Choosing to survey attitudes toward capital punishment in communities containing maximum security prisons would probably produce conclusions showing favorable attitudes toward capital punishment. To pursue the example further, a researcher might do a case study of the attitudes about public issues held by police officers in a rural community. Once again, attitudes favoring capital punishment would probably be expressed. By choosing both a rural community and a police organization, it is more probable that attitudes would favor capital punishment than if the study were done in other areas or with other work groups in the country.

3. Data Collection

There is an extensive literature in Psychology dealing with the problem of the *experimenter effect* in data collection. Robert Rosenthal and K.L. Fode, for example, did a series of experiments in which students were asked to collect data on the number of trials needed for rats to learn a maze.[1] The students were informed that a new breed of laboratory rat was being developed which had been bred for intelligence; the observations were to see if, in fact, there was any difference between the specially bred "smart" rats and ordinary laboratory rats. And so the students set to work, running the two types of rats through the maze.

It turned out that, indeed, the "smart" rats took fewer trials to learn the maze than the "ordinary" ones. Apparently the breeding program was working. There was just one problem. Dr. Rosenthal did not have any smart rats. The rats were simply randomly assigned to the smart and the ordinary categories. It was the students who were the "real" subjects of this study. Somehow their expectations about the outcome of the trials had an impact on the results of the study. If the experimenter expected a rat to learn quickly, somehow the data turned out that way. Rosenthal's findings indicate that there is a tendency to produce findings consistent with expectations.

The explanation for the so-called experimenter effect has been more difficult to identify. Did the students "fudge" the data to please the professor? Did they perceive "errors" differently for the two groups, perhaps being less likely to note an error made by the "smart" rats? Did they handle the rats differently? The current view is that the result is due both to expectations which influence behaviour and slight, but systematic, observer recording errors.[2] No matter what the explanation, Rosenthal's research is of critical importance to the experimentalist as well as to the survey researcher.

Before a discussion of the implications of Rosenthal's research for the survey researcher is presented, one other illustration is useful. A German mathematics teacher had a horse with unusual talents.[3] The amazing horse, known as Clever Hans, could solve simple mathematical problems by stamping his foot to indicate his answer. At first, skeptics thought that Clever Hans' trainer was signalling the horse, thus accounting for the horse's unusual ability. However, it turned out that even when the trainer was removed from the room, the horse could still do the trick with other people posing the questions to the horse.

When the audience did not know the answer, or when the horse was blindfolded, Clever Hans' mathematical skills declined dramatically. Apparently he was watching the audience. If the answer was three, the audience would gaze intently at the hoof clumping out the answer; after three stomps, members of the audience would raise their heads slightly, focussing their gaze to the horse's head. The horse simply watched the audience — they cued him when to stop. Quite a smart horse. Not much at mathematics, but a good observer of body language.

How is Clever Hans relevant to the survey researcher? Or, for that matter, what can the survey researcher learn from Robert Rosenthal's experiments?

Suppose you are conducting an interview. And suppose you have just asked the respondent how often she goes to church. The respondent replies, "I don't go to church." You say, raising your eyebrows slightly, "Oh, so you don't go to church?" In all likelihood, your respondent now feels slightly uncomfortable — your eyebrow movement and your comment have communicated a message. Future responses to religious issues may well encourage the respondent to express more interest in religion than she actually has. Respondents are often interested in figuring out what the survey is "really" all about and will look for cues, and probably be influenced by them. If Clever Hans noted a slight raising of heads in the audience, it is probable that most human subjects will be sensitive to a raised eyebrow, a change in voice tone, or to a shift in the body position of the interviewer.

Given the issue of expectancy that Rosenthal has raised, the survey researcher should avoid specifying the hypotheses of the study to either the respondents or the interviewers. Sometimes it is difficult, however, to withhold such information from one's interviewers. As a researcher, you want to make the interviewers feel part of the study and therefore to know what it is "really" all about. However, if you tell the interviewers what the hypotheses are, they may well inadvertently bias results toward the hypothesis (if they are friendly) or away from the hypothesis (if they are hostile).

Questionnaires or interview guides may provide cues to the respondent and, unless one is careful, responses may be distorted in the direction the respondent thinks the researcher prefers. Such distortions are due to *demand characteristics*. This term refers to a situation where people respond in terms of how they think they are expected to respond. It is as though the researcher is demanding a given response.

During the data collection phase, a research director must ensure that when a selected respondent refuses to participate, or is unavailable, a replacement is selected on an equal probability basis (see Chapter 9). If this is not done, there is a danger that the data collection personnel will simply choose the most convenient replacement, and this will tend to bias the study toward those people who spend more time at home.

4. Data Analysis

Particularly in survey research, a great amount of information is collected on a large number of variables. This data may be treated in a variety of ways —many of which may be viewed as alternative modes of analysis. Frequently, the researcher will analyze the data in a number of different ways, discard those results which are "less interesting" and keep those which make the most sense. Frequently the data are played with until the form of analysis producing the strongest association is retained. Such procedures violate the principles of objectivity but are, nonetheless, practiced in all disciplines. Scientific studies have their rituals and a range of approved methods of analysis. Playing with the data seems to be done often, but is rarely reported in formal presentations of research.

Using the modern computer, it is now possible to test many different relationships. There may be four or five different measures of a concept (such as SES for example) available to the researcher in a data set; the various hypothesized relationships might be tested using each of these possibilities. Finally, the one most congruent with the researcher's expectations is reported. A rationale for throwing out some of the results is readily available in terms of there being "poor measurement" on that particular item. It is likely that many researchers have, from time to time, engaged in some "selective" use of data. If the researcher "hunts" through a data set long enough, an acceptable — even interesting — finding will surely emerge. At that point, the hunt stops.

In the physical and in the social sciences, "hunting" is common.[4] What student in a Chemistry or a Physics laboratory has not checked with other students to see what answer they got? If different results have been obtained, then the procedure is redone on the grounds that something must have been done wrong. In short, if anticipated results are not obtained, the results are discarded. Even the mature researcher has a tendency to work with the data until the "right" finding is obtained. The search for "reportable" findings is a continuous process in all sciences. Yet few papers acknowledge this search.

For the survey researcher there is a special problem. Given many variables and many observations, it is possible to run every variable against every other one in a search for "significant findings." On a chance basis, using the .05 level of significance (see Chapter 8), it is conceivable to expect that 1 in 20 relationships examined would prove to be statistically significant. Unless the researcher reports the "hunting" that has occurred, the reader of a report will be in no position to regard the conclusions with the skepticism they deserve.

Research is social behavior. There are expectations of others to be met, there are norms of behavior to be followed, and there are findings which are anticipated. This social component of science is frequently at odds with the fundamental canons of science.

Finally, it should be pointed out that there is nothing inherently wrong with "exploring" data or looking at relationships which have not been hypothesized. But such analyses cannot be reported unless it is made clear that no hypothesis has guided the search. At least then the reader has been cautioned.

5. Reporting of Findings

In 1959, T.D. Sterling published an interesting paper in which he suggested that much of what is being published in the learned journals may represent fluke results.[5] His argument is that there are a lot of researchers and many may be working on similar problems at any time. The fluke result study, which produces a statistically significant relationship, is the one which will be published (journals ordinarily do not publish papers reporting "no relationship" findings). While Sterling's point is an interesting one, it no doubt overstates the problem.[6] Nonetheless, the argument needs to be kept in mind as one possible source of bias in what is published.

Sterling's argument can be extended into another area. There is a selection process whereby certain findings are viewed as reportable, others not. Indeed, it is unusual for one's first analysis of the data to make it through to the final report.

The key issue is this: what scientific principle determines when analysis is finished? Do we stop analysis when we get a reportable, respectable finding? If we stop analysis when we get the results we like, the bias will be toward confirming expectations. While some of the data may be consistent with expectations, some may not be. Frequently, inconsistencies are not reported.

The difficulty is that some non-scientific considerations come into play when reports are written. Are the findings culturally acceptable? Are the findings acceptable to one's peers? Since there is pressure to keep papers reasonably short, only the "major" finding is reported: this "major" finding, however, may not be representative of the findings of the whole research project.

6. The Use of Findings

Given the enormous confidence western culture has in science, it is no surprise that the findings of science are powerful tools. Courts, politicians, and the general public respect science. Scientific evidence is taken seriously.

Unfortunately, the findings of research can be misused. The potential for bias in reviewing the research literature is that there are many findings reported, some supportive of a particular view, others not. Thus, if only evidence supporting one side is presented, the scientific picture is distorted. To illustrate this point, a distinction can be made between a *debater model* and a *science model* of research. While the distinction is being made for the social sciences, it would not be wholly inappropriate in other disciplines.

a. Debater Model. The social scientist who is committed to some social cause, or to a particular theoretical perspective, may well be tempted to conduct research and review available scientific literature to help support a particular position. Debaters seek evidence to support a particular viewpoint, and because of their quest to support, are less interested in contrary evidence. Much like a lawyer defending a particular view, they report only the supporting evidence.

The problem with using the debater approach is that many people may think that the findings are objective, impartial ones, and that they represent a dispassionate, scientific view. But in fact, the result is really a conclusion seeking corroborating evidence. Debaters enjoy the credibility of science without having to work within its rules.

b. Science Model. Researchers who follow the science model seek to disconfirm; seek to rule out alternatives; seek to continually press a theory hard, trying to discover the limits of its ability to explain outcomes. Those who attempt to follow this model are trying to eliminate as much bias as possible in their research. This aim may never be perfectly achieved. Science is imperfect, but always on a quest for verifiable knowledge.

Unfortunately, it is often difficult to know which research model has been used. From time to time, researchers probably exhibit characteristics of both models. The sad part is that while researchers attempt to trade on their credibility as "scientists" they frequently violate the fundamental principles of science, slipping inadvertently into a variety of advocacy roles.

7. Conclusion

Science is social behavior. Science as practiced is neither value-free nor wholly objective. If the actual practices are observed, a whole host of nonscientific factors enter the picture. While the achievements of science have, indeed, been impressive, it is nonetheless true that there is a gap between the *ideal* and *actual* practices of science. An awareness of this gap, and of the sources of bias in research, can only benefit the beginning research methods student. Just as the good scientist is portrayed as a skeptic, so should we be skeptical of science itself.

C. A PERSPECTIVE

Realizing that there are many difficulties in doing research should not lead the student to despair. The social sciences deal with extremely difficult subject matter. So difficult, in fact, that some would argue that scientific social science is impossible. However, all disciplines have their difficulties and their challenges. A major problem for the social scientist, beyond the inherent complexity of the subject matter itself, is that as a human being he or she is part of the subject matter. The subject matter is such that the researcher has to continually deal with strongly held beliefs not only about how society works but how it ought to work. A science of society is a challenge, indeed.

The challenge, in Emile Durkheim's view, in developing a scientific sociology, is to treat the social world similarly to the way in which the physical scientist treats his subject matter. A central theme in Durkheim's 1895 work, *The Rules of Sociological Method*, is that the patterns of behavior exhibited by human societies may be treated as *social facts*.[7] These facts can be reflected through statistics collected by the state or by other appropriate measures. The key issue, and what Durkheim demonstrates in *Suicide*, is that these facts could be treated like those facts examined by the physical scientist.[8] The argument is that the subject matter of sociology can be treated with objectivity, even though not with the precision achieved by the physical scientist.

1. General Rules for Minimizing Bias

In order to work toward a more scientific sociology, while recognizing that bias is a problem in all science, the following general rules are suggested for the survey researcher:

Rule 4.1 Be skeptical of all reported research findings given the many sources of bias which may have influenced the conclusions. A healthy, questioning attitude toward one's own findings and those of others is appropriate, particularly in those disciplines where there is so much room for interpretation.

Rule 4.2 In reviewing literature, try to distinguish between those conclusions which appear to be demonstrated logically and/or empirically from those which are speculative. To avoid bias is also to recognize it. One must distinguish those conclusions which appear to have some scientific basis from those which are speculative and have not been tested.

Rule 4.3 Try to identify those researchers who are taking an advocacy stance. By being able to identify those who are essentially mounting the evidence to support a position, whether on theoretical or public policy issues, one can recognize a debater model operating in contrast to a science model. There is nothing inherently wrong with advocacy, but it must be recognized that its conclusions are not science. Where it is clear that a case is being mounted, the question to ask is: "But, Sir, what experiment could *dis*prove the hypothesis?"[9]

Rule 4.4 Orient research to disconfirmation. When studies are designed to rule out alternatives, to disconfirm theories, then the researcher is on the road to minimizing bias.

Rule 4.5 Use theory as a guide, a tool for generating testable hypotheses. A theory should be regarded as an efficient summary of findings and as a tool for deriving predictions about relationships between variables. Theories are attempts to make general, summary statements and are to be continually revised. Theories are for testing, not supporting.

Rule 4.6 Contemplate your own values. Recognizing your own preferences for the kind of society you would like to live in will help to alert you to potential bias you bring to a research project. Being sensitive to your own biases enables you to design studies which are more value-neutral, not predisposing the results to favor your own personal preferences.

2. Specific Rules for Minimizing Bias

Besides the general rules presented above, the following specific rules are suggested which may help minimize bias.

Rule 4.7 Do not reveal hypotheses to respondents or interviewers. This rule appears to be the safest course to follow to reduce expectancy bias. It may, however, be necessary to provide some general idea of what the study is about, but it is best not to provide either interviewers or respondents with the details.

Rule 4.8 To avoid demand characteristics, word questions to range across an attitudinal continuum. Where possible, present a variety of views. This will give the respondent a sense that all responses are acceptable. Be certain to offer a full range of attitudinal response categories so that no respondent is always forced to the extreme of the continuum.

Rule 4.9 Interviewers must be trained to be accepting of all responses and to convey a neutral response to questions. The ideal here is to create an impression of neutrality but, at the same time, a real interest in the respondent's answers. Interviewers should avoid coaching responses.

Rule 4.10 Just as hypotheses must be specified in advance, so must the data analysis procedures. To avoid bias and to avoid playing with the data, analytical procedures must be specified in advance of data collection. While this may be viewed as a restrictive rule, if followed, it prevents unwarranted massaging of the data.

Rule 4.11 Report the number of relationships that have been explored in the course of data analysis. Researchers should clarify the number of relationships that have been examined, and the rationale behind why certain findings are not reported.

D. ETHICAL ISSUES

Just as there are worrying sources of bias at every stage of the research process, so too are there problematic ethical issues throughout. Survey researchers have obligations to their respondents (those who complete questionnaires), to themselves, to their discipline, and to society. It is important that survey researchers recognize their different roles and role obligations. What are the different expectations of scientist, of citizen, and of advocate?

The special difficulty for the social researcher is that as a citizen he or she is a *valuing* member of society. That is, as a member of society, the researcher holds certain values; views, for example, about how society ought to work. The researcher may find that as a citizen he or she may be opposed, for example, to locating a sanitary landfill site in a nearby area; as a "neutral, objective, impartial" researcher the conclusion may be that the proposed site location is a good one.

Cross-pressures may also emerge in designing surveys where the researcher is torn between what represents the "ideal" design for a scientific study, and what is "ethically possible" given that human subjects are being researched. That which is convenient for research may not be ethically acceptable.

The following ethical rules are presented as guidelines and are organized around two themes: (i) the researcher's ethical responsibility to respondents; and (ii) the survey researcher's responsibility to his/her discipline and society.

1. Ethical Issues in the Treatment of Respondents

Rule 4.12 The confidentiality of responses to a questionnaire is a sacred trust. Most surveys and interviews are completed on the understanding that individual responses, or information which would permit the identification of the individual, will never be released. Researchers have not only an ethical responsibility to preserve the anonymity of respondents, but have also a practical interest in doing so: our ability to collect accurate information would be impaired if there was a public perception that responses were not kept in confidence.

Where it is necessary to identify individual names with particular questionnaires (as in longitudinal panel studies, for example), this should be done with number codes, not names. A master list of names and identification numbers can then be stored separate from the questionnaires themselves. Such master lists should be destroyed after the study has been completed.

If data are released to other researchers, steps should be taken to mask the individual identities of respondents. This can be achieved by simply removing the highly specific identifiers such as area of residence, specific job, or employer identification.

Rule 4.13 Completing a questionnaire or interview should be a painless experience for the respondent. Researchers must not expose respondents to needlessly long questionnaires, or ask questions which pry unnecessarily into personal matters. This constraint does not mean that the researcher should not examine certain areas of social behavior, but rather that unless the researcher knows precisely how the responses will be analyzed, the information should not be collected. Moreover, the researcher should consider using alternate, or indirect indicators, for those variables which may offend respondents.

Rule 4.14 Identify sponsorship. There must be no deception concerning sponsorship of a project. Respondents must know who is doing the study. On this basis alone, they may choose not to participate in the study.

Rule 4.15 Disclose the basis on which the respondent has been selected. It is the right of the respondent to know how he or she was selected for participation in a study. Has selection been through a probability sampling procedure, or is selection based on special characteristics (membership in a particular organization, the job one has, or any other qualities)? The prospective respondent must be given a reasonable amount of information in order to decide if he/she wishes to participate.

Rule 4.16 No pressure should be placed on the respondent to cooperate in a study. Respondents must feel free to refuse participation, withdraw at any time, or to refuse to answer any particular question. Researchers must never pressure, cajole, or harass respondents in an effort to coax cooperation with the study. While it is appropriate to follow-up non-responses with a letter or phone call, these contacts should be information-seeking opportunities, providing prospective respondents with a chance to seek additional information. Follow-up contacts must never pressure respondents to participate in a study.

Rule 4.17 No hidden identification codes may be placed on questionnaires. Researchers may not use hidden codes on questionnaires to assist in the identification of those who have or have not returned questionnaires. Such codes are sometimes used to enable the researcher to find out who has not returned a questionnaire: these respondents may be sent another request. While such codes may save the researcher time and money, they are unethical. If individuals are to be identified, this information should be placed directly on the questionnaire itself.

Rule 4.18 Where an offer to provide a research report to respondents has been given, the promise must be fulfilled. The relation between researcher and respondent should be a reciprocal one. As a practical matter, it is to the advantage of the researcher to fulfill such obligations because to do so will encourage continued cooperation of respondents in long-term projects.

Where individuals are offered the opportunity of receiving a report on the study, a separate, stamped envelope and request form should be provided for the respondent. The separate return envelope not only keeps the respondent's name disassociated from the questionnaire, but also conveys to the respondent that confidentiality is taken seriously by the researcher.

Rule 4.19 Where appropriate and feasible, respondents should be paid a fee for their participation. While there may be no ethical responsibility to pay respondents who volunteer their cooperation, such payments are to be encouraged to reinforce the idea of a reciprocal contract between researcher and respondent.

Rule 4.20 Informed consent is required. In dealing with competent adults, participation should be based on informed consent — that is, the potential respondent must be informed as to the nature of the study.

Where surveys are done involving children, the infirm, or incompetent adults, the organization or individual responsible for the prospective respondent should provide consent in writing.

2. Ethics and the Survey Researcher

The survey researcher has two special difficulties, not experienced to the same degree by researchers in other areas: (i) the researcher has frequently a theoretical and practical "vested interest" in the outcome of a study; and (ii) the social scientist typically works with a large number of indicators, providing many opportunities for alternate interpretations. Given the difficulties involved in replicating surveys, more than in other areas, we simply have to trust the findings reported by the survey researcher. This situation places an even greater ethical responsibility on the survey researcher to conduct unbiased studies.

Rule 4.21 Do not work on projects that set out to prove a point. Given the legitimacy of science in western culture, it should be no surprise that both scientists and non-scientists will be tempted to use this legitimacy to achieve personal or group goals. Evidence which is viewed as *scientific* carries a lot of weight in argument, hence, when a presentation is being prepared, collecting or referring to scientific evidence is tempting and sensible.

If you are hired to "develop a scientific case for..." then you have an ethical problem. You are, in this case, being asked to make others believe you have scientific evidence for some position. Such research should not be represented as science: to do so would be unethical.

Rule 4.22 Do not hunt through data looking for pleasing findings. The surest way to misrepresentation is to search for support for your own views. To do so would constitute bad science and unethical behavior. If data are being scanned for *interesting* findings, these cannot be reported unless the process by which they have emerged is made absolutely clear.

Rule 4.23 Be aware of potential sources of bias. Awareness of sources of bias may help you avoid them and will help you to spot bias in others' research reports. The researcher has an ethical responsibility to report fairly, attempting to avoid as much bias as possible.

Rule 4.24 Represent scientific literature fairly. For both ethical and scientific reasons one must attempt to accurately portray the body of literature in one's area of research. To selectively report findings is not acceptable.

Rule 4.25 Do the best research you can. Research must strive to be competent, impartial, and its results must be reported objectively. Use qualified personnel and consultants. Keep up with developments in your field and use the best techniques of data collection and analysis. Seek always to do the best research you can; do it with care.

Rule 4.26 Engage in research that will benefit society. The researcher should avoid trivial research and instead focus attention on those issues which may ultimately benefit society.

Rule 4.27 Acknowledge persons who have played a role in the research and acknowledge all literature sources which have directly influenced the study. All people who have assisted in the project should be acknowledged by way of a footnote. Similarly, where literature has been used in developing the project, each source should be cited.

Rule 4.28 If ethical issues arise, seek the advice of appropriate professional bodies or institutions involved in the project. Most surveys will not pose difficult ethical issues. However, where the research team identifies an ethical dilemma, outside consultations are appropriate. Such consultations would assess the benefits to society as against the costs that bending ethical guidelines may involve. Before any study begins, all such ethical dilemmas should be resolved by appropriate adjustments to the project.[10]

Two codes of ethics are included in Appendix E (Canadian Sociology and Anthropology Association) and Appendix F (American Sociological Association). The applicable code should be examined as each provides guidelines for the researcher.

E. EXERCISES

1. What is meant by "researcher affect" and how might it influence the conclusions to a study?

2. What are the fundamental differences between a debater model and a science model of research? What cues might be used to alert the student as to the type of research being encountered?

3. If you were designing a survey dealing with the sexual behavior of university students, what would you see as the major ethical problems? What steps would you recommend be taken before data collection begins?

4. Examine one of the ethics codes included in the Appendices. What additional rules would you think appropriate for social researchers to follow?

NOTES

[1] Robert Rosenthal and K.L. Fode, "The Effect of Experimenter Bias on the Performance of the Albino Rat." *Behavioral Science*, 1963, 8, pp. 183-89.

[2] Ronald W. Johnson and John G. Adair, "The Effects of Systematic Recording Error vs. Experimenter Bias on Latency of Word Association." *Journal of Experimental Research in Personality*, 1970, 4, pp. 270-75.

[3] For a discussion of Clever Hans and the role of expectancy in research see Robert Rosenthal, *Experimenter Effects in Behavioral Research*. New York: Century Books, 1966.

[4] Hanan C. Selvin and Alan Stuart, "Data Dredging Procedures in Survey Analysis." *Journal of the American Statistical Association*, 61 (June, 1966), pp.20-23. Reprinted in Dennis P. Forcese and Stephen Richer (eds.), *Stages of Social Research: Contemporary Perspectives*. Englewood Cliffs, New Jersey: Prentice-Hall Inc., 1970, pp. 326-32.

[5] T.D. Sterling, "Publication Decisions and Their Possible Effects on Inferences Drawn from Tests of Significance — or Vice Versa." *Journal of the American Statistical Association*, 1959, 54, pp. 30-34.

[6] A method for resolving the question (a systematic reporting of all findings and then locating a particular finding within the distribution of all findings on the particular relationship) has been suggested by Robert Rosenthal, "The 'File Drawer Problem' and Tolerance for Null Results." *Psychological Bulletin*, 1979, Vol. 86, No. 3, pp. 638-41.

[7] Emile Durkheim, *The Rules of Sociological Method*. New York: The Free Press, 1938. [Originally published in 1895]

[8] Emile Durkheim, *Suicide: A Study of Sociology.* Translated by J. Spaulding and G. Simpson. New York: The Free Press, 1951. [Originally published in 1897.]

[9] John R. Platt, "Strong Inference," *Science*, 1964, Vol. 146, Number 3642, p. 352.

[10] See the discussion, "Ethical Concerns in Social Science Research," in David Nachmias and Chava Nachmias, *Research Methods in the Social Sciences*, Second Edition. New York: St. Martin's Press, 1981. See also Paul Davidson Reynolds, *Ethics and Social Science Research*. Englewood Cliffs, New Jersey: Prentice-Hall Inc., 1982.

PART TWO

GETTING STARTED

CHAPTER FIVE

GETTING
THE PROJECT STARTED

Getting started is sometimes the most difficult part of a project. But care taken during the beginning stages will pay off. A carefully designed study that enables the researcher to come to conclusions about a dependent variable, includes some theory testing dimensions, and is informed by the existing literature, will provide the basis for an excellent project.

A. CHOOSING
A PROBLEM, A DESIGN, AND VARIABLES

An enormous variety of topics can be studied using survey techniques. To provide some sense of the range of topics which can be treated, a list of some projects carried out by students is given in Figure 5.1.

Figure 5.1 Some Student Projects

Territorial Invasions Among Students
Summer Employment and Economic Need
Community Size and Prejudice Level
Territorial Imperatives: the Elevator
Religiosity and Morality
Conformity Among University Students
Status Crystallization and its Application to Nurses, CNAs, Orderlies, and Aides
Professor-Student Exchange Relations
Energy Crisis: Attitudes and Concerns

Errors in the Self-Administration of Drugs
Desired Family Size
Factors Contributing to Alcohol Consumption
Cigarette Smoking: Patterns of High School and University
    Students Use
Religious Participation at Two Universities
Attitudes Toward Campus Medical Facilities
Residence Satisfaction: A Comparison of Two Residences
Factors Influencing Academic Achievement
Social Class and Educational Aspirations of Female Students
Spatial Invasion as a Function of Interaction Intensity
The Effect of Threat Upon Distance in an Interacting Dyad
University Students and Involvement in Voluntary Associations
Attitudes Toward Women and Faculty
Classroom Seating Location and Grade Performance
Satisfaction with the Nursing Program
Dress and Day of the Week
Patterns of Soap Opera Viewing
Attitudes Toward Separation of Quebec from Canada
Patterns of Superstitions
Survey of University Graduates
Pre-marital Sexual Patterns
Academic Performance and On- or Off-Campus Residence
Attitudes Toward Open Housing
Factors Influencing Liberalism
Grade Performance: What Causes Variation?
Factors Influencing Mother's Satisfaction with Birth Experience
Weight Gain Among Female University Students
Attitudes Toward the Police
Factors Influencing Program Selection Among Females Enrolled in
    Nursing and Physical Education Programs
Leadership Among University and Hospital Trained Nursing Students
Attitudes Toward Abortion, Euthanasia, and In Vitro Fertilization
Relative Status of University Departments
Attitudes Toward Campus Police
Class Attendance and Grade Performance
Factors Influencing Professional versus Traditional Career Orientations
Participation and Self Esteem
Effects of Contact and Attitudes Toward the Handicapped
Attitudes Toward Capital Punishment
High School Students' Attitudes Toward Alcohol Consumption
Attitudes Toward Abortion
Relation Between Sexual Knowledge and Sexual Behavior
Retirement and Life Satisfaction: A Study of Senior Citizens in Small
    Town Nova Scotia
Attitudes Toward Pre-marital Sex Among High School Students
Attitudes Toward the Elderly
Drug Use Among First Year University Students
Contraception Use: A Study of Female University Students
Factors Influencing Social Adjustment and Academic Achievement
Attitudes of Nurses Toward Student Nurses
Delinquent Compared to Non-delinquent Females
Attitudes Toward Sex Roles

Figure 5.1   (Continued)

An Analytical Comparison of Attitudes Toward Capital Punishment and
   Abortion
Choice of Non-traditional University Programs by Females
Wage Discrimination: Comparing Salaries of Male and Female
   Professors
Attitudes Toward the Male Nurse
Male Attitudes Toward Homosexuality
Factors Influencing Addictive Behavior
Fertility Expectations and Intended Labor Force Participation of Nursing
   Students
Factors Influencing Expected Age of Marriage
Attitudes Toward Primary Care Nursing
Comparing the Occupational Aspirations of High School Students in
   Antigonish and Dartmouth
Factors Influencing Maternal Confidence
Attitudes Toward Euthanasia
Suicidal Thought Among University Students
Attitudes Toward Homosexuality
Traditional and Non-traditional Program Choices
A Survey of Nursing Graduates of the Eighties
Liberal Attitudes Toward Pre-marital Sex
Shifts Between Freshmen and Seniors' Perceived Role of the Nurse

1. Choosing a Problem

The single most important consideration in choosing the topic for research
is genuine interest. Surveys involve considerable effort and it is especially
important for the first-time researcher to have a keen interest in the topic.

a. Current Issue. One method of selecting a problem is to choose one
which is the subject of public debate. Such topics might include capital
punishment, abortion, free trade, Japanese imports, unionization, poverty,
or the popularity of a political leader.

b. Variation in a Dependent Variable. Another method is to simply try
to understand variations in some dependent variable. What factors influence
grade performance? What influences the popularity of a teacher? What variables influence the choice of a non-traditional program among female students? The effort is directed toward understanding the causal factors
associated with variations in some phenomenon.

c. Testing a Theory. Those researchers who have theoretical inclina-
tions may wish to test a current theory of human behavior. The issue is to
examine a relationship between variables which is predicted by a theory but
which, at the same time, is not obvious in common sense terms. The most

convincing theory testing projects will be those that make a counterintuitive (against common sense) prediction which, if it turns out to be true, will be a convincing demonstration of the theory.

d. Testing Partial Theories. A review of the literature may reveal a consistent relationship between a set of variables, but alternative explanations for this relationship may not have been carefully tested. In such cases, it is reasonable to propose alternative explanations for the relationship, design a study, and then test which, if any, of the explanations best account for the relationship.

e. Applied Research. Another source for projects is to look at an "applied" problem. Perhaps through research, a specific social problem will be better understood, or even resolved. The applied researcher will often be asked to investigate social behavior issues. In the case of applied research, the problem has been provided by a sponsor. The researcher must decide, if the project is ethically acceptable (and the fee is right!), how to do the project. The applied researcher might be asked to figure out how to attract more students into a university program, or to describe the public's attitude toward some current issue.

f. Replication Study. Finally, one can choose to replicate, or repeat, some earlier study. But even if a replication is attempted, the researcher should attempt to add a new dimension to the study — try to answer some question left open in the previous project.

2. Determining the Precise Questions

Having selected the general area of research, the next step will be to articulate precisely what you wish to investigate. To illustrate the point further, suppose you wished to do a project on capital punishment. As you start to think about it, are you interested in:

a. describing public attitudes toward capital punishment;

b. the types of people who support capital punishment versus those who don't;

c. the relationship between other social attitudes (poverty, abortion, people in authority) and capital punishment;

d. whether there is a difference between the sexes in their support for capital punishment.

e. if women are less inclined toward capital punishment, what accounts for this tendency?

The list of dimensions concerning capital punishment needs to be extended. But as this short list suggests, once a problem has been selected, the work of pinning down the precise questions begins. Only after the problem has been discussed for some time do the particular dimensions emerge. It is at this point that a thorough review of the literature should be undertaken to find out what other researchers have discovered. The review will also help the researcher state, with greater precision, exactly what is to be investigated.

3. Reviewing the Literature

In reviewing the literature, you are trying to get a sense of the state of scientific knowledge about the topic. The first question is "Where do I start?"

> **a.** If you are part of a university, *ask instructors* who work in the area for any ideas they might have on where to get information.
>
> **b.** Check with a *Reference Librarian* for sources which may lead you to research done on your topic.
>
> **c.** Check *textbooks* for a lead.
>
> **d.** Check the appropriate discipline's *Abstracts* which provide brief descriptions of published papers dealing with a variety of topics. (Available in university libraries.)
>
> **e.** Check *journals* likely to publish work in the area. It is advisable to begin by checking through the most recent indexes; once you have found some articles that are somewhat close to your topic, check for references to other articles.
>
> **f.** You may not be able to find published results on the specific relationship, or category of individuals, you wish to study. If this is the case, focus on what *variables have been found to be related to the major dependent variable* you are proposing to examine.
>
> **g.** In some cases, it may also be appropriate to review research which uses *similar methodologies or theories.*

The goals of a review include: (i) identifying areas where there seems to be consensus among researchers and where there are inconsistencies in the findings; (ii) identifying variables others have found to be relevant to the problem at hand; (iii) identifying areas which, if explored, could lead to important new understandings of the phenomenon under examination; (iv) seeing how other researchers have made connections to theory;

and, (v) seeing how other researchers have measured variables and analyzed data.

Generally, when reviews are presented in a report they should try to summarize briefly the areas of agreement and disagreement in the literature. Article summaries may be useful to the researcher but are not generally appropriate in a final report. What is required is a sense of what the state of knowledge is on the topic under investigation.

Rule 5.1 Be certain to record the full bibliographic details of each article or book used. When the final report is being prepared, all the sources will be cited in the bibliography. If you have not recorded this information in full, you will have to retrace your steps to recover the information.

4. Choosing a Design

Many factors influence design selection. Some of these are dictated by the nature of the question being asked; some are pragmatic considerations, such as the amount of time available, or the kind of respondents available to the researcher. The researcher should begin by determining if the proposed research is primarily (i) a *descriptive study* (trying to estimate a larger population's characteristics from a sample); or (ii) an *explanatory study,* where relationships among variables are examined and there is less concern about extrapolating to some larger population. If the study is largely descriptive, then the design will need to ensure that all segments in the population have a known chance of inclusion in the study. On the other hand, explanatory studies, such as those testing alternative explanations or theoretically derived hypotheses, may be able to use quota or convenience sampling procedures. (See Chapter 8 on sampling techniques.) An exception to this, of course, would be those situations where a descriptive prediction is derived from the theory, such as Durkheim's prediction that the suicide rate in Spain will be low.

Assuming that the general design of the study involves a survey, the choice between personal interviews, phone interviews, mailed questionnaires, or questionnaires administered in a group setting can be determined by considering: (i) the nature of the sampling required; (ii) the type of information required (if the questions are many and complex, phone interviews will not work well); and (iii) if random sampling is required, then group administered questionnaires are probably inappropriate since they would ordinarily be of unequal probability in nature.

5. Choosing Variables

Variables may be identified by: (i) reviewing the research literature and identifying the variables other researchers have used in doing similar research; (ii) applying relevant theoretical models and identifying the variables implied by the theories; (iii) examining questionnaires for ideas about what variables should be measured; (iv) developing causal models and figuring out what *sources of spuriousness, intervening,* or *conditional variables* may be relevant for the project; and (v) simply thinking about what variables may influence the dependent variable.

At the beginning stages, the researcher should not worry too much about whether the identified variables can be measured. The relevant variables should simply be identified.

B. DEVELOPING CAUSAL MODELS

Clarity and precision are central to successful research. One way to force accuracy is to draw a picture or diagram of the causal connections proposed between variables. This section begins with a discussion of the simplest models and gradually moves toward the more complex ones. Common to all the models is the fact that each can be represented by a diagram; each shows causal direction; and each shows a picture of a hypothesis, or set of hypotheses. Procedures for analyzing these models are presented in Chapters 11 and 12.

1. Two Variable Models

In Chapter 1, the distinction between a dependent and independent variable was made: the dependent variable is the "effect" or the result of the influence of an independent variable. By convention, the dependent variable is referred to as the Y variable; the independent variable is known as the X variable. A simple way to describe the relationship is with a diagram:

$$> \quad \boxed{X} \longrightarrow > \quad \boxed{Y}$$

What does the diagram tell us? First, it describes a relationship between two variables known as X and Y. Note that there is an arrow pointing from X to Y: this tells us that X is the independent variable, Y the dependent one. The hypothesis reflected in this diagram argues that X influences Y. Next, note the > symbol before the X box. This symbol means "the greater;" the opposite symbol, <, means "the less." Putting it all together the hypothesis can be stated as: *The greater X, the greater Y.* An inverse relationship is expressed by reversing the second symbol. In that case, the hypothesis would be stated as: *The greater X, the less Y.* If X and Y are replaced by variable names such as participation and self-esteem, the following relationship would result: *"The greater the participation in social activities, the greater the self-esteem."*[1] The wording of the hypothesis indicates that participation is the independent variable, self-esteem the dependent one.

The advantage of drawing a diagram to represent the relationship is that the researcher is forced to indicate causal direction, and whether the relationship is inverse or direct. Drawing a picture forces precision.

There may be times when a problem cannot be formulated such that the researcher is able to say whether the relation is direct or inverse. In such cases, the researcher cannot speak in "greater than," "less than" terms. Where the nature of the relationship cannot be specified, a question mark ('?') is used to indicate that no prediction is being made.

Frequently, the researcher will not be in a position to set out a causal order: a situation can occur where variables exist together at the same point in time, and where the variables could be argued to be influencing each other. In this event, *reciprocal causation* can be indicated by placing arrows at each end of the line linking the two variables.

2. Three Variable Models

Now let us turn our attention to various three variable models. Besides independent and dependent variables, there are two additional types of variables: intervening and source of spuriousness variables.

An *intervening variable model* considers one or more variables which link X and Y. The goal is to understand the mechanism by which X is connected to Y. Frequently the researcher will be testing a number of alternative explanations for how X influences Y. In the case of one intervening variable, the relationship could be diagrammed as follows:

> ⟩ | X | ⟶ ⟩ | I | ⟶ ⟩ | Y |

In this diagram, I is the intervening variable. The hypothesis is that variations in X cause variations in I, which, in turn, influences Y. Typically, one would propose a number of possible intervening variables, so the following diagram would be more appropriate:

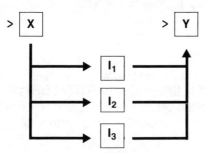

Here, three alternative explanations are suggested for the connection between X and Y. The researcher would collect data measuring each of the variables involved and then conduct the appropriate statistical tests to determine, which, if any, of the proposed alternative explanations or intervening variables explain the connection between X and Y. These matters will be further examined in Chapter 12.

The next major type of causal model is the *source of spuriousness* model. Here the researcher proposes that while there is a statistically significant relation between the variables X and Y, this relationship may be a non-causal one, only existing because some third variable is influencing both X and Y. The argument is that the only reason X and Y are related to one another is because of this third factor. Frequently, having observed a statistically significant relation, the researcher will want to ensure that the relationship is not spurious and therefore will run a number of spuriousness checks. The source of spuriousness model may be diagrammed as follows:

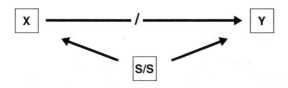

The statistical technique for examining such relations is examined in Chapter 12.

3. Multivariate Candidate Variable Models

Another model which may be used is a *candidate variable* model. Here the researcher proposes a number of independent variables which may be influencing the dependent variable Y. Such a model may be diagrammed as follows:

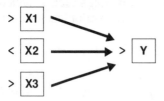

The variables X1, X2, and X3 are viewed as potential causes of variations in the dependent variable Y. Ideally, these variables will be at the same "level of analysis," and will be related to the dependent variable either one at a time, or simultaneously through procedures outlined in Chapter 12.

C. SPECIFYING HYPOTHESES AND PROCEDURES OF ANALYSIS

Having developed diagrams for the various relationships to be investigated, the researcher must now formally state the hypotheses of the study and specify how the analyses of the data will be done. The reason hypotheses and proposed methods of analysis are specified in advance is to ensure: (1) that the researcher is not inventing hypotheses after data have been analyzed; and (2) that data are not manipulated until they conform to expectations.

1. Stating Hypotheses

Frequently, good diagrams can replace formal hypotheses statements. Particularly in *candidate variable models*, which include a large number of variables, it is easier to diagram the hypotheses than to present each one individually. Similarly, where many alternative explanations are being tested for a particular relationship, a good diagram clearly shows the causal model and the implied research hypotheses.

In theory testing projects, it is important not only to state the derived hypotheses, but also to indicate the various steps that were taken in making the derivation(s). Only to the extent that such derivations can be traced, can one claim to have tested a theory.

2. Specifying Methods of Analysis

Specifying methods of analysis in advance forces the researcher to commit to particular procedures. The selection of these procedures will also determine how the variables will be measured. Thus if contingency tables (see Table 7.1 for an example of such a table) are to be used exclusively, it will not be necessary to achieve ratio level measurement on the variables. Although it is probably unreasonable to require a researcher to specify "cut-points" for contingency tables, it is reasonable to indicate the number of categories to be used and the principle used in making the cut-points. (Perhaps splitting the sample into thirds, or at the mid-point. See Rule 4.10, Chapter 4.)

D. ISSUES IN DEVELOPING MEASURES FOR VARIABLES

Information may be collected in a variety of ways: from unobtrusively observing people and recording their behavior, to getting information on behavior from public statistics, to observing people who are part of experiments, and through having individuals complete questionnaires or undergo telephone or personal interviews. But whatever the method of data collection, the researcher is attempting to measure variables.

1. Theoretical, Conceptual, and Operational Levels

Figure 5.2 presents the levels of a research project. As one moves down the figure, one progresses from the general to the specific: this is movement from the theoretical to the operational. At the *theoretical* level there are a number of interconnected propositions, assumptions, and statements of relationship between concepts. By employing axiomatic derivations and replacement of terms (see Chapter 2), it is possible to derive *conceptual* hypotheses. Such hypotheses may also be identified by reviewing the research literature, or from brilliant flashes of insight. A conceptual hypothesis is a statement of relationship between concepts. For example, *the greater the participation in campus life, the higher the self-esteem*. At this stage the researcher would proceed to the *operational* level, deciding how each of the concepts would be measured, and what procedures would be used to collect and to analyze the information.

Figure 5.2   Levels in Research Design

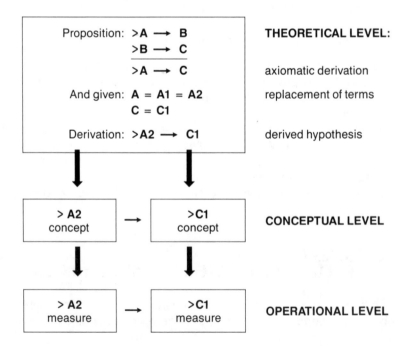

	THEORETICAL LEVEL:
Proposition: >A ⟶ B >B ⟶ C >A ⟶ C	axiomatic derivation
And given: A = A1 = A2 C = C1	replacement of terms
Derivation: >A2 ⟶ C1	derived hypothesis
> A2 concept ⟶ >C1 concept	CONCEPTUAL LEVEL
> A2 measure ⟶ >C1 measure	OPERATIONAL LEVEL

Measurement refers to the way in which numbers are assigned so as to reflect, or indicate, concepts. A concept is an idea which refers to a characteristic of an individual, of a group, or of a nation. Concepts help us to organize our thinking about the world. Sociologists use such concepts as socio-economic status, alienation, job satisfaction, organizational effectiveness, age, gender, poverty, and status consistency. There are hundreds of such concepts. The researcher must precisely define what is meant by each concept used. Precise definitions make clear what is included in the concept and also provide a guide to how the concept should be measured. The operational level of research refers both to those indicators used to reflect the concepts and to the procedures for collecting and analyzing data. Measurement, in essence, refers to the linkage between the *conceptual* and the *operational* levels. There are two key issues in this linkage: validity and reliability.

2. Validity

In Chapter 1, validity was defined as the *extent that a measure reflects the concept, reflecting nothing more or nothing less than that implied by the conceptual definition*. The validity issue has to do, then, with the congruence of concept and indicator. To illustrate, let us examine one possible conceptual definition of socio-economic status. If SES is defined as a "hierarchical continuum of respect and prestige," and we then choose to operationalize the concept by measuring each individual's annual salary, we will most certainly have problems convincing others about the validity of our measure.

On inspection, it becomes clear that annual salary would not adequately reflect an individual's place on a respect and prestige continuum. (Such inspections are generally referred to as *face validity*.) Among the reasons to doubt the validity of the proposed measures are: (i) the image of the local drug dealer who makes a fortune but enjoys little respect in the community; (ii) the best poker player in town who always seems to have lots of money, takes expensive trips, and is admired for his worldliness even though his salary at the legion hall is little above the minimum wage; (iii) the Protestant minister who is looked up to by almost everyone but his salary is a pittance; and (iv) Mrs. Bell Corden, the widow of good Dr. Corden who served the community with dedication for many years and who left his wife a substantial estate, and although she has no salary, she, along with the owner of the hardware store, probably has the most prestige in the community. The problem is that salary does not capture the concept adequately, and even if a measure of annual income rather than salary could be obtained, there would still not be a valid measure of the concept as defined.

Clearly, a definition of socio-economic status which stresses respect and prestige begs for a measure that would consider the extent to which different members of the community are looked up to. Perhaps a panel of community informants could estimate the relative prestige of known members of the community. Indeed, one might wish to examine the extent to which income and education are causally related to variation in prestige and then treat these as independent variables.

Ideally, in choosing indicators one should attempt to reflect the concept itself. The researcher should not select causes, consequences, or correlates of the variable. Given that important causes of variation in prestige may include annual income, one must not simply measure prestige by income. To do so would be to choose a correlate. Similarly, to measure the prestige of Mrs. Bell Corden by the success of her children would be to look at a consequence of her position and may not adequately reflect the prestige itself. Again it may correlate with it, but not reflect it adequately. Validity is controversial within the discipline of sociology. David Heise and George Bohrnstedt have argued that:

> "... validity is defined as the correlation between a measure and the true underlying variable. A high validity coefficient does not imply that one has measured that which he set out to measure. It means only that whatever the items are measuring, the composite constructed is highly correlated to it."[2]

It is not always feasible to get a direct measure of the concept and the researcher may therefore be forced to use indicators that are causes or consequences of it. But, in developing measures for an independent variable, the researcher must be careful to ensure that it is indeed independent of the measures used to reflect the dependent variable. If care is not taken, the result may be two different measures of the same phenomenon.

Figure 5.3 represents a way of thinking about validity. Diagram A shows a relationship between concept and indicator where the indicator misses the concept entirely; Diagram B shows the indicator reflecting part of the concept, but other things as well; Diagram C shows a situation where the indicator reflects part of the concept but not all of it; finally Diagram D represents perfect validity — the indicator reflects the concept, nothing more and nothing less.

While techniques for assessing the validity of measures are beyond the scope of this book, minimally the beginning survey researcher should be convinced that selected measures have face validity. Researchers use the term *criterion validity* to refer to the extent to which a measure is able to predict accurately. Thus, if one were attempting to develop a measure to predict success in university studies, one could then assess the validity of one's measure by correlating the measure with the grades achieved in university. A high correlation would indicate high criterion validity. Moreover, if a theoretically derived hypothesis turns out as predicted, this would constitute one piece of evidence for the validity of the measures. This latter type of validity is known as *construct validity*. Another way to think about construct validity is that it is based on inductive evidence. If one finds evidence to support one's theoretically derived hypothesis, then one's measures have construct validity.

Figure 5.3   Problems With Validity

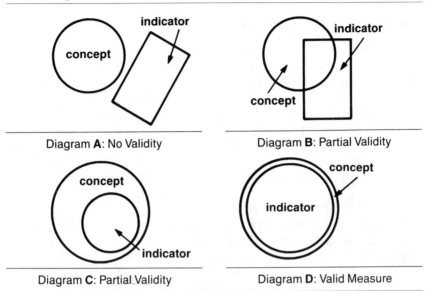

Diagram **A**: No Validity   Diagram **B**: Partial Validity

Diagram **C**: Partial Validity   Diagram **D**: Valid Measure

3. Reliability

In Chapter 1, reliability was defined as the *extent to which, on repeated measures, an indicator will yield similar readings.*

There are both simple and complex ways to test for reliability in a survey. Perhaps the easiest is to repeat a question that has already been posed. The idea of a *retest* procedure is that if the same question is posed twice, and the respondent is understanding the item the same way both times, then the two responses should be the same. A second simple, though not often feasible approach, is to independently verify the answers. Occasionally, for example, it may be possible to compare a student's self-reported grade to that "actually" received by the student. The issue is the extent to which students systematically over- or under-report grades.

Social scientists frequently combine several indicators to form an index. When one is assessing the reliability of the items being used to construct an index, one can randomly split the items into two groups, compute the indexes, and then correlate the resulting scores. Internal reliability would be indicated by a high correlation. This method is known as a *split-half* method for testing reliability. Another procedure is to compare an individual item's correlation to the total index score: if an item is consistent with the total score, it will correlate with it. This technique, known as the *internal consistency* approach to reliability, will be described when index construction is discussed. (See Chapter 11, section D.)

Whatever indicators are used, the effort is to reflect the concept precisely and, at the same time, reflect the reality being described.

4. Levels of Measurement

For the researcher designing a questionnaire, an understanding of levels of measurement is necessary since later analysis will be constrained by the nature of the measurement achieved in data collection. As a general rule, the most precise measurement possible should be achieved.

One way to begin to understand levels of measurement is to ask if the variable being measured has an underlying continuum (does it vary from low to high?). If the variable has an underlying continuum, then the level of measurement will be either ordinal, or ratio; if there is no underlying continuum, then the measurement will be at the nominal level.[3]

a. Nominal Measurement. Religious affiliation, by its nature, is a nominal variable. While there may be underlying continua related to religious affiliation (such as degree of religious commitment, or frequency of church attendance), by itself, the religious organization one belongs to is nominal; it may be Baptist, Lutheran, Roman Catholic, or Jewish. Whether the researcher asks the respondent to check which (if any) religious organizations he or she was associated with while growing up, or whether the respondent fills in a blank indicating religious affiliation, the measurement level attained is nominal. One category is neither higher or lower than any other — they are simply different categories. *Nominal Measurement* involves no underlying continuum and the numeric values assigned are arbitrary and have no arithmetic meaning. Other examples of nominal variables include program of study, gender, and ethnic origin.

b. Ordinal Measurement. Ordinal measurement involves an underlying continuum but the numeric values assigned are ordered so that low numbers mean a lower level on the continuum than high numbers; however, the distances between the assigned numbers and the underlying continuum are not in a one-to-one relation. For example, suppose a statement like the following is presented to respondents:

The United Nations keeps the world safe.
Strongly Disagree 1 2 3 4 5 6 7 8 9 Strongly Agree

This kind of item provides ordinal measurement. While we know that high numbers indicate greater agreement with the statement, we do not know that the distances between the values are equal: we do not know, for example, if the distance between 4 and 5 on the scale is of the same magnitude as between 8 and 9. Ordinal measurement *orders* values but does not assure equal gaps between the measurement points.

c. Ratio Measurement. Finally, there is ratio measurement. In the case of income, for example, the nature of the variable is such that it is possible to represent income with a number that exactly reflects the income of a person. In this case, it is also possible to use zero to reflect no income and other numeric values to reflect all others. With ratio measurement it is correct to say that an income of $50 000 is twice as much as $25 000. It is possible to add and subtract constants as well as to multiply or divide by them, without changing the proportionality among the values. Where communities are being studied, measures such as the proportion non-white, proportion of retired people in the population, and various rates and ratios (suicide rate, dependency ratio, sex ratio) all constitute ratio level measurements.

5. Measurement Error

Any time measurements are taken, there will be error. Measurement should be seen as a matter of probability: of being confident that most of the time the measures will be within a given margin of error. This implies that some of the time they will not be. There are two types of error: random and nonrandom. *Random* error is fluctuation around the "true" value, where higher or lower scores are equally likely; *nonrandom error* represents a systematic under- or overestimation of the value.[4] The survey researcher encounters both types of measurement error. In our culture, one might speculate, for example, that teenage males will over-estimate their weights (nonrandom error); teenage females, however, may slightly underestimate their weights (nonrandom error) but will probably show less variability in their estimates of their weight (random error). Researchers attempt to estimate the amount of error that is likely in their measurements. The specific procedures for doing this will be explained in Chapter 9.

E. EXERCISES

1. From a current issue, identify some relationship, or set of relationships, relevant to the issue, and draw a diagram(s) indicating the proposed relationships to be tested.

2. Choose a dependent variable that is of interest to you, and draw a diagram showing what variables may be influencing variations in the dependent variable.

3. Drawing on propositions of a social theory, derive a testable hypothesis and draw a diagram of the proposed relationship. You may combine

axiomatic and replacement of terms approaches in your derivations. Try for a counterintuitive prediction.

4. Propose and diagram a series of at least three alternative explanations for a proposed relationship.

5. Choose some "applied" problem and diagram relationships that you would explore to solve the problem.

6. Diagram the relationship(s) that would be explored if you were to replicate an existing study. Indicate and diagram one additional relationship you would explore in the replication.

7. Would it be possible to have a valid measure which is not reliable? Could you have a reliable measure which is not valid?

8. Discuss sources of random and nonrandom measurement error in survey designs. To what extent are such errors due to: (i) different perceptions of the question being posed; (ii) differences in image management? Is image management more likely to lead to random or nonrandom errors?

NOTES

[1] Andrea Brennan, "Participation and Self-Esteem: A Test of Six Alternative Explanations," *Adolescence*, Vol. 20, No. 78, Summer, 1985, pp. 445-66.

[2] David R. Heise and George W. Bohrnstedt, "Validity, Invalidity, and Reliability," in Edgar F. Borgatta and George W. Bohrnstedt, *Sociological Methodology 1970*. San Francisco: Jossey-Bass, Inc., Publishers, 1970, p. 123. Also see G.W. Bohrnstedt, "A Quick Method for Determining the Reliability and Validity of Multiple-Item Scales," *American Sociological Review*, 34, pp. 542-48.

[3] The conventional *equal interval* level of measurement is not presented here for the sake of simplicity: there are few variables measured at this level which are not ratio level. Most texts in the social sciences seem to use temperature as an example of equal interval measures. The distinction therefore may be left for more advanced treatments of the subject.

[4] An elementary discussion of measurement error is presented by Edward G. Carmines and Richard A. Zeller, *Reliability and Validity Assessment*, Sage University Paper series on Quantitative Applications in the Social Sciences, series no. 07-017. Beverly Hills and London: Sage Publications, 1979.

CHAPTER SIX

THE QUESTIONNAIRE

A well-designed questionnaire does not impose on the patience of the respondent. It should be possible to move through the questionnaire rapidly, without becoming bored, and without having to reread questions because of ambiguity. An easy-to-complete questionnaire is more likely to be properly filled out. This chapter presents a number of rules to help the beginning survey researcher prepare a questionnaire. We begin our consideration with some general issues, then deal with layout and format, and then pay attention to the phrasing of specific questions and to the development of indexes.

A. GENERAL GUIDELINES

The following list of rules for developing a questionnaire should be regarded as a guideline; there will be many situations where they cannot, or should not, be followed. Use them with intelligence and a good dose of common sense.

Rule 6.1 Consult the respondent. All surveys are something of an imposition on those who are asked to complete them. It is important, if you wish to have a high completion rate, to impose little on your respondents. Above all, the respondents must be made to feel that they are being consulted and should feel free to express their opinions.

Rule 6.2 Introduce the survey to respondents. Normally, questionnaires will contain a brief statement introducing the study to the respondent. It should be short (usually three or four lines is sufficient) and should tell the respondents who is doing the study, who is sponsoring it, and what the study is about. These few lines should attempt to establish the legitimacy of the project. By identifying who is doing the study and who is sponsoring it, the idea is conveyed that the survey is important. Such identification also provides the respondents with additional information to help them decide whether to fill out the questionnaire. The researcher should not identify the specific hypotheses of the study; to do so might well bias the responses. Finally, if the survey is an anonymous one, respondents should be assured that their anonymity will be protected. A good way to achieve the latter goal is simply to ask respondents *not* to write their names on the forms. (See Figure 6.1 for sample wordings.)

Figure 6.1   Sample Introductory Questionnaire Statements

The following is a Sociology 300 research project regarding attitudes toward some public issues. As all responses are confidential, please do not sign your name. Answer all questions as honestly as possible. Thank-you for your cooperation.

* * * * *

This is a survey of Nursing students with regard to their anticipated plans for managing both fertility and career expectations. The information will be kept confidential and your name is not required.

* * * * *

The following questionnaire has been prepared by Sociology 300 students from the university to compare the future plans of high school students. Your cooperation in completing this study by responding to the following questions would be greatly appreciated. Please do not put your name on the questionnaire since all responses are confidential.

* * * * *

This is a Sociology 300 survey. We would appreciate your cooperation in filling out this questionnaire to the best of your ability. Since your responses will remain anonymous, please don't write your name on the questionnaire.

In a mailed questionnaire, a letter describing the project and requesting the cooperation of the recipient is generally included. Ideally, this letter should be written on letterhead stationery and be signed by the head of the organization. The professional appearance of the material in the mailed package is important. Normally, a stamped return envelope is included for the convenience of the respondent.

Rule 6.3 Make a list of variables. Questionnaires can be thought of as consisting of four major groupings of variables: background characteristics, the dependent variable(s); the independent variables; and the other types of variables: intervening and source of spuriousness. Questions to measure variables in each of these groups will have to be developed. The first task is to create a list of variables; during this stage it is not necessary to worry about how the variables will be measured — a list is all that is required.

The list may be derived by: (1) applying relevant theoretical models and identifying variables which should apply; (2) reviewing the literature, paying particular attention to those variables measured by other researchers; (3) examining other questionnaires for ideas about variables to include; (4) reviewing the causal models which have been developed for the current project; and finally (5) deciding what variables "make sense," given the topic of the research.

Rule 6.4 Keep it short. Frequently projects involve a group of researchers and there may be considerable difficulty in keeping the questionnaire from becoming too long. Asking too many questions is not only an infringement on the respondent's time, but also creates additional work in data entry, and error detection and correction. To overcome this problem it takes a careful negotiator to persuade a colleague that some of his or her questions best be left for a later study. An acid test when such difficulties arise is to request individuals to indicate precisely how the variable will be used in analysis. Such discussions force some careful thinking about the survey and the analysis that will follow. All too often a number of variables remain unanalyzed either because they are viewed as being poorly measured or because their relationship to the study is unclear.

There cannot be any strict rules for the length of a questionnaire. If the questions are easy to answer, and the respondents have a particular interest in the survey, it is possible to extend its length. It is always wisest to use the fewest number of questions; never ask questions merely for interest's sake. Figure 6.2 suggests guidelines for maximum lengths of typical surveys.

Figure 6.2   Maximum Number of Questions for Surveys

Type of Survey	Maximum Length
Phone survey	20 questions
Mailed survey	60 questions
Group administered	100 questions
Interview	80 questions

The above table can only be approximate since there can be enormous variations in the complexity of the questions, the sophistication of the respondents, and in the respondents' interest in the survey.

Phone surveys have to be particularly easy to respond to; each question must have simple response options. The respondent will have difficulty trying to remember which option applies to him or to her if too many are presented.

Other surveys can involve more questions and greater complexity. Mailed surveys need to be kept somewhat shorter than group administered or interview questionnaires because the researcher is not present to provide encouragement. Interviews can safely be extended to about 80 questions, and may take as much as an hour to complete. It should be remembered, however, that many interviews will take much longer because of the tendency of respondents to stray off topic. Questionnaires administered to an assembled collection of individuals can involve 100 or more questions. As long as the questions are well designed, respondents can move through them rapidly and because of subtle group pressure, most respondents will complete the form.

But no matter how the data are to be gathered, the researcher should strive for brevity and simplicity. There is no point in gathering data that is beyond the researcher's theoretical or analytical skills.

Rule 6.5 Anticipate how data will be analyzed. After the list of variables is developed, it is important to discuss how the data will be analyzed once collected. Indeed, it is possible to establish dummy analysis tables showing what relationships are to be analyzed, and indicating what procedures will be used to examine each of them. It is critical to have some understanding of how the analysis is to proceed since the methods used to examine relationships are constrained by the level of measurement to be used in operationalizing each of the variables. This kind of discussion may also deal with how the analysis will proceed, given different outcomes of preliminary runs on the data. Frequently, important new variables will emerge as a result of this process.

Rule 6.6 Make certain you have all the variables. Finally, it is essential to ensure that all the variables which play a part in the hypotheses and models related to the project have been included. The list of variables must be checked and double checked. It is not unusual for a researcher to discover that some key variable has been lost in the shuffle. With checking completed, it is time to begin drafting the questionnaire. Once again, there are some rules to keep in mind as this process begins.

B. ISSUES OF LAYOUT, ORDER, AND FORMAT

Rule 6.7 Ease them into it. In deciding the order of questions, consideration should be given to starting with easy-to-answer ones. It is important not to start by asking questions which may be regarded as "too personal". Background information questions are usually placed at the end of questionnaires.[1] However, where students are being surveyed, or in situations where there is little problem with refusals, it is possible to begin with items such as the respondent's place of birth, gender, size of community, perhaps then moving to issues such as year-of-birth (don't ask age — that's too personal!). Whether one begins with background information or other questions, it is important that the respondent be able to move quickly through these first items, creating the impression that it will only take a few minutes to complete the whole questionnaire. Survey researchers are always concerned to do everything they can to increase the proportion of people who will successfully complete the form. If the backgound information involves questions that may be regarded as highly personal, then it is best to place them at the end of the questionnaire.

Another suggestion is to begin with questions the respondents will view as important. Respondents are more likely to complete a questionnaire if they view it as salient.[2]

Rule 6.8 Use consistent format for each type of question. By always presenting the "check-one-of-the-following" questions in the same manner, the respondent soon gets the idea that questions presented this way are to be responded to by choosing one of the options provided by the researcher. Later, when a "fill-in-the-blank" question is asked, by varying the format, the researcher can draw attention to the fact that something else is required. For example, if the respondent is to be asked to rank-order a list, or to choose the three most important items from a list, then a *different look* should be given to the question by varying the way in which the response categories are set up — perhaps a short line opposite each item rather than the open/close parentheses. (See Figures 6.3 through 6.6 for illustrations.) The key point is that different formats should be used consistently for different types of questions; this will help the respondent to answer the questionnaire rapidly.

Note that the formats in Figures 6.3 through 6.6 require the respondent to place a check mark in the appropriate space. Check marks are slightly easier to make than drawing a circle around appropriate responses and so they are preferable. Any device to make the task easy for the respondent should be incorporated.

Rule 6.9 Place key and repeated variables at the one third point. In most projects there will be a few variables absolutely central to the study. In most cases, these will include a major dependent variable. It is a good idea to place key variables at about the one third point in the questionnaire. One wants the respondent to be fresh, with maximum attention, when these key variables are presented.

If there are to be any "reliability checks" (repeated questions) then there should be as much separation as possible between the first and second presentation of such questions. The first presentation of any repeated questions should also be placed near the beginning of the questionnaire — after the respondent is warmed up — but before fatigue or boredom sets in.

Rule 6.10 Minimize the number of open-ended questions. An open-ended question asks the respondent to answer a question, or to offer some suggestion or opinion, but to do so without any pre-set categories being provided for the answer. Many researchers minimize the number of opinion seeking open-ended questions because they are time-consuming to code; moreover, there is a greater likelihood that such questions will be left blank. Indeed, respondents will frequently fail to complete a questionnaire that has too many such questions. Many respondents appear to feel that asking them to write a sentence or two is too much of an imposition.

Where a pilot study is conducted, and where the research team is uncertain about the appropriate response categories, it is a good idea to pose the question in an open-ended form, analyze the results, and then base the categories to be used in the final study on the categories suggested in the pilot study.[3]

Placing an open-ended question at about the two thirds mark of a long questionnaire may well provide the relief necessary to sustain the respondent through to the completion of the questionnaire.

If both open-ended and fixed choice questions are asked it is advisable to place the open-ended version first so that the respondent is not influenced by the fixed choice options.[4]

Rule 6.11 Anticipate computer data entry. Virtually all surveys of any size will be analyzed using a computer. To simplify the entry of the data, it helps enormously if the values to be entered are right on the questionnaire. Indeed, it is now quite common for researchers to avoid what was once referred to as "coding the data." Coding is the process whereby researchers go through the questionnaire and assign values to each response category, record this information on "code sheets," and then have the data entered into the computer. This process is expensive, time-consuming, and likely to introduce additional errors into the final data set. Where possible, avoid the whole coding process by placing the code values directly on the questionnaire. These numbers can then be used when the data are put into the computer. They can be placed unobtrusively on the questionnaire and will not distract the respondent.

Figure 6.3 illustrates a set of questions where such numbers have been used. Note that there are no blanks between the response category and the check-off space (usually open/close parentheses). Note, as well, that only question numbers are used, and response categories are numbered beside the place where the respondent makes his or her check mark. When the data are put into the computer, it is easy to enter the number immediately adjacent to the check mark made by the respondent.

Figure 6.3   The Simple Pre-coded Question

4. What year are you in?
           Freshman . . . . 1 ( )
           Sophomore . . . . 2 ( )
           Junior . . . . 3 ( )
           Senior . . . . 4 ( )

5. What is the highest education completed by your mother and father?

	Mother	Father
Grades 0 – 6	1 ( )	1 ( )
Grades 7 – 9	2 ( )	2 ( )
Grades 10 – 12	3 ( )	3 ( )
Some post secondary	4 ( )	4 ( )
University graduate	5 ( )	5 ( )

6. What was the approximate population of your home area prior to attending university?
    Rural area . . . . 01 ( )
    Small town under 999 . . . . 02 ( )
    Between   1,000 –   4,999 . . . . 03 ( )
    Between   5,000 –   9,999 . . . . 04 ( )
    Between 10,000 – 19,999 . . . . 05 ( )
    Between 20,000 – 29,999 . . . . 06 ( )
    Between 30,000 – 49,999 . . . . 07 ( )
    Between 50,000 – 74,999 . . . . 08 ( )
    Between 75,000 – 99,999 . . . . 09 ( )
    Between 100,000 – 249,999 . . . . 10 ( )
    Between 250,000 – 999,999 . . . . 11 ( )
    Over 1,000,000 . . . . 12 ( )

Figure 6.4 shows the formatting styles favored by Earl Babbie, by Don A. Dillman, and by this author. Babbie does not appear to favor the use of code values, uses square brackets for the check-off responses, and places the response brackets before the category.[5] Dillman favors the use of capital letters to identify response categories, and, in mail surveys, places the code values to the left of the response categories.[6] Dillman recommends placing the code values to the right of the categories in personal interview forms and telephone surveys. Both Babbie's and Dillman's styles are perfectly acceptable. This author prefers to include code values and place them to the right of the response categories, using a series of dashes to carry the respondent's eye out to the check-off brackets. Note that no space is left between the code value and the brackets.

Some researchers place the computer screen column numbers each variable will occupy on the questionnaire. These are placed on the right hand side of the questionnaire. The advantage of this is that errors can be avoided when entering the information into the computer. Certainly in the case of interviews or phone questionnaires it is advisable to include such codes. However, in cases where respondents are filling in the questionnaires themselves, such numbers add to the clutter on the questionnaire and should probably be avoided.

Figure 6.4   Three Format Styles Illustrated[1]

---

(1) Babbie Style Formats for Response Categories:

   23. Have you ever smoked marijuana?
     [   ] Yes
     [   ] No

(2) Dillman Style Formats for Response Categories:

   Q-22 Your Sex.   (Circle number of your answer)
              1   MALE
              2   FEMALE

(3) Jackson Style Format for Response Categories:

   23. Referring to my future job plans, I have given the subject:
        a lot of thought . . . . 1(   )
        some thought . . . . 2(   )
        little thought . . . . 3(   )
        no thought . . . . 4(   )

---

[1]See Earl Babbie, *The Practice of Social Research.* Belmont, California: Wadsworth Publishing Company, 1983, p. 212; and Don A. Dillman, *Mail and Telephone Surveys.* New York: John Wiley & Sons, Inc., 1978, p. 134.

Rule 6.12 Vary the placement of response categories. Figure 6.3 also illustrates how the appearance of a questionnaire can be improved by varying the placement of the response categories for each question. While this might be more in the area of aesthetics than science, the appearance of a questionnaire with response categories all lined up on the right margin is not pleasing to the eye, nor is it easy to see where one question ends and another begins. The rule, then, is to vary the location of the response category sets.

Rule 6.13 Group questions by type. Some grouping by type of item is advisable. Minimize the amount of shifting between open-ended and precoded questions. If there are a number of Likert-type items,[7] it is a good idea to group some of them together. The idea is to accustom the respondent to a particular format so that he or she will move through the items quickly. Continual shifting between types of questions will only slow the respondent down and increase the risk of error.

Rule 6.14 Clearly indicate any branching. Some questions are only to be answered by some respondents. In such cases, clearly guide your reader by using the technique shown in Figure 6.5. Note that those who respond positively to question 9 are directed to question 9a.

Figure 6.5   A Branching Question Illustrated

9. Have you consumed any beer in the past seven days?
         Yes . . . . 1 ( )
         No . . . . 2 ( )

> If yes: How much did you consume in the
>   past week:
> Less than 3 bottles . . . . 1( )
> 4 to 9 bottles . . . . 2( )
> 10 or more bottles . . . . 3( )

Rule 6.15 Achieve precise measurement. It is generally recommended to aim for the most precise measurement possible. Collect data in its rawest form: income to the dollar, precise occupation rather than a general category, age to the nearest year rather than a category spanning 10 years. This recommendation has to be moderated where other factors argue against precise measurement. Such factors might include being too personal, or asking for distinctions beyond those normally used by respondents, or where the technique would be too cumbersome.

Rule 6.16 Give the questionnaire a distinctive look. Besides paying attention to issues of layout, it is important to give the questionnaire a distinctive appearance. Using colored paper is one way to achieve this. Another useful tip is to have the questionnaire typed on 8½" x 14" paper and then have it reduced to the standard 8½" x 11" paper. With this method it is possible for the original typing to run closer to either edge of the paper (a wide margin will show up after the reduction is made).

Rule 6.17 Do not squeeze too much onto one page. Avoid trying to squeeze too much onto a single page: questionnaires should permit the respondent to move through each page rapidly. Squeezing material will only discourage the respondent.

C. RULES FOR WORDING QUESTIONS

Rule 6.18 Review conceptual definitions. When developing the wording for a particular question it is important to review its *conceptual definition*. The conceptual definition provides the key to what the question is to measure. To illustrate, suppose one is attempting to measure *socio-economic status* and suppose that in the conceptual definition of socio-economic status, reference is made to a *hierarchical continuum of respect and prestige*. Given this conceptual definition, the researcher should adopt a measure that particularly reflects the relative amount of prestige an individual has. In this case an occupational prestige scale such as those developed by Featherman and Stevens (U.S.A.) or Porter and Pineo (Canada)[8] might be used. While such a measure might be a valid measure of the concept in general, the experienced researcher would realize that the measure may be weak on the "respect" aspect of the definition, and might not include all respondents. Housewives and single parents at home are not assigned scores in occupational prestige scales. One might therefore choose to measure the "respect and prestige" an individual has by having a number of people rate each individual compared to others. Perhaps the latter approach would yield the most valid measure of the concept, even though it would only be the rare research design (probably a study of a particular group) that would allow for the use of this method.

Suppose, alternatively, that the proposed conceptual definition of *socio-economic status* stressed *variations in access to scarce resources*. In this case, the researcher might attempt to reflect the variable by collecting data on the total income of the individuals. Here the assumption is that total income would be a good reflection of ability to buy access to scarce items in society.

The more general point is that the researcher must pay careful attention to conceptual definitions — they provide invaluable and crucial guides to valid measurement.

Rule 6.19 Words must be understood. The words used in question-naires must be understood by all respondents. Err on the side of simplicity. If a survey is being done on high school students, play it safe. Use words that a grade seven student can handle. Furthermore, the words selected should be those that have one unambiguous meaning. Showing off an impressive vocabulary has no place in a questionnaire intended to produce valid and reliable data.

Rule 6.20 Avoid the word "and". Individual questions should be uni-dimensional. Avoid the trap involved in a question such as:

I get along very well with my mother and father.
Strongly Disagree 1 2 3 4 5 6 7 8 9 Strongly Agree

The problem with the question, as worded, is that some respondents will not "get along" equally well with both mother and father. As a result, some respondents may indicate a 1 or a 2 if they don't get along well with both; another with a similar relationship might indicate a 6 or 7 as a kind of average of the relationship they have with their parents. The point is that two dimensions have been introduced — the relationship with mother and the relationship with father. Such questions should be divided into two. It is always useful to scan one's questions to eliminate such unwanted confusion: double check any question with the word "and" in it.

Rule 6.21 Vary wording to produce variability. It is important that the items in a questionnaire produce varied responses. If most respondents provide similar answers to a question then the question will have little use during analysis. Try to ensure that the respondents will scatter themselves across the response continuum. A simple example will illustrate the point:

Mothers play an important role in our society.
Strongly Disagree 1 2 3 4 5 6 7 8 9 Strongly Agree

On a common sense basis, one could anticipate that most respondents will be in strong agreement with this statement and will circle 8 or 9. If, indeed, respondents do not vary their responses much, the question would not prove useful in discriminating between respondents in their views of the role of mothers. In this case, to produce more variability in response, the wording of the item should be strengthened so that more respondents will move toward the "disagree" end of the continuum: perhaps a statement such as, "Mothers play a more important role in society than fathers," or, "Mothers play the single most important role in our society." In both illustrations we have made it less likely that all respondents will remain at the "Strongly Agree" end of the continuum.

When variables such as job satisfaction are to be measured, a review of the literature will reveal that most respondents in surveys will report themselves relatively satisfied with their jobs. Knowing this, the researcher should strive to identify items which will induce some respondents to report themselves as less than fully satisfied — perhaps by asking if the respondents would like their child to have a job similar to their own or if they think they are paid the "right amount" for the responsibilities they have.

Similarly, questions which measure satisfaction with services delivered, such as patient services in a hospital, must be carefully written to allow for the slightest dissatisfaction, otherwise it is likely that virtually everyone will rate the service as "good" or "excellent."

The phrasing of questions in this manner is not an attempt to distort reality — to show dissatisfaction when none is present — but rather it is an attempt to develop highly sensitive measures. If the researcher is attempting to understand what leads patients to be relatively more, or relatively less, satisfied with their treatment in a hospital, highly sensitive measures would be needed. If all respondents simply reported that they were "satisfied" we would not be able to identify what factors influence levels of patient satisfaction.

Rule 6.22 Avoid complexity. Try to keep questions simple; avoid asking respondents to do difficult tasks. Where it is necessary, for example, to have respondents rank order a list, it is usually best to ask them to rank order the three most important items, rather than ask them to go through the whole list. In most cases, the slight reduction in discriminatory power will be offset by a higher response rate to the question.

Rule 6.23 Use existing wordings for comparative analysis. When a researcher wishes to compare his or her data with that reported by other researchers, it is important that wordings used be identical. Here the advantages of improving the wording of a question must be weighted against the advantage of using identical wordings to make comparative analyses easier.

Rule 6.24 Take the edge off sensitive questions. Using a combination of experience and common sense, the survey researcher soon learns that there are some issues respondents may be reluctant to report. Illegal activities, evaluating friends or neighbors, indicating age or income can all be sensitive issues. By asking year-of-birth rather than age, the question sounds scientific and is more likely to be answered; if age is asked, the respondent may feel some invasion of privacy. Similarly, questions about income must be carefully written. Often, researchers will ask respondents to indicate only the broad category of income into which they fall. Alternatively, if income level is important to the survey, the question may be located among others dealing with conditions of work, where respondents will generally provide precise information. However, if the income question is being used as a measure of socio-economic status, then other indicators, such as years of education or occupational prestige, might be considered in preference to income itself — simply to avoid prying unnecessarily into what may be perceived as a highly personal matter.

Rule 6.25 Avoid asking respondents to speculate about why they act the way they do. Generally, we are not interested in polling respondents for their opinions about the existence of certain relationships. For example, if you are studying the relationship between participation in student activities and levels of self esteem, you would not normally ask respondents if they think there is a relationship between these two variables. Instead, the researcher would get separate measures of the two variables (among others) and would analyze the data to determine if there is any relationship.

Rule 6.26 Be precise and highly specific when choosing wordings. If you wish to measure, for example, how much people drink, ask highly specific questions which pinpoint the type of drink and the time when it was consumed. Here the time period will have to be reasonable. It is useless to ask how many drinks someone has had in the past two years; few people could make a reasonable estimate without considerable thought. "In the past seven days how many beers did you drink?", would be preferable to:

>How would you describe your drinking?
>Abstainer . . . . 1 ( )
>Light. . . . . 2 ( )
>Moderate . . . . 3 ( )
>Heavy . . . . 4 ( )

The latter question would suffer considerably because of variations in what respondents consider light, moderate, or heavy drinking.

Rule 6.27 Pre-test the questionnaire. It is important to have a few individuals complete the questionnaire or the interview prior to settling on the final wordings of the questions. Start by filling it out yourself. Make any necessary corrections, then try it on a few other people. Generally, it is best to sit with the individual completing the questionnaire. Before they begin, tell them exactly what you are doing (trying to remove any ambiguity in the questionnaire), and encourage them to ask for any clarifications. If, as they complete the questionnaire, they ask "do you mean x or do you mean y in question 42?", you will know that the question has two or more possible interpretations and will need to be reworded. Or they might say "When you ask about the size of my family, do you mean the family I was born into or the one I have with my husband? Also, in that question, do you want me to include parents in the count?" Clearly, you will need to change how this question is asked. With experience you will learn to be very specific in how you word questions. The goal is to minimize differences in how respondents understand the questions. The goal, although impossible to achieve, is to have all respondents understand each and every question in an identical manner.

D. TYPES OF QUESTIONS ILLUSTRATED

This section will illustrate a variety of formats for typical questionnaire items. While it is not possible to anticipate all types of questions, many of the same principles could be applied to a great variety of questions.

1. Pre-coded, Single Choice Questions

In these questions, the respondent is asked to indicate with a check mark which category applies to him or to her. Figure 6.3 provides illustrations of such questions. In the first case, note that only the question is numbered; categories are not numbered, to reduce clutter. After the category label a dashed line is used so that the respondent's eye moves laterally to the correct check-off category; the number beside the open/close parentheses is the value that will be used when the data are entered into the computer. To avoid a cluttered look, there should be no space between the number and the open/close parentheses.

The next items in Figure 6.3 illustrate slightly more complex forms of the check-off question. Sample question 5 illustrates how a question can be set up to accommodate two columns of check-off categories; in this case, one for the mother's and one for the father's educational level. Once again, the computer codes are placed next to the categories to facilitate computer entry. Similar space saving can be achieved by splitting long category lists into two and placing them side by side.

The question on population size simply illustrates that when there are more than nine categories, it is important to place the leading zero in the computer codes. If the leading zero is omitted, data entry errors will almost certainly occur. The particular population categories would, of course, have to be altered, depending on the target population. The reader should also note that the population categories are mutually exclusive — that is, they do not overlap one another.

Two points also need to be mentioned that are not illustrated in Figure 6.3. Frequently, it is not possible to name all possible responses that would be appropriate (religious affiliation, for example) and the researcher will have a final category that says:

Other _____ 12(   )   Please specify _____.

The most obvious reason for using a "please specify" category is that there would not be sufficient room to list all possible religions. However, and even more important, you do not wish to insult your respondent by not having included his or her religion. In actual fact, if the major religious groupings have been included, the person who specifies a category not included will simply be coded as an "Other."

Finally, it should be noted that the response categories provided should cover the full spectrum of possible responses. (See Appendix G Sample Questionnaires, question 2.)

2. Open-Ended Questions

Open-ended questions simply pose a question and then provide space on the page for the response. There are at least five reasons why some open-ended questions are included in a survey. Such questions are used when: (1) there are too many possible responses (as in year of birth); (2) the researcher does not wish to impose response categories on the respondent; (3) the researcher wishes to create the impression that the respondent is *really* being consulted, by being asked to offer his or her suggestions; (4) a pilot study is being done and the appropriate response categories have not been determined; and, (5) to provide a change-of-pace for the reader. Such data are not always analyzed when writing the final report on a project, although they often provide rich sources for quotations.

Figure 6.6   Sample Open-Ended Questions

---

20. Approximately, what was your average in your final year of high school?

_____ _____ %

21. What is (or was) your father's occupation? (e.g., foreman, railway machine shop . . . supervises work of about 25 people.)

Job _____

Brief Job Description _____

_____

22. In what year were you born?   1 9 __ __ .

23. What is the one thing that you would like to see changed at the university?

_____

_____

24. In your opinion, what was the single best thing about attending university?

_____

_____

Figure 6.6 illustrates some variations in typical formats. Questions 20 and 22 are simple questions where the space for the response indicates that two numbers are expected. By providing two blanks, the respondent is being prompted for the entry of two numbers. The % symbol in question 20 also helps to indicate exactly what is expected. This technique can prevent frivolous replies like "average" in the case of question 20, or "a long time ago" in the case of question 22.

Question 21 illustrates a method of asking about occupation. The additional line "Brief Job Description" is added to ensure that sufficient detail is provided by the respondent to enable the researcher to attach an occupational rating code to the response. If such specification is not requested, some respondents will simply indicate the employer (for example, Sears) and the researcher will not be able to attach an occupational rating to that kind of response. Where detail is required, the researcher must be careful to request it.

Questions 23 and 24 simply seek the opinion of the respondent on two issues. Typically, the responses given would either be listed (simply typed) or coded. If they are coded, the code would be developed after the data have been collected and the responses examined.

Use opinion-seeking, open-ended questions sparingly; do keep in mind, however, that they are an excellent vehicle for providing a change of pace for the respondent, or for exploring new issues in detail.

3. Presence-Absence Questions

Figure 6.7 illustrates examples of these kinds of question. Of the two versions presented, the first one is preferable. In it, either a "yes" or a "no" answer is expected for each item. While this kind of question demands a little more work from the respondent, the researcher can be more confident that each item has been considered. In question 24, if an item is left blank the researcher cannot be sure if the respondent is opposed to capital punishment for that crime or if the respondent simply failed to consider that item.

Figure 6.7   Presence/Absence Check-Off Questions

Preferred format:
23. Have you ever had contact with handicapped people in any of these
groups?   (Circle a 1 for "yes", or a 2 for "no" for each category.)

	Yes	No
Community	1	2
Family	1	2
Relatives	1	2
Elementary school class	1	2
Junior high school class	1	2
Senior high school class	1	2
University class	1	2
As co-worker	1	2

Less preferred format:
24. After a guilty verdict, in which of the following situations would you
support the use of capital punishment?   (Check as many as
appropriate)

Manslaughter . . . . __ 1
Premeditated Murder . . . . __ 1
Rape . . . . __ 1
Murder of Police Officer . . . . __ 1
Murder of Prison Guard . . . . __ 1

In contrast to the check-one-of-the-following type questions presented in Figure 6.3, open/close parentheses are *not* used for the answer. Instead a short line leading to a 1 (Yes) and 2 (No) is provided, and this different style tells the respondent that a different kind of response is required.

The reader should also note that the computer codes used involve "1" for presence and "2" for absence. During analysis, the 2s will be converted to 0s and then a "total experience" variable will be created by simply adding the variables together. A total score of "5" on question 23 for example, would mean that the individual has had experience with handicapped people in five of the settings identified in the question.

4. Rank-Ordering Questions

Asking respondents to rank order a list has to be done with great care. In this case, detailed instructions should be provided for the respondent. Figure 6.8 provides a example of such a question.

Figure 6.8   Rank-Ordering Questions

---

31. <u>Rank order</u> the three most important things <u>you</u> want in the job you make your life's work.   (Place a 1 beside the most important one; a 2 beside the next important one; and a 3 beside the next most important one.)

Money . . . . ____

Security . . . . ____

Continued Interest . . . . ____

Power . . . . ____

Prestige . . . . ____

Excitement . . . . ____

First, note that the respondent is only asked to pick out the three most important items; in most cases, respondents will not be able to go meaningfully beyond the top three. These are difficult types of questions for respondents and they should be kept as simple as possible.

Second, it should be noted that the instructions are embarrassingly explicit. While "rank ordering" may be an obvious and simple idea for many people, detailed instructions will reduce the number of respondents who will simply place a check mark beside three items or who will check just one of the items.

Finally, note that the respondents are given a short line on which they are to write their answers. Again, it is important to provide a different look to the item in order to cue the respondent that this is not a "check-one" item.

It is generally unwise to use many rank-ordering items in a questionnaire. They slow the respondent down and increase the risk of losing the respondent's cooperation.

5. Likert-Type Questions

This type of question is widely used in social science research and was first devised by Rensis Likert. In his original format, a statement would be made, and the respondent would be asked to (1) strongly disagree, (2) disagree, (3) undecided or neutral, (4) agree, or (5) strongly agree with the statement. Such items were, and continue to be, popular in measuring both matters of fact and attitudinal issues. Figure 6.9 illustrates this kind of question.

Figure 6.9   Likert-Type Items

In the following items, <u>circle a number</u> to indicate the extent to which you agree or disagree with each statement.

52. I believe capital punishment represents the most effective deterrent to murder.

Strongly Disagree   1   2   3   4   5   6   7   8   9   Strongly Agree

53. I believe a murderer can be rehabilitated to become a responsible, functioning member of society.

Strongly Disagree   1   2   3   4   5   6   7   8   9   Strongly Agree

54. I believe a life sentence is a satisfactory penalty for murder.

Strongly Disagree   1   2   3   4   5   6   7   8   9   Strongly Agree

55. I would quit my present job if I won $1,000,000 through a lottery.

Strongly Disagree   1   2   3   4   5   6   7   8   9   Strongly Agree

56. I would be satisfied if my child followed the same type of career as I have.

Strongly Disagree   1   2   3   4   5   6   7   8   9   Strongly Agree

57. My mother would be upset if she knew I did drugs.

Strongly Disagree   1   2   3   4   5   6   7   8   9   Strongly Agree

Note that the items in Figure 6.9 deviate somewhat from the original format. Given a preference for increasing the variability in such items, the number of response categories has been increased from five to nine. This increase does not take more space on the questionnaire, or more space when coded into the computer.

The following tips may be helpful in constructing such items:

Tip 1. Avoid the word "and" in such items if such usage makes the item multidimensional.

Tip 2. Place the "Strongly Agree" on the right hand side of the scale, with 9 indicating strong agreement.[9]

Tip 3. Avoid negatives that may confuse respondents (statements such as: "I don't think the President is doing a bad job," will almost certainly confuse and slow down respondents).

Tip 4. Vary the "strength of wording" in each item to produce variation in response. (Some wordings should be highly positive, others negative.)

Tip 5. If there is uncertainty about where responses will fall, use more than one item with different intensities in the wordings.

Tip 6. Before the first Likert-type item, provide a brief explanation of how respondents are to indicate their answers.

Likert items result in an ordinal level of measurement. Frequently such items are combined to form indexes by adding together the values on individual items (after having reversed the scores on the negative measures). Index construction using such items will be discussed later in this chapter.

6. Semantic Differential Questions

There are numerous applications for this type of question. Originally these items were used to study stereotyping behavior; to measure how respondents view various out-groups. The format of such questions is shown in Figure 6.10.

Figure 6.10   Sample Semantic Differential Question

---

67. Circle a number to indicate where you think you fit on a continuum between the two opposites.

SHY	1	2	3	4	5	6	7	8	9	OUTGOING
PASSIVE	1	2	3	4	5	6	7	8	9	DOMINANT
CAUTIOUS	1	2	3	4	5	6	7	8	9	DARING
BOOKWORM	1	2	3	4	5	6	7	8	9	SOCIAL BUTTERFLY
QUIET	1	2	3	4	5	6	7	8	9	LOUD
SERIOUS	1	2	3	4	5	6	7	8	9	HUMOROUS
CONFORMIST	1	2	3	4	5	6	7	8	9	LEADER
COOPERATIVE	1	2	3	4	5	6	7	8	9	STUBBORN

These questions consist of a series of adjective extremes, placed at the margins of the page; the respondent is asked to indicate where, between the two extremes, he or she would place the group or individual being evaluated.

For example, respondents might be asked to indicate where a group would be placed on a honest/dishonest continuum, or on a hot/cold dimension. Respondents are encouraged to answer the questions quickly, hopefully letting their guards down, and revealing how they really "see" various categories of individuals.

There are a variety of uses for such items beyond the traditional ones. An examination of respondents' self-images is certainly possible, as shown in Figure 6.10. Such questions can be used to measure individual variables or can be combined to create indexes.

7. Magnitude Estimation Questions

Magnitude estimations are very useful when comparative judgments are required.[10] Ratio level measurement results from this technique and it should be in the arsenal of every survey researcher. This technique is best used in interview or group administered questionnaire situations. The instructions need to be reviewed carefully with the respondents. Therefore, the researcher should be present when the instrument is completed.

Typically, one of two methods is used to do magnitude estimations. The first approach is to have respondents provide numerical estimates. If one were doing estimates of the relative popularity of different students in a residence, for example, one might begin by having respondents compare the popularity of each student to that of a student identified as being about average in popularity and to whom the researcher has assigned 100 units of popularity. The respondent would be asked to proceed through a list of students, indicating in each case the amount of popularity each has, relative to that of the "average student." If the respondent thinks that Joan is $2\frac{1}{4}$ times as popular as the average, a value of 225 would be assigned. Alternatively, if the respondent thinks that Joan has $\frac{3}{4}$ the popularity of the "average student," then a value of 75 would be assigned.

The second method is to have respondents draw lines of different lengths to indicate their perceptions of the differences between stimulus objects. In this case, a standard line is given, and the respondent is asked to draw lines relative to the standard line. (Sample instructions for using the "line method" are presented in Figure 6.11.)

Some tips for employing magnitude estimations are:

Tip 1. Magnitude estimations should only be used where a researcher is present to explain the method. The mailed questionnaire is not generally suitable for this technique.

Tip 2. Magnitude estimations are applicable to situations where comparative judgments are required.

Figure 6.11 Sample Magnitude Estimation Instructions

Now we would like to have you rate the various local universities on a number of dimensions. The way you will do it will be to draw different lengths of line to indicate how each of the universities compare to one another. If you draw a line twice as long as the 'standard' line, it means you think that particular university is twice as good as average for the particular dimension being rated. For example, suppose you were asked to indicate how far each institution is from your home. You would then draw lines indicating the relative distances from your home. You might draw the following lines:

IF THE AVERAGE UNIVERSITY IS _____ THIS FAR
AWAY, HOW FAR AWAY IS: (suppose you then drew the following lines)

    Acadia   _____
    Dalhousie   _____
    Mount Allison   _____
    Mount St. Vincent _____
    St. Francis Xavier _____
    St. Mary's   _____

We would interpret your lines to mean that you think that Acadia is about 1½ times further away than the average Nova Scotia university; Dalhousie, Mount St. Vincent, and St. Mary's about average, while St. F.X. is about ¾ as far as the average university.

Now we would like you to give us estimates on the following 25 aspects, using the technique described above.

How good are the residence accommodations?
                Standard = _____
            Acadia
            Dalhousie
        Mount Allison
    Mount St. Vincent
    St. Francis Xavier
        St. Mary's

How good an academic reputation do you think each university has?
                Standard = _____
            Acadia
            Dalhousie
        Mount Allison
    Mount St. Vincent
    St. Francis Xavier
        St. Mary's

Tip 3. Use as a *standard* a category somewhere near the middle of the range used. Avoid choosing a standard that is near the extreme high or low.

Tip 4. After the standard has been assigned, leave the respondent free to assign all other values.

Tip 5. Randomize the order of presentation, and avoid starting with the extremes of the continuum.

Tip 6. Before the session begins, tell the respondent how to indicate a "zero" response or a "non-applicable" one.

Tip 7. Data derived from magnitude estimations will generally require three columns of space for each variable entered in to the computer. When lines or numbers are used, the value "999" is used to indicate an item that has not been answered; "001" generally is used to indicate a zero response. Lines are generally measured in millimeters, while numerical estimates are entered directly without change.

E. SELECTING INDEX ITEMS

Indexes are constructed by combining several individual questions and are an attempt to summarize, in one score, a measure of a variable. Indexes are used when dealing with a single dimension variable, but where one question might not adequately measure the variable. Indexes can be constructed by combining a number of similarly formatted questions, or by using combinations of questions with different formats. In all cases, the indicators are combined, and possibly weighted, to sum to a single index score. The steps involved in developing an index are identified below.

Step 1. Review Conceptual Definition. As in developing other measures, the first step is to review the conceptual definition of the variable. Some sense of the "range", or the dimensions, involved in the variable should be developed. The chances are that several questions can then be developed to measure the variable, reflecting each of the dimensions in the conceptual definition.

Step 2. Develop Measures for Each Dimension. Here the same principles apply as for the development of individual measures, discussed earlier. For example, in measuring attitudes toward capital punishment, one might identify which, if any, offences would lead a respondent to favor capital punishment. Items may be initially selected on the basis of *face validity*. That is, if the item appears, on the face of it, to represent a part of the theoretical continuum being measured, then an effort should be made to get a measure of that item. Three capital punishment items which could be part of an index might be:

> I support capital punishment for convicted child molesters.
> Strongly Disagree 1 2 3 4 5 6 7 8 9 Strongly Agree

> I support capital punishment for a murderer of a policeman.
> Strongly Disagree 1 2 3 4 5 6 7 8 9 Strongly Agree

> I support capital punishment for drug smugglers.
> Strongly Disagree 1 2 3 4 5 6 7 8 9 Strongly Agree

Step 3. Pre-test Index. If time permits, indexes should be pre-tested. This is done to see if the index items discriminate. However, if time is not available to do a pre-test, ensure minimally that a full range of possible variability is represented by the measures. During data analysis, the various items can be tested using the SPSS^x procedure, RELIABILITY.[11]

F. EXERCISES

1. Develop a series of background information questions that would be appropriate for a study you would like to do. Be careful to obey as many of the rules for questionnaire construction as you can.

2. Develop a series of items for an index that is of interest to you. Define the conceptual aspects of the index and suggest indicators.

NOTES

[1] Don A. Dillman, *Mail and Telephone Surveys*. New York: John Wiley & Sons, Inc., 1978, p. 125. The Dillman book is an excellent presentation of many of the issues involved in doing mail or telephone surveys. Also see Paul L. Erdos, *Professional Mail Surveys*. Malabar, Florida: Robert E. Krieger Publishing Company, 1983.

[2] Thomas A. Heberlein and Robert Baumgartner, "Factors Affecting Response Rates to Mailed Questionnaires," *American Sociological Review*, 43, August, 1978, p. 457.

[3] For an excellent discussion of the issues involved in the choice of open- or fixed-choice questions see Howard Schuman and Stanley Presser, *Questions and Answers in Attitude Surveys*. New York: Academic Press, 1981.

[4] See Seymour Sudman and Norman Bradburn, *Asking Questions*. San Francisco: Jossey-Bass, Inc., Publishers, 1983.

[5] See Earl Babbie, *The Practice of Social Research*. Belmont, California: Wadsworth Publishing Company, 1983, p. 212.

[6] See Don A. Dillman, *Mail and Telephone Surveys*. New York: John Wiley & Sons, Inc., 1978, p. 133-36.

[7] A Likert-type item refers to a type of question whose response categories are modeled after those originally developed by Rensis Likert (1932). In such an item, respondents are asked to respond to a statement by indicating if they (1) strongly agree, (2) agree, (3) undecided or neutral, (4) disagree, or (5) strongly disagree.

[8] See David L. Featherman and Gillian Stevens, "A Revised Index of Occupational Status: Application in Analysis of Sex Differences in Attainment," Chapter 7 in *Social Structure and Behavior: Essays in Honor of William Hamilton Sewell*. New York: Academic Press, 1982. Peter C. Pineo and John Porter, "Occupational Prestige in Canada," *Canadian Review of Sociology and Anthropology,* 1967, pp. 24-40. B.R. Blishen, "A Socio-economic Index for Occupations in Canada," *Canadian Review of Sociology and Anthropology,* February, 1968, pp. 41-53.

[9] Some researchers prefer to vary the response categories by reversing the order in which the agree/disagree items are presented. This is done to prevent "response set," a situation where the respondent tends to answer similarly to all items. While switching the order of agree/disagree categories may reduce the tendency to respond in a set manner, it may also introduce additional errors in response. My preference is to maintain a uniform presentation.

[10] See Robert L. Hamblin, "Ratio Measurement for the Social Sciences," *Social Forces*, 50, 1971, pp. 191-206; also see Robert L. Hamblin, "Social Attitudes: Magnitude Measurement and Theory," in H.M. Blalock, Jr., *Measurement in the Social Sciences*. Chicago: Aldine Publishing Company, 1974, pp. 61-120; also see J.E. Winston Jackson and Nicholas W. Poushinsky, *Migration to Northern Mining Communities: Structural and Social Psychological Dimensions.* Winnipeg: Center for Settlement Studies, University of Manitoba, 1971.

[11] Additional readings on the topic of questionnaire construction should include: Norman M. Bradburn and Seymour Sudman, *Improving Interview Method and Questionnaire Design.* San Francisco: Jossey-Bass, Inc., Publishers, 1980; Don A. Dillman, *Mail and Telephone Surveys.* New York: John Wiley & Sons, Inc., 1978.

PART THREE

STATISTICS

CHAPTER SEVEN

STATISTICS FOR SURVEY RESEARCH

This chapter reviews the statistical concepts necessary for the beginning survey researcher. While the elementary view presented here will be helpful for the beginning student, a more profound understanding will be necessary for those students attempting more advanced work.[1]

For those with a background in statistics, this chapter may be skipped or quickly reviewed; those with no background should work through the material carefully and will then have a foundation upon which to build an understanding of advanced techniques. SPSS^x commands are included after each statistic is introduced so that the reader will realize how simple it is to have a computer calculate them.

The social researcher asks questions about many kinds of phenomena: some of them are about individuals (age, type of job, income, and job satisfaction); some questions are about communities (how much deviance occurs, how many new houses have been built in the past year, has there been a change in the proportion of low income people living in the community?); and some questions may be about nations (how many births were recorded, how many deaths, and have the incomes of the people increased or gone down over the past 10 years?).

Typifying a sample's characteristics may be achieved by a variety of *descriptive statistics*. Such statistics include various tools, conventions, and procedures for describing variables. (Means, standard deviations, normal distributions, and Z scores are of particular concern to the survey researcher.) In addition to describing individual variables, the social researcher is also interested in examining relationships between variables (is there a relationship between gender and income? Does this relationship persist when males and females in similar occupations are compared?). Once again, the researcher wishes to decide what, if any, relationship exists, and if there is one, does it hold up in virtually all circumstances? Once again, there are a variety of conventions used to describe such relationships. (Cross-classifications, means across categories, correlations, and regressions are important tools.)

A second group of statistics are known as *inferential statistics*; these deal with making extrapolations from samples to the population from which the sample was drawn. Both types of statistics are of relevance to the survey researcher. An introduction to inferential statistics will be presented in Chapter 8.

The student should keep in mind that statistics are tools to help in describing and understanding social relationships. Be a master of these tools—but treat them as tools—they are no substitute for theory and cannot make up for poorly designed studies or sloppy measurement.

A. DESCRIBING AN INDIVIDUAL VARIABLE

In this first section, we will consider how individual variables may be described; included will be measures of central tendency, how variation within a variable is measured, and approaches to standardizing variables.

1. Measures of Central Tendency

Measures of central tendency attempt to reflect, with one number, a distribution of values. Just as baseball fans attempt to summarize a player's hitting ability by citing the batting average, the survey researcher uses various simple statistics to convey a sense of the data. There are three commonly used measures of central tendency.

a. The Mean. The mean is a measure which typifies a set of observations with a single value. Suppose, for example, we wished to examine grades in two first year sociology tests. The grades are listed in Figure 7.1.

Figure 7.1   Two Test Grades for a Sociology Class

Test A   Results:

60	60	82	71	60	58	64	81	58	58	70	57	56
56	69	58	55	82	46	54	62	61	77	70	59	74
87	47	57	63	37	67	55	59	63	59	55	52	58
63	72	54	54	62	69	66	58	53	73	57	68	52
75	47	52	73	72	65	64	63	59	57			

Test B   Results:

53	64	83	60	61	61	61	83	54	58	68	55	49
60	59	55	53	69	44	56	48	54	74	71	49	54
86	51	67	63	59	63	55	40	65	63	62	55	49
53	72	59	59	54	69	73	57	59	72	26	65	70
60	45	60	69	66	63	51	59	63	63			

Examine the grades. If you were asked to indicate the test on which students did best, what would you say? The task is a frustrating one. It is difficult to answer. The mass of detail is overwhelming. Quickly, the need for some method of summarizing the grades becomes apparent. You need a way to compare the results in each of the two tests — a way to simplify the reporting of the mass of numbers contained in Figure 7.1. It is too inefficient to read an unordered listing of numbers; to do so would fail to convey to your reader any sense of the results. You would simply have a boring list of numbers. Your job as a data analyst is to put some order into the data, helping your reader to understand the results of the two tests. Presenting only the grades would not help the reader to detect if the performance in the two tests was very different.

Computing averages might be a first step in putting some order into the list of grades in the two sections. The average (more formally known as an *arithmetic mean*) is computed by summing the values of a variable and dividing the result by the total number of cases. A mean is properly computed when *ratio level* data are available. To find the mean grade in each test we would simply sum the grades and then divide by the number of students. This would result in a mean grade for each section of the course.

Figure 7.2   Summary Statistics for Student Grades

Summary Statistics	Test A Grades	Test B Grades
Central Tendency:		
Mean	62.02	60.02
Mode	58.00	59.00
Median	60.00	60.00
Variation:		
Range	50.00	60.00
Standard Deviation	9.53	10.13
Number of Cases:	62	62

Figure 7.2 reports the means, showing that the average performance was somewhat higher in Test A. Students scored 2.0 points higher on the first test than on the second one. That difference is not easily apparent in looking at the raw scores.

b. The Median. The median represents the mid-point of a distribution. It is that point in a distribution such that one half the cases fall above this value, one half below it. The median is used for *ordinal level* variables or in cases where the use of a mean would be problematic because a few extreme values would give an inappropriate impression of the typical case. The steps in determining the median are:

Step 1. Arrange the cases in order from highest to lowest, or lowest to highest;

Step 2. Assign a number to the values (ignoring no response or missing data);

Step 3. If there is an odd number of cases, then the middle value is identified, and that value is the median for the distribution;

Step 4. If there is an even number of cases, then the mean of the middle two is calculated, and that value represents the median.

Figure 7.3 Computing the Median

Odd Number of Cases			Even Number of Cases		
#	Value	Median	#	Value	Median
1.	1		1.	4	
2.	1		2.	4	
3.	1		3.	5	
4.	2		4.	6	
5.	3		5.	6	
6.	3		6.	7	
7.	4	◀— 4 is	7.	7	◀— 7.5 is
8.	4	median	8.	8	median
9.	5		9.	8	
10.	5		10.	8	
11.	6		11.	9	
12.	8		12.	9	
13.	9		13.	9	
			14.	9	

Figure 7.3 illustrates medians on a 9-point attitude item for both odd and even numbered sample sizes. Note that the values have been ordered and the middle-most figure has been identified as the median.

Figure 7.4 Median for Extreme Values

Case #	Income	Case #	Income
1.	5 400	9.	19 000
2.	6 600	10.	20 000
3.	7 700	11.	20 500
4.	10 200	12.	22 900
5.	13 400	13.	24 600
6.	16 400	14.	31 500
7.	16 700	15.	580 000
8.	18 300	◀— $18 300.	median value
		$54 213.	mean value

Figure 7.4 illustrates a situation where a median would be a better description of a sample than would a mean. Here the data are for the annual incomes of 15 musicians in Montreal. Given the extreme case of $580 000 in comparison to the more modest incomes of the other musicians surveyed, the mean would falsely give the impression that the incomes of musicians are typically quite high. The median value of $18 300 is a much better description of the income distribution than is the $54 213 mean. When atypical values are present, it is preferable to use the median as a better summary description of the data.

c. The Mode. The mode is the most frequently occurring response to a nominal variable. If one wishes to describe an "average" respondent in terms of community type, then the mode would be the appropriate statistic. In the case of home community, it might be "Small Town." This would simply mean that "Small Town" was the most frequently occurring response to the question asking respondents to indicate the type of community they grew up in. Figure 7.5 presents a frequency distribution (showing the number of respondents who fall into each category) of respondents who report themselves to be from each of the eight different types of communities.

Figure 7.5   Distribution of Respondents by Community Type

Community Type	Number	Percent	
Rural Farm	37	6.9	
Rural Non-farm	72	13.5	
Small Town (under 5000)	126	23.7	◄——— mode
Town (5000 to 19 999)	103	19.4	
Large Town (20 000 to 49 999)	121	22.7	
Small City (50 000 to 99 999)	23	4.3	
Medium City (100 000 to 499 999)	36	6.8	
Large City (Over 500 000)	14	2.6	
TOTAL	532	99.9	

From Figure 7.5 the modal category can be identified by looking at the "Number" column, and picking out the one with the highest frequency: in this case, the category is "Small Town."

d. SPSSˣ Commands for Measures of Central Tendency. For ratio level variables, to get the mean simply run the CONDESCRIPTIVE procedure and the mean is automatically computed:

CONDESCRIPTIVE Var1, Var2, Var3, Var6

For nominal or ordinal variables, use the FREQUENCIES procedure to get the mode or median values as well as the distribution of the variable. The commands are:

FREQUENCIES VARIABLES = Var7, Var11/
STATISTICS = MEDIAN MODE DEFAULT/

2. Measures of Dispersion

Besides describing a variable in terms of central tendency, it is helpful to know something about the variability of the values. Are most of the values close to one another, or are they spread out? To illustrate, suppose we have two students, Mary and Beth. Their grades are indicated in Figure 7.6.

Figure 7.6 Two Grade Distributions

Subject	Mary	Beth
Sociology	78	66
Psychology	80	72
History	82	88
English	82	90
Philosophy	88	94
Mean Grade[1]	82	82
Range[2]	10	28
Standard Deviation[3]	3.35	10.95
Variance[4]	11.22	120.00

[1]Mean = Sum of values divided by number of cases.
[2]Range = Highest value − lowest value.
[3]See computation in Figure 7.7.
[4]Variance = sd²

While both students have an identical 82% average, the distributions are quite different. Mary's grades vary little, Beth's vary considerably. We will explore three ways of describing the dispersion in the two students' grades.

a. Range. The range is an elementary measure which simply indicates the gap between the lowest and highest value for an individual. It is computed by subtracting the lowest value from the highest one. Figure 7.6 indicates that the range of Beth's grades is 28, while for Mary the range is 10.

b. Standard Deviation. Researchers rely heavily on standard deviations to give them a sense of how much dispersion there is in a variable. Essentially, this measure reflects the average amount of deviation from the mean value of the variable. The formula is:

$$sd = \sqrt{\frac{\Sigma\,(X - \overline{X})^2}{N}}$$

Figure 7.7 shows how the standard deviation for Beth's grades may be computed. An examination of Figure 7.6 reveals that the standard deviation of Mary's grades is 3.35, considerably less than Beth's 10.95. An examination of the actual grades indicates that, indeed, there is much more variability in Beth's than in Mary's grades. The standard deviation reflects the variability in a set of values.

Figure 7.7   Computation of Standard Deviation, Beth's Grades

Subject	Grade	$X - \bar{X}$	$(X - \bar{X})^2$
Sociology	66	66 – 82 = – 16	256
Psychology	72	72 – 82 = – 10	100
History	88	88 – 82 = 6	36
English	90	90 – 82 = 8	64
Philosophy	94	94 – 82 = 12	144
MEAN	82.0	TOTAL	600

$$sd = \sqrt{\frac{\Sigma (X - \bar{X})^2}{N}}$$

$$sd = \sqrt{600/5} = 10.95$$

The beginning researcher should be familiar with how standard deviations are computed; this statistic is probably the single most important one to be encountered. It will be relevant for a number of other statistics. Once data have been entered into the computer, it will not be necessary to hand compute standard deviations; nonetheless, it is crucial to understand what they measure.

   c. **Variance.** The third measure of dispersion is variance, which is simply the standard deviation squared. Or:

$$\textbf{Variance} = \textbf{sd}^2 = \frac{\Sigma (X - \bar{X})^2}{N}$$

In the illustration using Mary's and Beth's grades, the variances are 11.22 and 120.00 respectively.

   d. **SPSSx Procedures for Measuring Dispersion.** To have the computer calculate these values, the following SPSSx commands will produce measures of the range, standard deviation, and variance:

```
CONDESCRIPTIVE Var1 TO Var6, Var27 TO Var33
STATISTICS 5 6 9
                        OR

FREQUENCIES VARIABLES = Var7, Var10/
STATISTICS = STDDEV VARIANCE RANGE/
```

3. Standardizing Data

To standardize data is to make adjustments so that comparisons between different sized units may be made; data may also be standardized to create variables which have similar variability in them (Z scores).

a. Rates. The incidences of social phenomena are often presented in the form of a rate. *Rates indicate the frequency of some phenomenon for a standard sized unit* (such as incidence per 1000 or per 100 000). This allows us to easily compare the incidence of a phenomenon in different sized units. To know for example that there were 27 suicides in a city of 250 000 (Middle City) in one year and in another city of 110 000 (Small City) there were 13, does not allow quick comparison unless we compute a suicide rate. A suicide rate may be computed in the following manner:

$$\text{Suicide Rate} = \frac{\text{Number Suicides/Year}}{\text{Mid-year Population}} \times 100\ 000$$

When calculated, we find that the suicide rate for Middle City is 10.8, while for Small City the rate is 11.8. This means that Middle City has 10.8 suicides in the year for every 100 000 people in the city; in Small City the rate is 11.8 per 100 000. We see that the smaller of the two cities has a slightly higher suicide rate. Rates can also be computed for specific age categories, or on other bases; the only adjustment required is that the number of suicides in the category must be compared to its total size. Rates are computed for many things including births, marriages, divorces, deaths, and crime.

Figure 7.8   Suicide Rates for Canadian Provinces, 1985, and the United States, 1982

A. Canada	Number of Suicides	Population	Suicide Rate[1]
Atlantic:	189	2 307 400	8.19
Newfoundland	23	580 400	3.96
P.E.I.	3	127 100	2.36
Nova Scotia	90	880 700	10.21
New Brunswick	73	719 200	10.15
Quebec:	879	6 580 700	13.35
Ontario:	790	9 066 200	8.71
Western:	708	7 404 100	9.56
Manitoba	102	1 069 600	9.53
Saskatchewan	106	1 019 500	10.39
Alberta	243	2 348 800	10.34
British Columbia	238	2 892 500	8.22
Yukon & N.W.T.	19	73 700	25.78
CANADA	2 566	25 358 500	10.11

Figure 7.8 Continued

B. United States	Suicide Rate[2]	United States	Suicide Rate[2]
Region:		District of Columbia	11.8
Northeast	9.1	Virginia	13.9
Midwest	11.3	West Virginia	11.7
South	12.9	North Carolina	13.3
West	15.4	South Carolina	11.4
New England:	9.9	Georgia	13.2
Maine	13.0	Florida	17.0
New Hampshire	11.7	East South Central:	11.7
Vermont	16.0	Kentucky	13.5
Massachusetts	9.4	Tennessee	12.6
Rhode Island	11.3	Alabama	10.9
Connecticut	7.7	Mississippi	8.7
Middle Atlantic:	8.8	West South Central:	12.5
New York	7.6	Arkansas	12.0
New Jersey	7.8	Louisiana	12.5
Pennsylvania	11.3	Oklahoma	14.1
East North Central:	11.2	Texas	12.2
Ohio	11.9	Mountain:	17.4
Indiana	11.4	Montana	15.7
Illinois	9.5	Idaho	14.1
Michigan	12.1	Wyoming	18.9
Wisconsin	12.3	Colorado	16.4
West North Central:	11.4	New Mexico	19.8
Minnesota	11.4	Arizona	17.6
Iowa	10.6	Utah	12.9
Missouri	11.8	Nevada	29.0
North Dakota	10.9	Pacific:	14.7
South Dakota	13.7	Washington	13.4
Nebraska	10.3	Oregon	14.7
Kansas	11.5	California	15.2
South Atlantic:	13.7	Alaska	12.2
Delaware	12.7	Hawaii	9.7
Maryland	10.1	UNITED STATES	12.2

[1]The Canadian data were computed by drawing on data from: Statistics Canada, *Mortality: Vital Statistics.* Vol. 3, 1985. Statistics Canada, *Postcensal Annual Estimates of Population by Marital Status, Age, Sex, and Components of Growth for Canada, Provinces and Territories, June 1, 1985.* Vol. 3, Third Issue.

[2]The United States data were derived from Table 116, *Statistical Abstracts of the United States, 1986,* 106 Edition, U.S. Department of Commerce, Bureau of the Census, p. 75.

Figure 7.8 presents provincial and state suicide rates for Canada and the United States. Note that the data are standardized; permitting easy comparison between the units. If the absolute number of suicides were presented, the impression that there is a much more serious problem with suicides in the larger provinces would be created.

SPSS^x procedures for computing rates are presented in Chapter 13.

   b. Ratios. Ratios are used to compare rates or other measures across categories. For example, suppose one wished to compare U.S. and Canadian crime rates. Suppose the burglary rate in the U.S. is 200 per 100 000 while the comparable Canadian rate is 57 per 100 000. The American/Canadian burglary ratio could be represented as:

$$\text{American/Canadian Burglary Ratio } = \frac{\text{U.S. Burglary Rate}}{\text{Canadian Burglary Rate}}$$

$$\text{American/Canadian Burglary Ratio } = \frac{200}{57} = 3.51$$

This ratio suggests that the American burglary rate is 3.51 times higher than the comparable Canadian rate. Many ratios can be computed which, like rates, facilitate comparison between categories.

Figure 7.9   Male/Female Suicide Ratios, by Province, Canada, 1985

Province	Suicide Rate Males	Suicide Rate Females	Ratio Male/Female Suicides
Newfoundland	8.1	–	–
P.E.I.	4.4	2.6	1.69
Nova Scotia	18.6	3.2	5.81
New Brunswick	18.5	3.2	5.78
Quebec	23.8	6.4	3.72
Ontario	15.5	4.7	3.30
Manitoba	17.7	3.9	4.54
Saskatchewan	19.5	5.3	3.68
Alberta	19.0	4.2	4.52
British Columbia	14.7	3.9	3.77
CANADA	18.2	4.8	3.79

In this table the Male/Female suicide ratio is computed for each province by dividing the male suicide rate by the female rate. The result indicates how many male suicides there are for every female suicide.

Figure 7.9 presents the ratio between male and female suicide rates for Canadian provinces. Note that nationally males commit suicide 3.79 times more frequently than females. The ratios facilitate comparison between the provinces.

In some cases, ratios are reported so that they are standardized to a base of 100. For example, if we had a community with 27 304 males and 31 216 females, we might compute a sex ratio. The ratio for the community could be calculated as follows:

$$\text{Sex ratio } = \frac{\text{Number of males}}{\text{Number of females}} \times 100$$

$$\text{Sex ratio } = \frac{27\ 304}{31\ 216} \times 100 = 87.5$$

This sex ratio would indicate that there are 87.5 males in the community for every 100 females. Such a ratio allows us to quickly compare the sex ratios of communities, nations, age groups, or any other category. SPSS^x procedures for computing ratios are presented in Chapter 13.

c. Proportions and Percentages. A proportion may be calculated to show, for example, how many females there are in a population compared to the total population. Suppose we wished to compute the proportion female in the community noted above:

$$\text{Proportion female } = \frac{\text{number females}}{\text{total persons}}$$

$$\text{Proportion female } = \frac{31\ 216}{58\ 520} = .533$$

The females represent .53 of the population. If we wish to represent this value as a *percentage* we would simply multiply the proportion by 100. By doing this, we find that females constitute 53.3 percent of the population.

Table 7.1 presents the relationship between size of home community and whether or not the respondents plan to attend university. Note that in this table we cannot simply say that 69 rural students and 102 small town students plan to attend university. Percentages are used to adjust for the fact that there are different numbers of students involved in each of the categories. By computing the percentages, we are able to say that of the rural students, 52.3 percent are planning-to-attend university in contrast to 73.9 percent of the high school students from towns over 5000.

4. The Normal Curve

The normal distribution is another key concept used by researchers. Many of the observations researchers make about individual or group characteristics will approximate what is referred to as a normal distribution. What does this mean?

If a graph is made showing the distribution, for example, of the weight of male university students, it would approximate a bell-shaped curve. There will be few cases on the extremes—the very light and the very heavy; most of the cases will be found clustered toward the middle of the distribution.

Another way to illustrate the normal curve is to plot the outcomes of a series of 10 coin flips. Suppose we flip a coin 10 times, record the number of heads, repeat this operation 1024 times, and then plot the number of times we got 0, 1, 2, ... 10 heads in the trials. The outcome will approximate that shown in Figure 7.10, which is a graph of the theoretical probabilities of getting each of the 11 possible outcomes (i.e., 0 through 10 heads).

Figure 7.10   Distribution of Number of Heads Flipped in 10 Attempts, 1024 trials

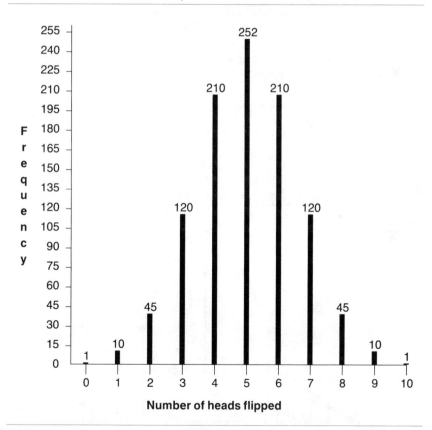

A further characteristic of the normal distribution is its connection to the standard deviation. By definition, a fixed proportion of cases will fall within given standard deviations of the mean (see Figure 7.11). About two thirds of

the cases will fall within one standard deviation of the mean; just over 95 percent of the cases will fall within two standard deviations of the mean. More precisely, the properties of a normal distribution include that:

a) it will form a symmetrical, bell-shaped curve;

b) the mean, mode, and median values will be the same; half the cases will fall below the mean, the other half above the mean;

c) as the number of observations and the number of measurement units become finer, the distribution curve will become smoother;

d) 68.28 percent of the observations will be divided equally between the mean and one standard deviation to the right of the mean (34.14), and one to the left of the mean (34.14);

e) 95.46 percent of the observations will fall $\pm$ two standard deviations from the mean;

f) 95 percent of the cases will fall $\pm$ 1.96 standard deviation units from the mean;

g) 99 percent of the cases will fall $\pm$ 2.58 standard deviation units from the mean.

Figure 7.11   Normal Distribution Curve

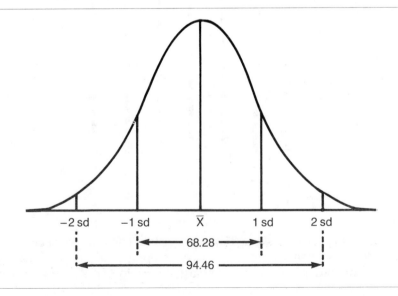

5. Z Scores

Z scores measure the distance, in standard deviation units, of any value in a distribution. Thus, if someone's income has a Z score of +1.43 it would mean that the income is 1.43 standard deviation units above the mean of the distribution. Suppose that the mean income is $25 000 and the standard deviation $12 000: the Z score +1.43 would indicate an income of $42 160. How is this value computed? The formula for Z scores is as follows:

$$Z = \frac{X - \overline{X}}{SD}$$

Where: X is the observation; $\overline{X}$ is the mean of the distribution; and where sd is the standard deviation of the distribution.

By plugging the values into the equation and solving it, the value $42 160 is obtained, as in:

$$1.43 = \frac{X - 25\,000}{12\,000}$$

$$X = (1.43 \times 12\,000) + 25\,000$$

$$X = 42\,160$$

One of the consequences of being able to report a value in terms of its Z score, is that we now have a powerful comparative tool. Suppose we wanted to compare individuals' relative income positions in two countries: we could simply report the incomes in Z score terms and this would tell us where each individual stands in terms of his or her country's income distribution. This result would permit us to compare a British family's income of 12 000 pounds to an American family's income of $20 000.

The student should recognize that whole sets of variables can be standardized by computing Z scores, and the resulting distributions will have means of 0 and standard deviations of 1. Thus, instead of just having variables with income scores, educational levels, and occupational prestige, we might have standardized variables containing the Z scores for each variable. Such standardization can be accomplished easily in SPSS[x] with the following command:

```
CONDESCRIPTIVE Var1,Var22,Var30
OPTIONS 3
```

6. Z Scores in Index Construction

A major use of Z scores is in combining indicators to create an index. Suppose, for example, that we have measures on income and years of education and we wish to combine them to form a socio-economic index. Clearly, it does not make sense to simply add a respondent's years of education to the annual income of that person. The reason is that incomes might vary from $5000 to $500 000 while years of education might vary from 0 to 20, and by adding them together the income component would totally dominate the index. Someone earning $40 000 with 8 years of education would have a score of 40 008 while a person with a B.A. and $30 000 income would end up with a score of 30 016. Somehow, we need to weight the components so that income and education will equally influence the outcome. One easy way to do this is by using Z scores.

Figure 7.12   Computing an Index Score Using Z Score

	Income	Years Education
Given population values:		
Mean	25 000	11
Standard Deviation	12 000	4
Suppose five individuals:		
A.	35 000	7
B.	21 000	12
C.	10 000	8
D.	44 000	16
E.	56 000	9

Compute an Index equally weighting income and years of education. The general equation is:

$$Z = \frac{X - \overline{X}}{sd}$$

Case **A.**	Income:	(35 000 − 25 000) / 12 000	=	.83
	Education:	(7 − 11) / 4	=	− 1.00
	Socio-economic index score			− .17
Case **B.**	Income:	(21 000 − 25 000) / 12 000	=	− .33
	Education:	(12 − 11) / 4	=	.25
	Socio-economic index score			− .08
Case **C.**	Income:	(10 000 − 25 000) / 12 000	=	− 1.25
	Education:	(8 − 11) / 4	=	− .75
	Socio-economic index score			− 2.00
Case **D.**	Income:	(44 000 − 25 000) / 12 000	=	1.58
	Education:	(16 − 11) / 4	=	1.25
	Socio-economic index score			2.83
Case **E.**	Income:	(56 000 − 25 000) / 12 000	=	2.58
	Education:	(9 − 11) / 4	=	− .50
	Socio-economic index score			2.08

Figure 7.12 shows the computations of socio-economic index scores using Z scores. Notice how either a lower-than-average income or a lower-than-average education will lead to a reduction in the total socio-economic score. In analyzing a survey, these indexes can be calculated quickly using the computer and the components weighted any way the researcher likes. The Z scores, for example, may be added together resulting in a value that can be taken to represent the relative socio-economic position of the various respondents, with income and education making equal contributions to the final score. Such computations can be done rapidly within SPSS^x. (See Chapter 11.)

7. Areas Under the Normal Curve

Another useful property of the normal distribution is that it is possible, with the help of a table (see Table A in the Appendix), to calculate the proportion of cases that will fall between two values, or below or above a given value.

To illustrate, suppose we wished to know what percentage of incomes will fall above $40 000, given a population standard deviation of $12 000, and a mean of $25 000. The steps in solving this problem are as follows:

Step 1. Draw a normal curve, marking below it the mean and standard deviation values, and drawing a line through the curve at the point where you expect $40 000 to fall. Since the question asks about the percentage above this point, shade the curve to the right of the $40 000 mark.

Step 2. Calculate the Z score to determine how many standard deviation units $40 000 is above the mean. As in:

$$Z = \frac{X - \bar{X}}{sd}$$

$$Z = \frac{40\,000 - 25\,000}{12\,000}$$

$$Z = 1.25$$

Step 3. Look up the value 1.25 on the table in Appendix A. Move down the Z score column until you come to the value 1.2, then read across to the column headed by .05, and read the value. You should have found the number 3944. This number should be understood as ".3944", a proportion.

Step 4. By definition, we know that one half of the cases will fall above the mean. Expressed as a proportion, this would indicate that .5 of the cases will fall above the mean. The question we are trying to answer is what proportion of the cases fall above $40 000? Looking at the diagram we made in step one, we realize that if the right side of the curve contains .5 of all the cases, and if the value $40 000 is .3944 above the mean, then the cases above $40 000 would have to be:

.5000 – .3944 = .1056

Step 5. As a proportion, .1056 of the cases will fall above $40 000. Or, another way of expressing the same thing is to say that 10.6 percent of the cases will fall above $40 000.

Suppose we wish to determine the proportion of cases that will fall between $20 000 and $40 000, given the same population mean and standard deviation. Similar procedures to those above should be followed. This time, however, the diagram will show a shaded area between two points on either side of the mean. This time, also, two Z scores will need to be computed, the values looked up in Appendix A, and the proportions between the mean and each cut-point determined, and then added together to reach the final answer. The computations may be done as follows:

Step 1. Proportion between mean and $40 000:

$$Z = \frac{X - \overline{X}}{sd} = \frac{40\,000 - 25\,000}{12\,000} = 1.25$$

Proportion covered by Z score of 1.25 = .3944

Step 2. Proportion between $20 000 and mean:

$$Z = \frac{X - \overline{X}}{sd} = \frac{20\,000 - 25\,000}{12\,000} = -.42$$

Proportion covered by Z score of - .42 = .1628

Step 3. Adding the proportions together:

.3944 + .1628 = .5572

The computation indicates that just over one half of all the cases, 55.7 percent, fall between the incomes of $20 000 and $40 000. The proportion between the mean and the respective Z scores is shown in Figure 7.13. In this case, the values are added together to determine the proportion of cases that fall between $20 000 and $40 000.

Figure 7.13   Areas Under the Normal Curve

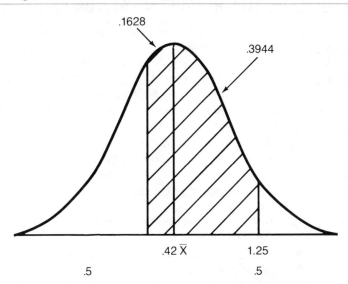

Total area between −.42 and +1.25 is the proportion between
X̄ and +1.25 = .3944; between X̄ and −.42 = .1628 Total = .5572

There are other types of normal curve problems which can be solved. Just keep in mind the above examples, draw a diagram shading in the area you need to determine, and remember that each side of the normal curve contains one half, or .5 of the cases. With these things in mind, it should be possible to solve most normal curve problems.

8. Other Distributions

Not all variables will be normally distributed. If, for example, we were to plot the weights of our freshman students we would almost certainly find that the result would be a *bi-modal* distribution. The reason for this is that female students will have lower average weights than the males. Essentially we would end up combining two normally distributed plots, one for women and men, and one which would have two peaks and a lot of overlap between the male and female weights.

If a set of values has little variability — a small standard deviation relative to the magnitude of the values — then the distribution will be peaked and is said to be *leptokurtic;* on the other hand, if the distribution has a great deal of variability, the distribution curve will tend to be flat and wide, and is called a *platykurtic* distribution.

B. DESCRIBING RELATIONSHIPS BETWEEN VARIABLES

The survey researcher is primarily concerned with describing and understanding relationships among variables. Typically, in dealing with simple relationships, one of the variables will be treated as a dependent variable; the other(s) as independent variable(s), or control variable(s). Recall that the dependent variable is the effect, the independent variable the cause, while a control variable is either an intervening, source of spuriousness, or conditional variable.

This section of the chapter will describe some of the major procedures used to examine relationships between variables. The first step in any analysis is to decide which variable is the dependent one; second, an appropriate procedure for examining the relationship must then be selected; and finally, the analysis is performed.

Since the researcher typically is trying to understand what causes variations to occur in a dependent variable, the designation of a variable as dependent is generally obvious on a common sense basis. However, there will be other cases were it is not obvious. In such cases, the researcher must try to decide which variable occurs last in a temporal sequence. It is entirely possible that the two variables mutually influence one another. If this is the case, one will nonetheless have to be designated as the "dependent" variable.

Having decided which variable is to be treated as the dependent one, the researcher must next identify the level of measurement of each of the variables. Then, using the information provided in Figure 7.14, the SPSS^x procedures which would be most appropriate for the analysis must be identified. Let us explore each of the procedures identified in Figure 7.14.

Figure 7.14   Basic SPSS^x Procedures for Different Levels of Measurement

	INDEPENDENT VARIABLE		
DEPENDENT	Nominal	Ordinal	Ratio
Nominal	CROSSTABS	CROSSTABS	CROSSTABS BREAKDOWN*
Ordinal	CROSSTABS	CROSSTABS NONPAR CORR	CROSSTABS NONPAR CORR
Ratio	BREAKDOWN	BREAKDOWN	PEARSON CORR SCATTERGRAM PARTIAL CORR REGRESSION

*In this case, one must run the independent variable as though it were the dependent variable (i.e., name it first); the interpretation of the test of significance would be standard.

1. CROSSTABS: Contingency Tables

Contingency table analysis presents information so that a nominal-level dependent variable can be related to an independent variable. Table 7.1 presents findings on the relationship between the educational plans and the sizes of the home community of 360 students in rural Nova Scotia. We will examine this table in detail as it typifies the crosstabs table.

Table 7.1   Plans to Attend University by Size of Home Community

University Plans?	Rural		Town up to 5 000		Town over 5 000		TOTAL	
	N	%	N	%	N	%	N	%
Plans	69	52.3	44	48.9	102	73.9	215	59.7
No Plans	63	47.7	46	51.1	36	26.1	145	40.3
TOTAL	132	100.0	90	100.0	138	100.0	360	100.0

If appropriate, results of a test of significance are entered here.

A contingency table cross-classifies cases on two or more variables. In this example, the data are first sorted into categories representing community size; next, each of these categories is sorted into whether the person does, or does not, plan to attend university. This sorting allows us to see if those from rural areas are more likely to have university plans than their urban counterparts.

Rules for presenting such tables will be discussed in Chapter 11, but note that *the dependent variable is placed on the vertical axis, and that the percentages are run toward the independent variable and total 100.0 percent.* In interpreting such tables, one compares percentage distributions in adjacent columns, as in: "while about one half of the respondents from rural and small town areas plan on postsecondary education, some 73.9 percent of those from larger centers have such plans."

The SPSS^x command for CROSSTABS, which will generate the appropriate percentages and a test of significance, is as follows:

```
CROSSTABS TABLES = depend BY independ
OPTIONS 4
STATISTICS 1
```

2. BREAKDOWN: Comparing Means

When the researcher has a ratio-level dependent variable, and either a nominal or ordinal independent variable, then it is appropriate to compute the mean values of the dependent variable for each category of the independent variable. Table 7.2 presents the kind of data that would be appropriate for this kind of analysis. Note that the dependent variable (income) is measured at the ratio level, while the independent variable is nominal (gender).

Table 7.2   Mean Income by Sex

Sex	Mean Income	Number of Cases
Male	37 052	142
Female	34 706	37
COMBINED MEAN	$36 567	179

If appropriate, test of significance values entered here.

The above table presents a model for the presentation of a comparison of the mean values of a dependent variable (income) by categories of an independent variable (gender).

SPSS^x commands for running BREAKDOWN are as follows:

BREAKDOWN TABLES = income BY sex
STATISTICS 1

The BREAKDOWN procedure requires that the dependent variable be named first. This will cause the program to compute the mean value for the first variable (income) for each of the categories of the independent variable (gender). In cases where there are many categories in the independent variable, these will have to be regrouped into two or three before the analysis is run (RECODE procedure).

In interpreting the outcome of an analysis, the mean values should be compared. In Table 7.2, for example, the average incomes of the males are compared to those of the females.

3. PEARSON CORR: Correlational Analysis

In cases where variables are to be measured at the ratio level, various correlational procedures may be used. A variety of statistical procedures are based on correlational analyses. Once the fundamentals of this family of statistical techniques are understood, the beginning researcher is in a position to grasp such procedures as partial correlations, multiple correlations, multiple regression, factor analysis, path analysis, and canonical correlations.

One of the major advantages of using correlational techniques is that it is possible to examine a number of variables simultaneously without running out of cases. Multivariate (many variable) analysis, whose computations have been made easier through the use of high-speed computers, rely heavily on correlational techniques. But the cost of using these powerful statistical tools is that more attention must be paid to the problems of measurement. Correlational techniques assume measurement at the ratio level. While this assumption may be relaxed, the cost of doing so is that the strength of the relationships between variables will tend to be underestimated.

Given the importance of correlational techniques it is crucial that the beginning researcher understand the fundamentals of the procedure. Once the fundamentals are understood, the more sophisticated procedures are extensions of the simple ones.

In simple correlation analysis we have two basic concerns: (i) What is the equation that describes the relation between the variables?; and (ii) What is the strength of the relation between the two? An attempt will be made to show how each may be visually estimated; in addition, a simple, intuitively obvious approach to each computation will be presented.

a. The Linear Equation: A Visual Estimation Procedure. Our first concern will be to determine the equation that describes the relation between two variables. The general form of the equation is:

$$Y = a + b(X)$$

The components of the equation are Y, the dependent variable, and X, the independent variable; a is a constant which identifies the point at which the regression line crosses the Y axis; b refers to the slope of the regression line which describes the relation between the variables. The terms "Y axis," and "regression line" are discussed below.

For purposes of illustration we will use the following data set:

Table 7.3 Sample Data Set

X	Y
2	3
3	4
5	4
7	6
8	8

Step 1. The first step in visually estimating the equation that describes the relation between the variables is to plot the relation on graph paper. Figure 7.15 shows what such a graph would look like.

Note that the dependent variable (Y) is plotted on the vertical axis, the independent variable (X) on the horizontal axis.

Figure 7.15   Scatterplot of Sample Data

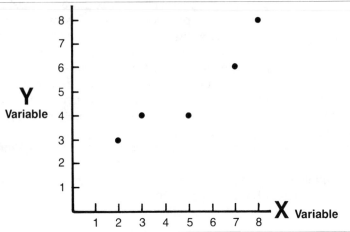

Step 2. Insert a straight *regression line* such that the vertical deviations of the points above the line equal the vertical deviations below the line. There need not be the same number of points above as below the line, nor do any of the points need to fall right on the line. The regression line offers the best linear description of the relation between the two variables. From the regression line one can estimate how much the independent variable has to be changed in order to produce a unit of change in the dependent variable. (See Figure 7.16)

Figure 7.16   Estimating the Equation

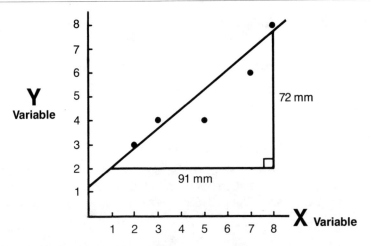

Step 3. Observe where the regression line crosses the Y axis; this point represents the constant, or the *a* value in the regression equation. Note that in Figure 7.16 we have estimated that it crosses the Y axis at 1.33.

Step 4. Draw a line parallel to the X axis and one parallel to the Y axis, similar to that shown in Figure 7.16. Measure the lines in millimeters. (In Figure 7.16, the vertical measures 72 mm, the horizontal 91 mm.) Divide the horizontal distance into the vertical distance: this computation will provide our estimated *b* value. (In our figure, 72 ÷ 91 = .79.)

Step 5. The visual estimation of the equation describing the relation between the variables is determined by simply adding the *a* and *b* values to the general equation:

$$Y = a + b(X)$$

In our illustration the values would be as follows:

$$Y = 1.33 + .79(X)$$

The above formula is the estimated equation for the relation between the two variables. Let us now perform a simple computation to see what the "real" equation is.

b. The Linear Equation: A Simple Computational Procedure. Table 7.4 presents the data and the computations necessary to determine the actual equation.

Table 7.4 Computing a Linear Equation

Step 1		Step 2	Step 3	Step 4	Step 5
X	Y	$X - \bar{X}$	$(X - \bar{X})^2$	$Y - \bar{Y}$	$(X - \bar{X})(Y - \bar{Y})$
2	3	−3	9	−2	6
3	4	−2	4	−1	2
5	4	0	0	−1	0
7	6	2	4	1	2
8	8	3	9	3	9
25	25	0	26	0	19

$\bar{X} = 5$

$\bar{Y} = 5$

General Equation: $Y = a + b(X)$ where:

$$b = \frac{\Sigma(X - \bar{X})(Y - \bar{Y})}{\Sigma(X - \bar{X})^2} = \frac{19}{26} = .73$$

$$a = \bar{Y} - b(\bar{X}) = 5 - .73(5) = 1.45$$

Hence, $Y = 1.45 + .73(X)$

The following steps are required:

Step 1. Determine the mean value for the X and Y variables. This can be done by summing the values and dividing by the number of cases.

Step 2. Subtract each value of X from the mean of X.

Step 3. Square the values determined in the previous step.

Step 4. Subtract each value of Y from the mean of Y.

Step 5. Multiply the value determined in Step 2 by those determined in Step 4.

Step 6. Sum all columns.

Step 7. To determine the *b* value, divide the column total determined in Step 5 by the column total in Step 3. As in:

$$b = \frac{\Sigma\,(\,X - \overline{X}\,)\,(\,Y - \overline{Y}\,)}{\Sigma\,(\,X - \overline{X}\,)^2}$$

$$b = 19 \div 26$$

$$b = .73$$

Step 8. To determine the *a* value apply the formula:

$$a = \overline{Y} - b(\overline{X})$$

$$a = 5 - .73(5)$$

$$a = 1.45$$

Step 9. The values may now be applied and the final equation determined. In the illustration, the formula is:

$$Y = 1.45 + .73(X)$$

We can now compare the actual (computed) formula to the estimated one. The estimated equation is:

$$Y = 1.33 + .79(X)$$

Note that the estimate comes fairly close to the computed figures. In a research project, the computer would generate the *a* and the *b* values, as in:

```
REGRESSION VARIABLES = Y X /
       DEPENDENT = Y/
       BACKWARD/
```

Estimating equations is a good exercise for becoming familiar with the different values involved in regression analysis.

In some cases, the *a* value will turn out to be negative and this simply means that the regression line crosses the Y axis below the X axis. It should be noted as well that as the *b* value increases, the regression line is steeper, thus smaller increments in the X variable lead to increments in the Y variable. A negative value of *b* indicates a negative slope, a situation where the data are indicating a relationship where *the greater X, the less Y.*

The beginning researcher should recognize that with a linear equation it is possible to *predict* the value of a dependent variable given a value for the independent variable. When social scientists speak of prediction this is usually the sense in which they are using the term. That is, a predicted value is computed using an equation where the values of the independent variable(s) is(are) plugged into the equation. Suppose, for example, we attempted to predict the values of Y given X values of 1, 4, and 6. To solve the problem we would simply use the equation computed above and then determine the predicted values of Y, as in:

computed equation:	$Y = 1.45 + .73(X)$	
with X value of 1:	$Y = 1.45 + .73(1)$	$= 2.18$
with X value of 4:	$Y = 1.45 + .73(4)$	$= 4.37$
with X value of 6:	$Y = 1.45 + .73(6)$	$= 5.83$

In situations where there are multiple independent variables, determining the predicted values of a dependent variable is the same, except that there are more values to be plugged into the equation.

Figure 7.17   Estimating a Correlation

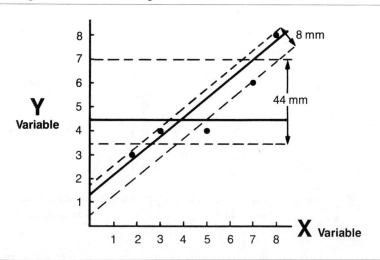

Figure 7.17 shows how it is possible to visually estimate the predicted value of Y, given a value of X. The procedure simply involves locating the X value on the X axis, moving vertically to the regression line, then moving horizontally to the Y axis. Where the Y axis is intersected represents the visual estimate of the Y variable.

c. Correlation Coefficient: A Visual Estimation Procedure. In learning to visually estimate a correlation it is important to develop some sense of what correlations of different magnitude look like. Figure 7.18 presents graphs of four relationships, where the correlation coefficients vary from .99 to .36. Note that if the correlation dropped below the .36 level, it would be difficult to determine where the regression line should be drawn. At the other end of the continuum, note that correlations drop fairly slowly as the scatter around the regression line increases.

Figure 7.18   Scatterplots of Four Correlations

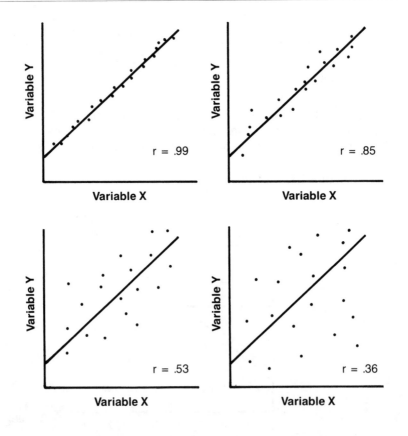

The correlation coefficient (r) is a measure of the strength of the association between two variables. The correlation may vary from + 1 to -1. Perfect correlations are rare, except when a variable is correlated with itself; hence almost all correlations will be represented by values preceded by a decimal point, as in: .98, .37, or –.56. Negative correlations mean that there is a negative slope in the relation.

There is an intuitively simple way of estimating the strength of the relation between two variables. An examination of the various correlations on Figure 7.18 reveals that as the correlations increased, the plotted points tended to be closer to the regression line. And, as the correlation dropped, the points diverged more from the regression line.

In estimating the correlation coefficient, there are two kinds of variability to be concerned with: (i) explained variation (the variations around the regression line) and (ii) unexplained variation (variations around the mean of Y). If we set the total variability to be equal to 1, we can then try to determine what proportion is explained and what proportion is unexplained. Essentially, the correlation coefficient (r) reflects this ratio so that the higher the proportion of explained variation, the higher the correlation. Indeed, we can represent the relation as follows:

$$\textbf{Explained Variance} \; = \; r^2 \; = \; 1 \; - \; \frac{\textbf{Explained Variation}}{\textbf{Unexplained Variation}}$$

As an exercise in trying to visually estimate the strength of a correlation, the following steps may be taken:

Step 1. Plot the data on graph paper, and draw in an estimated regression line.

Step 2. Draw in a line, parallel to the X axis, that will cut through the estimated mean value of Y.

Step 3. To estimate the deviations around the regression line (explained variance), draw in an additional regression line, parallel to the original one, for the points on or above the existing regression line. (You may want to cover the points below the regression line to avoid confusion.) Now draw in yet another regression line, parallel to the other two, for those points below the original regression line. Measure and record the perpendicular distance between the two new regression lines.

Step 4. To estimate the deviations around the mean of Y (unexplained variation), two additional lines parallel to the mean of Y line must be drawn: the first for those points above the line, the second for those points below the line. Once again, the perpendicular distance between these new lines should be measured and recorded.

Step 5. To estimate the correlation simply enter the values recorded above (also see Figure 7.18) into the following equation:

$$\text{Explained Variance} = r^2 = 1 - \frac{\text{Explained Variation}}{\text{Unexplained Variation}}$$

$$r^2 = 1 - \frac{8}{44}$$

$$r^2 = .82$$

$$r = .91$$

Such estimations indicate that a correlation is a measure of the ratio between explained and unexplained variation. As the explained variation becomes relatively smaller, the correlation rises. Conversely, as the explained variation starts to approach the measure of the unexplained variation, the correlation approaches zero. Correlations estimated in the above way are never reported because they are not exact. Instead, the computations are made by computer. However, if there are only a few cases, it is possible to hand compute a correlation using the steps outlined below.

d. Correlation Coefficient: A Simple Computational Procedure. Table 7.5 presents the information necessary to hand compute a correlation using a method which parallels the estimation procedure outlined above. The steps are simple and can be quickly performed if there are only a few observations.

Table 7.5   Computing the Correlation Coefficient

X	Y	$(Y - \bar{Y})^2$	Y_p	$Y - Y_p$	$(Y - Y_p)^2$
2	3	4	2.91	.09	.0081*
3	4	1	3.64	.36	.1296
5	4	1	5.10	−1.10	1.2100
7	6	1	6.56	.56	.3136
8	8	9	7.29	.71	.5041
		16			2.1654

*The Y_p value is computed by substituting each value of X into the equation determined in Table 7.4. In the first observation the computation would be: $Y_p = 1.45 + .73(2) = 2.91$

$$r^2 = 1 - \frac{\Sigma((Y - Y_p)^2 \div N)}{\Sigma(Y - \bar{Y})^2 \div N}$$

$$r^2 = 1 - \frac{.433}{3.2} \qquad r^2 = .86 \qquad r = .93$$

Step 1. The first step is to determine the variation around the regression line. For each observation of X, we will need to compute the predicted value for Y. To do this, we simply go to the equation determined in section c, plug in the value for X, and solve. The first observation would be calculated as follows:

$$Y_p = 1.45 + .73(X)$$

$$Y_p = 1.45 + .73(2)$$

$$Y_p = 2.91$$

The predicted values for Y are determined for each case in the manner described for the first observation.

Step 2. The second step is to compute how much each observation deviates from its "predicted" value. $(Y - Y_p)$

Step 3. The third step is to square the results of the previous step. After this is completed, this column should be summed. $(Y - Y_p)^2$

Step 4. The previous three steps provide us with a measure of the variations around the regression line. To get an estimate of the deviations around the mean of Y, we need only look at the sum for the column:

$$(Y - \overline{Y})^2$$

Step 5. We are now able to plug the values into the formula:

$$r^2 = 1 - \frac{\text{Variations Around Regression}}{\text{Variations Around Mean of Y}}$$

$$r^2 = 1 - \frac{\Sigma\,(\,Y - Y_p\,)^2 \div N}{\Sigma\,(\,Y - \overline{Y}\,)^2 \div N}$$

$$r^2 = 1 - \frac{.433}{3.2}$$

$$r^2 = 1 - .14$$

$$r^2 = .86$$

$$r = .93$$

Note that the computations have led to roughly similar results as were achieved using the estimation procedures. (Usually the results will not be so close.) Having done a few visual estimations, and a few hand calculations of correlations, the student should have a good understanding of simple correlations. Many statistical techniques are extensions of correlational techniques. Once the basics are understood, then we can turn the drudgery of computation over to a computer. The SPSSˣ command for computing a correlation coefficient is:

PEARSON CORR V16, V18 TO V22

4. SCATTERGRAM: Plotting the Data

If the researcher wishes to have a look at the plot of the data, then the computer can produce such plots by using the SCATTERGRAM procedure in SPSSˣ. The command is as follows:

SCATTERGRAM depend WITH independ

When producing a scatterplot of the data, name the dependent variable first and it will be plotted on the vertical axis. The axis values may be specified by the researcher. See the SPSSˣ manual for details.

5. NONPAR CORR: Computing Spearman Correlations

The beginning researcher may wish to run a correlation on ordinal data but may not wish to violate the measurement assumptions of a Pearson Correlation, discussed previously. In cases where one or both of the variables are ordinal, then a Spearman Correlation may be calculated. The details of such computations may be checked in any elementary statistics text and will not be presented here. Think of them as being similar to the correlation procedures just discussed. In order to have the computer calculate Spearman rs, the following SPSSˣ command is used:

NONPAR CORR V34, V37.V42 TO V45

6. PARTIAL CORR: Computing Partial Correlations

A partial correlation is a special type of correlation which may be used with ratio level variables. It measures the strength of association between two variables, while simultaneously controlling for the effects of one or more additional variables. In partial correlations we adjust the values of the dependent and independent variables in order to take into account the influence of other independent variables. The advantage of partial correlations over contingency table analysis is that: (i) we make use of all of the data (by not recoding variables into two or three categories as would be done in CROSSTABS); and (ii) we can work with fewer cases without running into cell size problems as happens frequently with contingency table analysis.

Like ordinary correlations, partial correlations take on values from + 1.0 through to − 1.0. Partial correlations control, or take into account, one or more independent variables. If there is one control variable, the correlation would be known as a *first-order partial*; one with two controls is a *second order partial*, and so forth. Incidentally, ordinary correlations are sometimes referred to as *zero-order correlations* which simply means that there are no control variables in the analysis.

The strategy involved in partial correlations is that regression equations can be used to express the relation between each pair of variables in the equation. For any value of an independent variable, it is possible to predict the value for the dependent variable, while adjusting for the influence of the control variables.

The idea of residuals is also useful for understanding partial correlations. In the three variable case, if the possible combinations (X–Y, Z–Y, and X–Z) are plotted, and a regression line is entered for the X–Y relation, deviations from the line are thought to be the result of the influence of factor Z plus that of other known, and unknown, factors. These deviations are called *residuals*. They arise when one variable is allowed to explain all the variation it can in another variable; variations left unexplained (deviations from the regression line) are the residuals. The correlating of residuals gives a measure of the amount of influence a third variable has on the first relationship (X–Y), independent of the second relationship (X–Z).

The notational convention used in referring to partial correlations shows the numbers of the two major variables and these are separated from the numbers of the control variables by a "." as in:

$$r_{12.3} = .56$$

In this case, there is a first-order partial reported, with a value of .56. This value represents a measure of the strength of association between variables 1 and 2, controlling for variable 3. A third-order partial simply designates three control variables, as in:

$$r_{12.347} = .28$$

Partial correlations will be used in testing causal models where the variables involved are measured at the ratio level of measurement. The SPSS^x command is set up in the following manner:

PARTIAL CORR jobsat WITH pay BY fringe (1)

In this case, the request has been made for a partial correlation between the variables Jobsat (job satisfaction) and Pay (salary), controlling for the variable Fringe (fringe benefits). To specify higher-order partials the additional control variables are simply listed after the BY part of the command.

7. REGRESSION: Regression Analysis

In multiple regression analysis the idea is to predict variations in a dependent variable using two or more independent ones. As in correlational analysis we are interested in both the equation that describes the relation and a measure of the strength of the association. We will only consider the simplest version of regression — that of an additive or linear relationship among the variables. Once again, the measurement assumption of regression analysis is for ratio measurement. Special procedures, however, do permit the inclusion of variables not achieving ratio measurement.

a. The Linear Regression Equation. The form of the linear multiple regression equation is as follows:

$$Y = a + b_1x_1 + b_2x_2 \dots B_kx_k$$

In the equation, *a* is a constant which, if the values were multiplied out and plotted, would represent the point where the regression line crosses the Y axis. The *b* coefficients refer to the non-standardized slopes of the regression lines. If standardized slopes are of interest, these will be referred to as *ß* weights (pronounced beta weights). In this case, think of all the variables in the equation as being standardized (recall Z scores?). The Xs refer to the independent variables.

The strategy of multiple regression involves determining the slopes for each of the independent variables while simultaneously holding constant, or adjusting for, the other independent variables. The *ß*s represent the amount of change in Y (the dependent variable) that can be associated with a given change in one of the Xs, when the influences of the other independent variables are held constant. The slopes are computed to maximize our ability to predict variations in the dependent variable.

b. The Multiple R. The slopes and constant are computed to maximize the prediction of variations in the dependent variable. The measure of the amount of variation explained is reflected by the statistic, R^2. Recall that when two variables are involved, the measure is r^2. The two statistics are directly comparable and would yield identical results if, in the multiple independent variable case, one simply took the values for each variable, plugged them into the equation, and then computed the "predicted value" for the dependent variable. If the predicted and actual observations of the dependent variable are then correlated, the problem is reduced to a simple two variable correlation, and the r^2 would equal R^2. The R^2 is a measure of the amount of variation in the dependent variable that is explained by the combination of independent variables.

The SPSS^x command for regression is:

```
REGRESSION VARIABLES = depend, V33, V46 TO V49/
DEPENDENT = Depend/
BACKWARD/
```

Regression analysis is a powerful technique if the researcher wishes to assess the relative influence of independent variables on a dependent one. It is an important technique for both applied and pure research. The applied researcher will be particularly interested in identifying those independent variables which combine significant influence on the dependent variable with the possibility for manipulation through policy changes. The applied researcher will also be concerned with the b coefficients, for they will indicate how much change in the independent variable will be required for a unit change in the dependent variable. The pure researcher, on the other hand, will almost certainly focus on the β values since generally he or she will be more concerned with the relative impact of each independent variable.

Given that βs represent standardized slopes, a useful procedure which takes advantage of this fact is to estimate the percentage of the explained variance which is controlled by each of the independent variables. The following equation may be employed:

$$\% \text{ variance explained by each variable} = \frac{\beta^1 \times R^2}{\Sigma \beta s} \times 100$$

The above formula was reported by Robert L. Hamblin[2] and is most useful for estimating the relative importance of independent variables. However, caution must be exercised since any change in the variables included, or in the sample selected, may render these values unstable. Hand computations are required since SPSS[x] does not have an option which will produce these values.

C. EXERCISES

Student Grades in a Test:

Student	Grade	Student	Grade	Student	Grade
A	80	J	80	S	53
B	57	K	50	T	80
C	67	L	70	U	50
D	63	M	57	V	70
E	67	N	53	W	57
F	77	O	63	X	67
G	73	P	50	Y	53
H	60	Q	73	Z	57
I	70	R	57		

1. Calculate the mode, median, mean, range, standard deviations, and variance for the grades.

2. Using the mean and standard deviation calculated above, use Z scores to estimate the percentage of the students you would expect to score 58% or below. What percentage would you expect to score over 65 percent? What percentage between 70 and 80 percent?

3. Equally weighting income and education, use Z scores to calculate each person's socio-economic status from the following data set:

Subject	$ Income	Years Education
1	40 000	14
2	30 000	10
3	51 000	19
4	16 000	8
5	20 000	12
6	26 000	12
7	37 000	16
8	42 000	18
9	30 000	11
10	32 000	14

Assume that the mean for the population on income is $32 000 with a standard deviation of 8000; assume a mean of 11 years for education with a standard deviation of 4 years.

4. Using the data given below on respondent's, father's, mother's, and sister's years of education, plot the data (treating respondent's education as dependent) and go through the procedures to visually estimate the correlation and the equation that describe the relationship between respondent's and father's educational levels. Compute the r and the equation. How close were your estimates to the actual value?

Sample Data for Years of Education

Respondent	Father	Mother	Sister
1	3	1	4
2	3	4	3
3	4	3	5
5	4	7	2
6	7	5	8
8	8	10	12
9	7	6	6
10	10	10	8
12	11	9	14
14	13	15	8

5. Using the formula computed in question 5, what would you predict the respondent's education to be if father's education was 9, 11, and 15 years of education respectively?

6. Using visual estimation procedures, estimate the correlation between mother's and sister's educational levels.

7. Using visual estimation procedures, estimate the linear equation that describes the relation between respondent's (dependent) and mother's educational level.

NOTES

[1]See particularly Hubert M. Blalock, Jr., *Social Statistics*, Toronto: McGraw-Hill Ryerson, 1979.

[2]Robert L. Hamblin, "*Ratio Measurement and Sociological Theory: A Critical Analysis.*" St. Louis: Social Science Institute, Washington University (mimeo), 1966.

CHAPTER EIGHT

ON TESTS OF SIGNIFICANCE

A. INTRODUCTION

Beneath most tables a number of values are reported. Almost certainly one of these will indicate whether the differences reported in the table are statistically significant. What does this mean? *A test of significance reports the probability that an observed association or difference is the result of sampling fluctuations, and not reflective of some "real" difference in the population from which the sample has been taken.*

This chapter will explore two common tests of significance. Other such tests are based on similar principles and, therefore, need not be explored in detail by the beginning student. The two that will be explored are the Chi-Square test and the *F* test. Since tests of significance are often badly misunderstood, this chapter will also review the conditions under which such tests are inappropriate.

1. The Research and the Null Hypotheses

Tests of significance are used to test hypotheses. These are set up in a "research" and in a "null" form. The *research hypothesis* is simply the statement of a relation between variables; the *null hypothesis* states that there will be no relation between the variables. It is the null hypothesis that is tested. In short, the proposition that there is no relation between the variables is what is tested. The test will lead us to either accept or reject the null hypothesis.

If the null hypothesis is accepted, the conclusion is that the association or the difference may simply be the result of sampling fluctuations and may not reflect an association or difference in the population being studied. If the null hypothesis is rejected then the belief is that there is an association between the variables in the population and that this association is of a magnitude that probably has not occurred because of chance fluctuations in sampling. If the null hypothesis is rejected, the data are examined to see if the association is in the predicted direction; if it is, then this is one piece of evidence consistent with the research hypothesis.

There is frequently a tendency among students to think that they have somehow failed if they do a project and find out that they have to accept the null hypothesis. Such should not be the case. Acceptance of the null hypothesis is a research finding and it may well be just as important to find out that two variables are not associated, as it is to find out that they are. It might be extremely important to discover, for example, that among people under 25 there is no difference between Catholics and Protestants in their attitude toward the use of birth control; perhaps among those over 50 there is less inclination among Catholics, in comparison to Protestants, to support the use of birth control.[1]

The following statements illustrate research and null hypotheses:

Research Hypothesis #1: "The greater the participation, the higher the self-esteem."

Null Hypothesis #1: "There is no relation between levels of participation and levels of self-esteem."

Research Hypothesis #2: "Controlling for qualifications, achievements, and experience, male university faculty members are paid more than their female counterparts."

Null Hypothesis #2: "Controlling for qualifications, achievements, and experience, there is no difference in the earnings of male and female faculty members."

Tests of significance report whether an observed relationship could be the result of sample fluctuations or reflect a "real" difference in the population from which the sample has been taken.

2. The Sampling Distribution

Perhaps the best way to begin to understand tests of significance is to recognize that one sample group (containing 50 individuals, for example), is a unique collection of respondents who are taken to represent the larger population from which the sample was selected. If another sample is drawn from that same population the result would be another unique collection of individuals, slightly different from the first sample. If 1000 such samples were drawn and then the means of the same variable for each of the samples were plotted, a normal distribution curve would result, albeit a peaked, or leptokurtic, one. Suppose, for example, that the means of the weights of respondents are plotted. While these weights might range from 159 to 169 pounds for the males, the majority of the samples would cluster around the true mean of 164 pounds.

The distribution is quite peaked because we are plotting mean weights for samples. The measure of the dispersion of these means of samples is known as the *standard error of the means*. If the standard deviation of the population was 14 pounds, with repeated samples of size 50, the standard error of the mean would be given by the following formula:

$$\text{Standard Error of Means} = \frac{\text{Sd population}}{\sqrt{N}}$$

$$\text{Standard Error of Means} = \frac{14}{\sqrt{50}}$$

$$\text{Standard Error of Means} = 2$$

When a sample is drawn, the sample mean will fall somewhere within a normal distribution. Although the beginning researcher is not likely to be doing methodological research and selecting repeated samples, it is necessary to understand such distributions in order to fully understand sampling and related tests of significance. There are four key points to be made about probability sampling procedures where repeated samples are taken:

Point 1. Plotting the means of repeated samples will produce a normal distribution. Note that this distribution, however, will be more peaked than that achieved when raw data are plotted.

Point 2. The larger the sample sizes, the more peaked the distribution, and the closer will the sample means be to the population mean.

Point 3. The greater the variability in the population, the greater the variation in the samples.

Point 4. Where sample sizes are above 100, even if a variable in the population is not normally distributed, when repeated sample means are plotted, the means themselves will be normally distributed. For example, weights of a population of males and females will be bi-modal but after repeated samples, the means of sample weights would be normally distributed.

3. One- and Two-Tailed Tests of Significance

An understanding of tests of significance requires knowledge of the difference between one- and two-tailed tests. If the direction of the relation is predicted in the research hypothesis then the appropriate test will be one-tailed; one-tailed because we are predicting which particular tail of the normal distribution curve the result will fall into if the null hypothesis is to be rejected.

If no prediction about the direction of the relationship is made, then a two-tailed test is in order. An example of a one-tailed research hypothesis is: "Females are less approving of physical conflict than males." A two-tailed version would be: "There is a significant difference between males and females in their approval of physical conflict."

A test of significance measures the likelihood that an observed difference (for example, the difference in "approval of conflict" scores between males and females) is of a magnitude within normal sampling fluctuations, given no real difference between the males and the females in the population. If the probability of an observed difference would occur less than 5 percent of the time, then the null hypothesis is rejected: we are concluding that there is *probably* a real difference between the male and female tolerance of conflict. If we predict the "tail" of the normal distribution curve that the difference will fall into, then we have made a one-tailed prediction; if we simply hypothesize a difference without specifying into which tail the difference will fall, we then would do a two-tailed test.

Figure 8.1   Five Percent Probability
Rejection Area: One-and Two-Tailed Tests

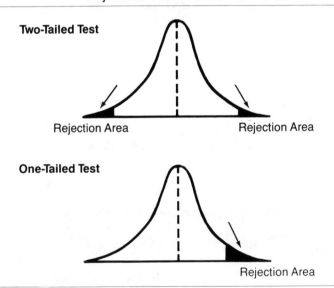

Figure 8.1 shows two normal distribution curves. The first one has the 5 percent rejection area split between the two tails — this would be used for a two-tailed test; the second one has the 5 percent rejection area all in one tail, indicating a one-tailed test is being done. The same principle applies to tests at the 1 percent level — only now the difference between the males and the females would have to be greater in order to fall into the null hypothesis rejection area.

4. A Simple Problem: Are There More Red Balls in the Container?

Suppose that we have a huge container filled with a mixture containing thousands of red and white balls. Now suppose that we draw a sample of 200 balls from the container and we get 114 red ones and 86 white ones. Can we safely conclude that there are more red balls in the container than white ones? Perhaps if we drew another sample we would find more white than red balls. Let us introduce the Chi-Square test to try to answer this question.

B. THE CHI-SQUARE TEST OF SIGNIFICANCE

The Chi-Square test is associated with analyses produced by the CROSS-TABS procedure, where the dependent variable is a nominal one. Essentially, the Chi-Square is based on a comparison of "actual frequencies" that show up in the sample with "expected frequencies" which would occur if there were no difference between the categories in the population.

The null hypothesis we wish to test is that there is no difference in the proportion of red and white balls in the container. We are testing whether the sample selected could have come from a population containing 50 percent red balls and 50 percent white ones. The Chi-Square test (also known as X^2) is defined by the following equation:

$$x^2 = \sum \frac{(f_o - f_e)^2}{f_e}$$

Where f_o is the frequency observed and f_e is the frequency expected. Note that the formula reflects the amount of deviation from the expected values, in relation to the magnitude of the expected values.

1. Hand Computing a Chi-Square of Red/White Ball Example

Table 8.1   A Sample Chi-Square Computation

Color	Step 1 f_o	Step 2 f_e	Step 3 $f_o - f_e$	Step 4 $(f_o - f_e)^2$	Step 5 $\frac{(f_o - f_e)^2}{f_e}$
Red	114	100	14	196	1.96
White	86	100	− 14	196	1.96
				TOTAL	3.92

Chi-Square = 3.92   df = 1   Significant at the .05 level.

Required Critical Value to reject the null hypothesis is 3.841 (two-tailed test, 1 degree of freedom, at .05 level); see Appendix B.

Decision: Since the Chi-Square value is 3.92 and this exceeds the Critical Value, the null hypothesis is rejected.

Let us now analyze the red/white ball example using the Chi-Square test. The computations are shown in Table 8.1.

Normally, Chi-Squares will be computed by the computer; in the particular example under consideration it is actually easier to hand compute the value than to try to enter the data into a program to do it for you. The steps in computing a Chi-Square are as follows:

Step 1. Create a table with the headings shown in Table 8.1. Enter the observations that have been made for each of the cells included in the original table. The convention for naming cells is to label them by starting in the top left corner of the table, naming them a, b, c, etc. across the table, then continuing at the beginning of the next line.

Step 2. Compute the expected frequency for each of the cells. There are four basic techniques for doing this: (a) you can theoretically determine what the expected frequency would be, if the null hypothesis is correct (in the red/white ball example, the theoretical expectation would be that one half would be red, the other half, white; (b) in contingency tables, a cell's expected frequency can be determined by multiplying the row total (row marginal) by the column total (column marginal) and dividing this result by the total number of cases; (c) alternatively, the expected frequency would have the same number as the percentage distribution of the margin column; and (d) having computed the expected frequency in some columns, it is often possible to compute the remaining ones by subtraction, knowing that the margin totals for expected and observed frequencies must be identical.

Step 3. Subtract the expected from the observed frequencies for each of the cells.

Step 4. Square the values determined in Step 3.

Step 5. Divide the result of Step 4 by the frequency expected.

Step 6. Sum the column of values determined in Step 5. This value is the raw Chi-Square.

Step 7. Determine the degrees of freedom. (The number of cells where the expected frequency would have to be computed before the remaining cells could be determined by subtraction, given that the total expected must equal the total observed.) In contingency tables with two or more categories in both the dependent and independent variables, the degrees of freedom may be determined by the following formula:

$$df = (\# \text{ rows} - 1)(\# \text{ columns} - 1)$$

Step 8. Decide the "level" of risk you wish to take; usually you will choose either the .01 or .05 level. This means that you are willing to accept that a difference is statistically significant with a 1 percent or 5 percent chance of being wrong.

Step 9. Determine whether you are doing a one- or a two-tailed test of significance. Remember that if the direction of the relation is predicted then the appropriate test will be one-tailed; one-tailed because we are predicting the tail of the normal distribution the result will fall into if the null hypothesis is to be rejected. If no prediction about the direction of the relationship is made, then a two-tailed test is required.

Step 10. Look up the raw Chi-Square value on the Chi-Square Table (Appendix B) to determine if the difference between the expected and the observed frequencies is statistically significant. The raw value must exceed that listed (the "Critical Value") in order for the relation to be considered statistically significant.

Step 11. Below the table report the raw Chi-Square value, degrees of freedom, and whether the difference observed is statistically significant, and at what level (.05 or .01 generally).

Step 12. If the difference is statistically significant, then the null hypothesis is rejected. The data must then be inspected to see if they are consistent with the research hypothesis. (It is possible, of course, that the difference could be statistically significant, but in the opposite direction predicted by the research hypothesis.) If the difference is not statistically significant then the null hypothesis is accepted.

The results reported in Table 8.1 would lead us to reject the null hypothesis since the difference observed would occur on a chance basis less than 5 percent of the time. We can then conclude that there are more red balls than white balls in the container. The risk we take in making this conclusion is that we may, by chance, just happen to have over-selected red balls. A difference of the magnitude observed, (114 red and 86 white) however, would occur less than 5 percent of the time if the container held the same number of each color.

To help understand tests of significance more clearly, note that if repeated samples were taken and the results plotted (say, the percentage of red balls), the plot would resemble a normal distribution curve. We would also find that the larger the sample size, the more peaked would the distribution be (leptokurtic). Most times when we do a survey only one sample is drawn and we don't know if we have a truly representative sample. We may simply have an atypical sample where we just happened to draw a preponderance of red balls and we might, therefore, wrongly conclude that there are more red balls in the container. But since we cannot easily observe all cases, we simply take the chance of being wrong. We can reduce that risk by increasing our confidence limit to .01 or even .001. That would reduce, but not eliminate, the chance of coming to an incorrect conclusion. If we reject a null hypothesis which should be accepted we have made what is referred to as a *Type I* error. If we accept a null hypothesis which should be rejected we have made a *Type II* error.

2. A One Sample Chi-Square Test

There are situations where one wishes to compare a cohort of respondents to some known distribution. For example, suppose that one did a survey of university students and found the following family income distribution reported by them:

Table 8.2 Sample Student and General Population Family Incomes

Income	Student Sample N	%	General Population %
Over $50 000	30	15.0	7.8
$20 000 to $49 999	160	80.0	68.9
Under $20 000	10	5.0	23.3
TOTAL	200	100.0	100.0

In Table 8.2 we have an illustration of a situation where the income distribution is reported for the sample, and a comparative regional distribution is also reported (source would be federal government statistics). In this case, the research hypothesis is that "university students come from the wealthier families in the region." Note that this hypothesis predicts the direction of the relationship and therefore requires a one-tailed test. The null form of this hypothesis would be that "there is no difference between the income distribution of university students' families and that of the region served by the university." Table 8.3 presents the steps in computing the Chi-Square value for this example.

The critical value that must be exceeded in order to reject the null hypothesis is 4.605 (see Appendix B; note that we look up the value for 2 degrees of freedom under the .10 column, since we are predicting the direction of the relationship). Since the observed X^2 value is 45.61 we reject the null hypothesis and conclude that university students indeed come from the wealthier families in the region.

Table 8.3   Computing Chi-Square for Student Family Income Data

Income Category	f_o	f_e	$f_o - f_e$	$(f_o - f_e)^2$	$\dfrac{(f_o - f_e)^2}{f_e}$
Over $50 000	30	15.6*	14.4	207.36	13.29
$20 000 – $49 999	160	137.8	22.2	492.84	3.57
Under $20 000	10	46.6	– 36.6	1 339.56	28.75
TOTALS	200	200			45.61

* The expected frequencies are computed on the presumption that if there is no difference between the general population and the families of university students, the income distribution would have similar proportions in the various categories. In the first cell, where there were 30 students, we would have expected 15.6. (200 × .078 = 15.6) In the general population 7.8 percent of the families had incomes above $50 000.

Degrees of Freedom = 2 (two cells would have to be computed before the final one could be calculated by subtraction as in:

$$f_o \text{ cell c} = (200 - (30 + 160))$$

Required Critical Value to reject the null hypothesis is 4.605 (one-tailed test, 2 degrees of freedom, at the .05 level); see Appendix B.

Decision: Since the Chi-Square value is 45.61 and this exceeds the Critical Value, the null hypothesis is rejected.

3. Typical Chi-Square Illustration

Table 8.4 presents a typical contingency table showing the relationship between frequency of drug use and gender. Beneath the table, the computational procedures are presented for the computation of the Chi-Square. It should be noted that there are 2 degrees of freedom in this table (rows – 1)(columns – 1). Note that the computations excluded the "no responses" from the analysis. Note, too, that since the critical value is not exceeded, the decision is to accept the null hypothesis. However, had we been doing a one-tailed test, we would reject the null hypothesis. (The critical value would be 4.605.)

To have SPSS^x generate the Chi-Square values simply use the following command:

```
CROSSTABS TABLES = depend BY independ
OPTIONS 4
STATISTICS 1
```

C. THE F DISTRIBUTION

The test of significance used with the BREAKDOWN procedure in SPSS^x is known as *Analysis of Variance*. The distribution associated with this test is the F distribution and it is used to test whether there is a significant differ-

Table 8.4 Frequency of Drug Use, by Sex

Frequency of Drug Use in Lifetime	SEX Male No.	Male %	Female No.	Female %	TOTAL No.	TOTAL %
No Experience	47	34.8	63	48.1	110	41.4
Once or Twice	51	37.8	39	29.8	90	33.8
Three or More Times	37	27.4	26	19.8	63	23.7
No Response	–		3	2.3	3	1.1
TOTALS	135	100.0	131	100.0	266	100.0

Chi-Square = 5.689   df = 2   Not significant at .05 level.

The Chi-Square could be hand computed in the following manner:

Cell	f_o	f_e	$(f_o - f_e)$	$(f_o - f_e)^2$	$\dfrac{(f_o - f_e)^2}{f_e}$
a	47	56.5	−9.5	90.25	1.597
b	63	53.5	9.5	90.25	1.687
c	51	46.2	4.8	23.06	.499
d	39	43.8	−4.8	23.06	.526
e	37	32.3	4.7	21.72	.673
f	26	30.7	−4.7	21.72	.707
				Σ	5.689

Required Critical Value to reject the null hypothesis is 5.991 (two-tailed test, 2 degrees of freedom, at the .05 level); see Appendix B.

Decision: Since the Chi-Square value is 5.689 and this does not equal or exceed the Critical Value, the null hypothesis is accepted.

ence in the means of various categories. It is useful for the beginning researcher to understand something about this test since it is used not only in Analysis of Variance, but it also plays a role in tables created through the BREAKDOWN procedure and is utilized in regression analysis. Much of this material will not be new since some of the ideas discussed in presenting the Chi-Square test and correlations will be used.

1. Faculty Ages: An Illustration of a Simple Analysis of Variance

Suppose that we had data on the ages of male and female faculty members at a university. For purposes of illustration we will suppose that the random sample involves 20 faculty members, evenly divided between males and females (it is not necessary to have an equal number).[2] Our research hypothesis is that male faculty are older than female faculty. The null hypothesis is that there is no difference between the ages of the male and the female faculty.

The procedures for testing the above hypotheses involve: (i) determining the appropriate procedure to run; (ii) stating the null hypothesis; (iii) deciding the level of confidence we wish to employ (normally specifying whether we risk being wrong 5 percent or 1 percent of the time); (iv) determining whether the observed difference is, or is not, within the range of normal sampling fluctuations; and (v) deciding whether we accept or reject the null hypothesis.

Table 8.5   Analysis of Variance of Age Distribution by Sex

	Male Ages	Female Ages	Total
	24	24	
	26	27	
	30	30	
	35	31	
	36	33	
	40	38	
	42	40	
	45	42	
	48	42	
	51	44	
Sums	377	351	728
Means	37.7	35.1	36.4
N of Cases	10	10	20

Table 8.5 presents the results from our survey of faculty ages. Various computations are made and the resulting test of significance, the F test, indicates that the null hypothesis must be accepted. The difference of 2.6 in the mean age is within the range of normal sample fluctuations. We conclude, therefore, that there is no statistically significant difference between the ages of the male and the female faculty members.

This test of significance is based on the idea that when a sample is drawn there will be fluctuations in the mean ages of the male and the female faculty. What the test does is assess the chance, if the true difference between the males and the females in age is zero, of getting a sample fluctuation of the magnitude shown in the sample data. In the case under examination, there is a difference of 2.6 years. The test of significance reveals that the amount of fluctuation is within the range of normal sample variability. In other words, if there was no "real" age difference between the sexes, a sample would reveal a difference ± 2.6 years more often than 5 percent of the time simply due to sampling fluctuations. On the other hand, if the observed difference could occur less than 5 percent of the time, we would reject the null hypothesis and conclude that the females are indeed younger than the males — the difference being statistically significant.

To repeat, a statistically significant relationship is one where the observed difference would occur less than 5 percent of the time on a chance basis. If the test were set at the 1 percent level, it would simply be more difficult to reject the null hypothesis; here the difference would be statistically significant only if it could occur on a chance basis less than 1 percent of the time.

2. Computational Details for a Simple Analysis of Variance

Like the computational procedure involved in determining the correlation between two variables, the procedures involved in doing an Analysis of Variance require a measurement of two kinds of variation: variations within a column (for example, differences within the column for males); and variations between columns (differences that show up between the male and female columns). An Analysis of Variance involves computing a ratio which compares these two kinds of variability — within column and between column variability.

On examining the data within each column of Table 8.5, it should become intuitively obvious that the variation within each column cannot be explained by a connection to the independent variable. (In the first column the male data is reported and since all the cases are for males, gender cannot explain variations within this column.) Differences between the columns, however, may be associated with the independent variable (gender). In the case under examination, perhaps recent hiring practices have favored the appointment of female faculty and therefore the females will tend to be younger; or perhaps more women are attending graduate school and are now competing effectively for any new university positions.

Table 8.6 goes through the computation of a simple Analysis of Variance for the sample data. In this particular case, the estimates of variance indicate more variation within the columns than between them; as a result, the F ratio is less than one. After the F ratio is computed, and the critical value is looked up in the F Distribution Table, Appendix C, the decision is made to accept the null hypothesis since the computed F ratio is less than the value looked up in the table.

Table 8.6 Steps in Computing a Simple Analysis of Variance

Three measures of variation are required to compute the Analysis of Variance:

Total Variation = Between Variation + Within Variation

The Total Variation may be computed by summing the squares of all the age values and subtracting from that value the square of the sum divided by the total number of cases. As in:

Step 1. $24^2 + 26^2 + \ldots + 44^2 = 27\,730$
minus
Step 2. $728^2 \div 20 = 26\,499$
equals
Step 3. $27\,730 - 26\,499 = 1\,231$
Total variation = $1\,231$

The Between Variation may be computed by squaring the column totals, dividing this value by the number of cases, then summing the result, and finally subtracting the value in Step 2 above. As in:

Step 4. $((377^2 \div 10) + (351^2 \div 10)) - 26\,499 = 34$

The Within Variation may be determined by simply subtracting the Between Variation from the Total Variation. As in:

Step 5. $1\,231 - 34 = 1\,197$

Step 6.   An F Ratio table may be computed as follows:

	Sums of Squares	Degrees of Freedom	Estimate of Pop. Variance	F
Total Variation	1 231	N − 1 = 19		
Between Variation	34	k − 1 = 1	34.00	.51
Within Variation	1 197	N − k = 18	66.50	

Step 7.   Determine the value which has to be exceeded in order to reject the null hypothesis by looking up the value on the F table (Appendix C). The F table requires the use of two values for degrees of freedom: the Between Variation df are placed across the top of the table (in the sample case df = 1); the Within Variation df are arranged along the vertical column (in our table df = 18). We will test the hypothesis at the .05 level. The value given in the table is 4.41.

Step 8.   Since the F ratio for the sample data is .51, the null hypothesis is accepted. Variability of the magnitude reported in faculty ages could simply reflect sampling fluctuations and we cannot reasonably conclude that there is a "real" difference in the age distribution of the males and the females.

Normally, all such computations will be made by computers. The survey researcher will encounter F distributions in using the BREAKDOWN procedure in SPSS[x], and in doing REGRESSION analysis. In the latter case, the F is produced automatically with all analyses. To do a one-way Analysis of Variance of a BREAKDOWN analysis would require the use of an optional statistic, as in:

    BREAKDOWN TABLES = depend BY independ
    STATISTICS 1

The student must recognize that the presentation here is the least complex one possible. Analysis of Variance is a major analytical tool used particularly by experimental researchers. While it is used extensively in survey research, it is not as frequently used as multiple regression in multivariate data analysis.

D.   WHEN TESTS OF SIGNIFICANCE ARE NOT APPROPRIATE

Tests of significance are often inapplicable when non-experimental research designs are employed. Yet they are widely used, often improperly.[3] Why is this the case?

One motivation for the inclusion of tests of significance no doubt has to do with the attempt to be scientific, or to appear to be scientific. If the researcher's data turns out to be "statistically significant," then this is taken to demonstrate the importance of the finding and to confer scientific legitimacy on the work. Such tests help to create the impression that the God of science — that independent, unbiased arbiter of truth — has blessed the research with approval.

A second motivation perhaps has to do with the fact that such tests are routinely — even if inappropriately — reported in the literature. Hence, to produce a report which meets the standard of the discipline is to report tests of significance.

A third possibility is that tests of significance are poorly understood by social scientists, and they are inappropriately used because of such misunderstandings.

Probably well over half of the surveys completed should not make use of tests of significance. The following rules indicate when such tests are inappropriate.

Rule 8.1 Tests of significance are not applicable when total populations are studied. If a study is being done on the wage differences between male and female faculty members and data are analyzed including all faculty, then a test of significance would not be in order. If a $1500 difference is observed after the appropriate controls are introduced, this difference is absolute. The researcher must decide whether the difference is to be characterized as substantial, modest, or trivial. To say that it is statistically significant is simply wrong!

Arguments have been advanced that a study like the one above represents a sample out of a universe of possible samples which might be taken. The problem with this argument is that not all institutions were given an equal chance of being included; second, if the argument is that this is but one case in many, then the unit of analysis has been shifted to the institutional level (a university) and there is now one case represented by one difference. You would be left with a difference of $1500 but with no knowledge of what differences are present in other institutions.

Rule 8.2 Tests of significance are not appropriate when nonprobability sampling procedures are employed. Data gathered using convenience or quota samples are not properly analyzed using tests of significance. Since tests of significance only provide a measure of the probability of a given difference being the result of sampling fluctuations, assuming probability sampling procedures, such tests are not appropriate if those methods are not used.

Rule 8.3 Tests of significance are to be regarded as suspect where there is a substantial non-participation rate. If substantial numbers of respondents have refused to participate (for argument's sake let's say 40 percent), then tests of significance become problematic, for it is difficult to assume that non-participants are similar to those who agree to participate in the study. Hence the extent to which such data can be regarded as representative can be called into question.

Rule 8.4 If one is exploring a relationship shown to be statistically significant, it is not appropriate, when controls are applied to check for spuriousness or for an intervening variable, to once again employ a test of significance. The issue in evaluating causal models is to assess the impact of the control on the original relationship, and to observe whether the differences have remained the same, increased, decreased, or disappeared. Frequently, they may change from being statistically significant to no longer being statistically significant. This change may simply represent the fact that the data have been partitioned (perhaps cut in half) and therefore fewer cases may be involved, and the switch from significance to non-significance may simply reflect this adjustment

The researcher should note how much the original relationship has shifted, not simply note whether the relationship is still statistically significant. To avoid confusion, do not employ tests of significance when causal models are being evaluated beyond the stage of the initial relationship. For example, if the relationship between X and Y is being explored, and if sampling and other conditions are appropriate, then a test of significance for the relation between X and Y is legitimate. However, a test of significance would not be appropriate if after having established that there is a statistically significant relation between X and Y one is then testing to ensure that the relationship is not spurious because of its connection to some third variable.

Rule 8.5 Tests of significance may not be applied to relationships which were not formulated as hypotheses prior to the collection of data for the study. Survey researchers routinely collect data on many variables — it is not unusual for data to be collected on 100 or more variables. If one simply runs every variable against every other one, one will not only generate enormous piles of computer output, but will also generate results for many thousands of theoretically meaningless relationships as well as generate many "statistically significant" relationships. Indeed, one would expect that 1 in 20 tables will prove to be significant, providing the .05 level is used for the tests. Unfortunately, researchers rarely report how many relationships were analyzed, what confounding data have been discarded, and which causal models were not fully developed prior to data collection.

An exception to the above rule has to be made for those analyzing secondary data. In such cases, hypotheses need to be formulated prior to data analysis.

The survey researcher may use tests of significance only with the greatest of care. Above all, the beginning researcher must appreciate what such tests really measure. All too often it is not recognized that a finding is equally important whether the relationship is statistically significant or not. Social scientists are in the business of trying to understand and to describe the social world, and to have discovered that there is no relationship between A and B is as important as to have discovered that there is a relation between A and B. And, to the extent that one is involved in theory testing, it is especially important to find that a predicted relationship does not hold, for this will cast doubt on the theory, and perhaps lead to a refinement or refutation of it. In short, do not despair if your survey does not yield statistically significant results. Science proceeds through disconfirmation, through ruling out alternatives, through rejecting, modifying, and continually re-thinking theoretical formulations.

E. EXERCISES

1. Test the null hypothesis that there is no difference in parental identification by those women enrolled in sex-traditional versus non-traditional university programs. Test the hypothesis at the .05 level. The data are as follows:

Table 1. Sex Traditional or Non-traditional Program Enrollment by Sex of Parent Identified with, Female Students

PROGRAM TYPE	Identify Mother		Identify Father		Total	
	N	%	N	%	N	%
Traditional	31	47.0	21	34.4	52	40.9
Non-Traditional	35	53.0	40	65.5	75	58.1
TOTAL	66	100.0	61	100.0	127	100.0

2. You have examined the salaries of all the clerks working in a department store. What is the appropriate test to determine if there is a statistically significant difference in the male versus female salaries? (Caution: This is a trick question!) The data are as follows:

Table 2. Income List by Sex, Bigtown Department Store

Males	Females
6 200	6 600
7 300	6 800
8 800	9 100
10 200	8 700
9 600	7 700
8 800	8 600
7 900	7 700
11 100	10 400

NOTES

[1] In reference to accepting or rejecting null hypotheses, psychologists seem to prefer the terms "reject" or "fail to reject". While this usage is correct, I avoid it since the term "fail to reject" encourages students to think that they have somehow failed, if they do not find a statistically significant relationship.

[2] This sample size of 20 is used for computational simplicity; normally surveys will have much larger sample sizes and hence the distributions may be assumed to be normal. With small sample sizes one would consider using a t test.

[3] Some of the major references to the controversy over tests of significance are as follows: Hanan C. Selvin, "A Critique of Tests of Significance in Survey Research," *American Sociological Review*, October, 1957, pp. 519-27. David Gold, "Comment on 'A Critique of Tests of Significance,' *American Sociological Review*, February, 1958, pp. 85-86. James M. Beshers, "On 'A Critique of Tests of Significance in Survey Research,' " *American Sociological Review*, April, 1958, p. 198. Robert McGinnis, "Randomization and Inference in Sociological Research," *American Sociological Review*, October, 1958, pp. 408-14. Denton E. Morrison and Ramon E. Henkel, eds., *The Significance Tests Controversy*. Chicago: Aldine Publishing Company, 1970. James K. Skipper, Jr., Anthony L. Guenther, and Gilbert Nass, "The Sacredness of .05: A Note Concerning the Uses of Statistical Levels of Significance in Social Science," *American Sociologist*, 2 (1967): pp.16-18.

DATA COLLECTION

CHAPTER NINE

SAMPLING AND ADMINISTRATION

This chapter reviews fundamental sampling procedures and sample size determination, and offers practical suggestions for the administration of different types of surveys.

A. FUNDAMENTAL SAMPLING PROCEDURES

Social scientists, market researchers, political parties, and media people all have a need to describe — and sometimes even to understand — variations in public opinion. They also aim to examine the differences between individuals or groups. The interest may be in getting an accurate profile of categories of individuals or groups, or in trying to understand how variables are related to one another.

One way to approach such problems is to take measures on the relevant variables for all people in a population. This solution is possible if one is studying a few individuals (perhaps employees who work in a nursing home). When the concern is to understand how people from larger aggregations such as a community, region, or country feel about certain issues, then it is necessary to get a sense of their feelings without having everyone complete a questionnaire, or agree to be interviewed. In such cases, a sample is drawn which can reflect, or represent, the views of the larger population. Sampling is done to save time and money.

There are two categories of sampling procedures, known as probability and nonprobability sampling techniques.

1. Probability Sampling Techniques

Probability sampling procedures involve techniques for selecting sampling units so that each unit has a known chance of being included. The sampling units usually are individuals, but may also refer to other levels of analysis, such as communities or countries. The procedures for selecting each of the major types are listed below.

a. Simple Random Sample. This procedure requires that a list of the potential respondents be available to the researcher. Such lists might include student lists, lists of eligible voters used for elections, lists of employees, lists of companies, and so forth. The steps involved in random sampling are:

Step 1. Number the units on the list.

Step 2. Using a Table of Random Numbers, select the required number of units. (Sample size determination is discussed later in this chapter.) This procedure is done by shutting one's eyes and stabbing a pencil into the table of random numbers. The point where the pencil has struck is used as the starting point. From this point one reads down the column, placing a check mark beside those cases whose number shows up on the random number table. This process continues until a sufficient number of cases for the survey has been selected.

Step 3. Additional replacement units should be selected and kept on a separate list, so that when a unit cannot be contacted, or if an individual or company does not participate, then that unit will be replaced by the first replacement unit. Replacements should be identified and numbered since they will be used in the order in which they have been selected. R1, R2, etc. is a convenient way of noting them.

b. Systematic Sample. The systematic sample is a somewhat easier way of selecting cases from a list of potential respondents. Names listed in phone books, directories, street maps, dormitory diagrams, student lists, or elector lists are all sources from which a systematic sample can be drawn. It is even possible to proceed with sampling even though no list exists prior to sampling. For instance, students living in every fourth residence room could be chosen and, so long as the rooms are numbered systematically, sampling could proceed without a list of the students. The critical issue is that every person must have a known (usually equal) chance of being selected. The steps in selecting a systematic sample are as follows:

Step 1. Get a list, map, or diagram as appropriate.

Step 2. Having determined the sample size required, plus the additional number for replacements (for the refusals, or for those with whom contact cannot be made), these two figures should be added together and will be regarded as the *total sample requirement.*

Step 3. Divide the total sample requirement into the total number of units in the population being surveyed. This number should then be rounded to the nearest, but lower, round number. (E.g., if the number you get is 8.73, round it to the nearest, lower, whole number; in this case, 8.) This number represents what is known as the *skip interval.*

Step 4. Using a Table of Random Numbers, select a number between 1 and the value of the skip interval. The number selected becomes the starting case, the first one selected to participate in the survey. Suppose we were doing a survey of students living in campus dormitories and we have determined the skip interval to be 8 and the starting case to be 3. In this case, we would develop a systematic procedure for numbering the dormitory rooms and for moving from floor to floor, dormitory to dormitory. We would begin with the 3rd door, then go to the 11th, 19th, and 27th rooms. In rooms with two student residents, we would ask both to participate (otherwise students in double rooms would have less chance of being selected for the study).

When systematic samples are being selected from lists, it is a rather straightforward matter to go through the list, placing check marks beside cases that have been selected, perhaps marking every 5th one (if you need 20 percent for use as replacements).

c. Stratified Sample. There are times when a simple random or systematic sample would not provide an appropriate solution to sample selection. Suppose, for example, that a survey of attitudes toward capital punishment according to political party preference in a city is to be done. While it would be possible to do a random sample of individuals in the community, such a procedure might be somewhat wasteful because the community might be made up predominantly of those who support one of the parties. As a result, a very large sample would be required in order to provide a sufficient number to allow generalizations about supporters of each of the parties. In situations such as this it is useful to draw a stratified sample, a sample which will give supporters within each party an equal chance of selection, but will, at the same time, ensure that an equal number will be selected from each of the parties.

The researcher might decide, for example, that 150 respondents should be chosen from each of the political parties. The steps in selecting a stratified sample are:

Step 1. Determine the sample size required from each of the categories.

Step 2. Develop a list for each of the categories from which you wish to draw the sample.

Step 3. Using either a systematic or random sampling procedure, choose the cases for the sample, along with the required number of replacements.

Samples may be stratified by more than one variable. In order to achieve more precise estimates, the above sample might also have been stratified by sex and by socio-economic levels. The procedures are identical: simply identify the stratification dimensions, then using an equal probability procedure, select respondents. Unless appropriate weighting procedures are used, however, the results of such surveys can only be used to compare different subgroups and do not represent the community in general. This is because such samples overrepresent smaller categories and underrepresent larger ones.

d. Multi-Stage Area Sample. When the task involves developing a sample to reflect a large unit such as a state, province, or country and no list of the population is available, then the researcher develops a sample by stages. The key point is that at each stage of the sampling process, every individual (or unit) must have a known chance of being selected. In a simplified form, the procedures for a national survey may be summarized as follows:

Step 1. Identify primary sampling units (these may be census tract areas, or other similar units, normally several hundred of them); these units are numbered, and a selection of at least 30 units is made from them, using an equal probability technique.

Step 2. Within the selected areas, identify the city blocks (in urban areas) or square miles (rural areas). From these, using an equal probability technique, choose an appropriate number of units.

Step 3. Within the selected areas, number the housing units and randomly select from among these which units will be used.

Step 4. For each household, list the people who fall within the desired sampling parameters (perhaps adults, over the age of 18, who have lived in the community for one month or more).

Step 5. From the list of eligibles use an equal probability procedure to select respondents.

Rule 9.1. No sampling choices are to be made by interviewers. All choices are to be made by probability procedures. When a selected respondent is not available (moved away, not home after three callbacks, or refuses to cooperate) then a replacement is used, in the order selected. It is critical that interviewers *not* simply replace the unavailable respondent with the nearest, most convenient, replacement. This would bias the sample toward those who are at home, or are more cooperative. Whatever rules are established, these should be communicated clearly to those doing the data collection, and should also be made clear in any technical reports on the research project.

2. Nonprobability Sampling Techniques

There are two additional sampling procedures frequently used by survey researchers. While these procedures do not provide potential respondents with a known chance of being asked to participate in a study, they are, nonetheless, important to know.

a. Quota Sample. In quota sampling, respondents are selected on the basis of meeting certain criteria. No list of potential respondents is required; the first respondent to meet the requirement(s) is asked to participate; sampling continues until all the categories have been filled — until the quota for each has been reached. Suppose one were asked to compare food preferences of the young versus the elderly. One might do a survey of supermarket customers, selecting the first 75 who meet the "young" criteria, and the first 75 who meet the criteria for inclusion in the comparison group.

The steps are as follows:

Step 1. Define precisely the criteria for inclusion into each of the categories.

Step 2. Select participants on a first-come-first-included basis until the quota for each category has been met.

b. Convenience Sample. Convenience samples involve selection on the basis of ease or convenience. If you were to "poll" people entering a shopping mall on their attitudes toward an upcoming election you would be selecting a convenience sample. Such samples may involve, however, particular categories of individuals. For example, asking a couple of classes of grade ten students to complete questionnaires would constitute a convenience sample of the students present.

Convenience and quota samples are reasonable approaches to sampling when a researcher is investigating relationships among variables (say the relationship between participation and self-esteem), where the interest is not

in generalizing to the general population, but, rather, is in trying to understand the conditions under which there is, or is not, a relation between the
major variables under investigation. Explanatory studies, in fact, frequently
use nonprobability sampling procedures. However, when tests of significance are an important tool for the research it is to be noted that such tests
assume probability sampling procedures and therefore tests of significance
are not appropriate when quota or convenience samples have been used.

B. SAMPLE SIZE DETERMINATION

A variety of factors influence the size of the sample appropriate for any
study. Sample size determination is no simple matter and involves a series
of trade-offs between accuracy, cost, and the numbers needed to do the
selected analyses.

1. Six Steps in Determining Sample Size

Sample size determination involves six basic steps; some of these are
statistical, some pragmatic. It is usually best to begin with the statistical ones,
estimating the required sample size, and to then modify this number in terms
of practical considerations.

Step 1. Decide on the confidence level to be used. If you would
like to be confident that your result will be within a given accuracy
95 percent of the time, then you will choose the Z score value which
includes 95 percent of the cases. This value is 1.96. (Ninety-five percent of the cases fall $\pm$ 1.96 standard deviation units from the mean).
If you wish to be 99 percent confident, a larger sample will be required. Here the appropriate Z score value will be 2.58. Most social
science researchers use the 95 percent level of confidence in determining sample size. With this level you can be confident that your
sample mean will be within a given accuracy 19 out of 20 times.

**Step 2. Select a major variable in your study and estimate the
population standard deviation.** The variable chosen should be
measured at the ratio level since it will be easier to determine sample size requirements with such a variable. Such a variable might
include weight, percent voting for a given party, or an attitude scale
score. Next, the population standard deviation (sd pop) for this variable must be estimated. This estimate can be made by examining
results from other surveys, or, failing that, by simply estimating the
number on a common sense basis, noting the mean and the range

within which two thirds of the cases are expected to fall. Another suggestion for estimating an unknown population standard deviation is to approximate it by taking the range of values (excluding extreme cases) and dividing this value by two. This method will generally provide a reasonable estimate. Finally, it must be acknowledged that in most surveys a large number of variables are involved and it is therefore impossible to make claims, with any certainty, about the accuracy of all of the variables. Most of these variables will have unknown sampling distributions.

Step 3. Determine the minimum accuracy which would be acceptable. Do you want to be within 3 pounds of the true mean if estimating weight; within 2 percentage points in predicting a vote; or within 3 points on a scale with a maximum score of 75? The measure of accuracy will have to be expressed in the same units as the standard deviation.

Step 4. Compute sample size. Compute the required sample using the following formula:

$$\text{Required Sample Size} = \left[\frac{\text{(Confidence Limit) (sd pop)}}{\text{Accuracy}} \right]^2$$

Suppose, for example, that you wished to determine the sample size required to estimate the average weight of male university graduates. You wish to be 95 percent confident ($Z = 1.96$), and be within 2 pounds of estimating the true weight. The estimated standard deviation of the population is 14.0 pounds. The values would be plugged into the equation, as in:

$$\text{Required Sample Size} = \left[\frac{1.96 \, (14.0)}{2.0} \right]^2 = 188$$

The indicated sample size is 188 and should result in an estimate of the population's average weight within 2 pounds, being confident that the estimate will be within this margin 95 percent of the time.

Step 5. Ensure that there are sufficient cases for the analysis. The required sample size must now be scrutinized to ensure that it will provide a sufficient number of cases for the most complex analysis to be done. For example, if one intends to do a series of cross-tabulation tables with three categories in each of the independent and dependent variables, with a maximum of one control variable with two categories, then one is proposing a number of 18 cell tables (3 x 3 x 2). With 188 cases, the maximum expected frequencies would be just over 10 cases per cell ($188 \div 18 = 10.44$).

This would hardly prove to be adequate and therefore one would want to increase the sample size, or else rethink the proposed types of analyses to be performed. Correlational techniques place less stringent demands on a sample. Therefore, to the extent model testing can be done using those techniques, fewer cases will be required.

Step 6. Adjust sample size for cost and time factors. A final step is to adjust the sample in terms of what is feasible from a time and a cost point of view. If a sample of 3000 is required but there are only the resources to deal with 1000, then some rethinking about the accuracy that will be possible will have to be done. If, on the other hand, there are sufficient resources to increase the sample size, then this is usually done since some additional precision is likely to result.

2. Sample Size and Accuracy

The relationship between sample size and accuracy of estimations is a simple one. *To double accuracy, sample size must be quadrupled.* In the illustration concerning the weights of graduating university males, if we wished to be within 1 pound of estimating the true value of the population we would need a sample 4 times as large as the one proposed for a sample which would get us within 2 pounds. This is shown by:

$$\text{Required Sample Size} = \left[\frac{1.96\,(14.0)}{1.0} \right]^2 = 753$$

The original sample size required was 188 or one quarter of 753. "Accuracy" will be referred to in statistics texts as the *confidence interval*. In the above illustration, with a sample size of 753 we can be 95 percent confident that the true population mean weight is within 1 pound of the sample mean.

3. Sample Size and Confidence Limits

The relationship between accuracy and confidence limits is that to move from the 95 percent confidence limit to the 99 percent level, the sample size is simply multiplied by 1.73. Thus, in the illustration on graduating males, to be within 2 pounds but to be 99 per cent confident, the original sample size of 188 would have to be multiplied by a factor of 1.73. (188 x 1.73 = 325) A sample of 325 will be required to be 99 percent confident that the estimate will be within 2 pounds of the true population mean. Conversely, to move from the 99 percent confidence limit to the 95 percent one, the sample size determined for the 99 percent level may be multiplied by .58.

4. The Impact of Refusals

Little is known about the impact of refusals on the outcomes of surveys. While the evidence from studies examining different response rates under controlled conditions shows little variation in descriptive accuracy independent of response rate, tests of significance assume probability sampling techniques and also assume that there is no systematic bias in who chooses to complete the form.[1] Such tests also assume that any measurement error is random. Given that we cannot know what impact refusals and measurement error have on our data, researchers make every effort to get as complete and accurate a response from respondents as possible. It is not clear what conclusions can be legitimately arrived at if the response rate is only 20 percent.

5. Confirming Representativeness

Steps, however, may be taken to confirm that the sample is indeed representative of the population about which one is attempting to make generalizations. For example, one might compare the age distribution of one's sample to known age distributions for the population from census data. If the sample is not wholly representative, there are techniques for weighting results to better reflect the population for which one is trying to make estimations. Where, however, there has been a high nonparticipation rate, even though the sample may appear to be representative in terms of age or sex distributions that have been checked, this would not in any way ensure that the sample is representative in terms of other key variables.

C. ADMINISTRATION OF SURVEYS

In this section, rules will be provided for questionnaires administered individually and completed in group settings, and for mail surveys, phone surveys, and interviews. In all cases, the suggestions should be used with common sense, since there will be times when they should be violated.

Given that permissions to distribute questionnaires will frequently be required, researchers must allow the time needed to obtain them when planning a survey. Permission requests usually will require a statement of the problem under investigation and a copy of the proposed questionnaire. Plan for extra time.

1. General Rules for the Administration of Surveys

The following rules are intended to increase response rates for all types of surveys. Sections following this one will suggest approaches for particular types of surveys.

Rule 9.2 Keep it simple. Keep questionnaires, interview guides, or phone interviews as simple to complete and as nonthreatening as possible.

Rule 9.3 Establish legitimacy. Establish the legitimacy of the research by noting who is sponsoring it, noting why it is being done, and presenting it in such as way as to reflect that it is a competent piece of research.

Rule 9.4 Provide a report to the respondent. Where individuals are to be interviewed more than once in a study (as in a panel study), report findings to respondents; in all cases where a report has been promised to the respondent it must be provided. Otherwise, future cooperation will be thrown into doubt.

Rule 9.5 Pay respondents. Where reasonable and financially possible, pay respondents for their time and cooperation. The fee helps establish the legitimacy of the study and establishes a reciprocal relationship with the respondent. Such payments appear to have a modest impact on the willingness of respondents to participate.[2] Payments help establish reciprocity between researcher and respondents and help to avoid the respondents' perception that they have been "ripped off" by giving their data.

Rule 9.6 Do not pressure respondents to participate. Although the researcher has a powerful interest in getting everyone selected to complete the survey, it must be indicated that while cooperation in completing the questionnaire or interview is appreciated, it is, nonetheless, optional. Particularly in face-to-face encounters there may be considerable pressure placed on individuals to participate in the study. In the case of questionnaires administered to a gathering of individuals, there is considerable informal pressure on those present to cooperate by staying in the room and completing the survey. The researcher must exercise self-discipline to avoid putting undue pressure on individuals in an attempt to coax participation. (See the discussion on research ethics in Chapter 4.)

2. Individually Completed Questionnaires

An individually completed questionnaire is delivered to a respondent by a researcher. A brief explanation is offered, any questions answered, and arrangements are made for the return of the completed questionnaire. This method of handing out questionnaires will typically be used in community surveys where the form is dropped off at selected houses; in campus dormitories where questionnaires are handed to selected respondents (usually systematic sample of campus dormitory rooms); in studies in organizations (such as hospital staff, university faculty, employees of a private firm) where target respondents are approached to complete the survey.

In cases where a survey of students is being conducted, and a systematic sample of students in residence is being used, if there is a mixture of double and single rooms, remember that you wish to provide everyone with an equal chance of being in the survey. This will mean that in cases of double rooms, both residents should be asked to complete the questionnaire.

Rule 9.7 Make personal contact with the respondent. Where feasible contact respondents in person to explain the survey and to let them know when you will pick up the completed form. In a door-to-door survey, it should be possible to get over 80 percent to agree to complete the forms. Avoid having third parties handing out your questionnaires: a member of the research team can better explain the survey and answer any questions that might be raised. In particular, try to avoid having workers' supervisors, teachers, or co-workers hand out questionnaires. The extra effort to have a member of the research team hand out the questionnaires will avoid many problems associated with a third-party delivery.

Rule 9.8 Avoid mailed and drop-box return method. Where possible, avoid mailed returns or having respondents drop their completed questionnaires into a box left in a dormitory or other convenient spot. If at all possible, completed forms should be picked up by the researcher at an agreed upon time. Such arrangements will encourage the respondent to complete the form by the prearranged time.

Rule 9.9 Record place and time information. It is critical to record where questionnaires have been dropped off, and when they are to be picked up. Pick the questionnaire up on time: respondents will be quite properly annoyed if they complete a questionnaire and it is not picked up at the agreed upon time.

Rule 9.10 Use a slotted return box. In order to help convey the sense of anonymity, it is a good idea to use a box with a slot cut in one end (a box measuring 9″ x 12″ is a good size) into which respondents' completed questionnaires can be slipped. In especially sensitive studies, this return procedure can be pointed out when the questionnaire is given to the respondent.

3. Questionnaires Administered in Group Settings

Questionnaires administered in group settings almost always have good response rates. In such situations the person administering the questionnaire can briefly explain what it is about and answer any questions which may be raised. Normally between 95 and 100 percent of potential respondents will complete questionnaires in group settings. They generally do not, however, meet probability sampling requirements (unless the units of analysis are the groups being surveyed, and these have been selected on a probability basis).

Rule 9.11 Arrange to administer the questionnaire well in advance and also remind the person in charge that you will be coming, shortly before the event is to take place. Frequently it will be necessary to gain permission to have a questionnaire administered.

Rule 9.12 Explain the survey to those present. In addition to answering any questions, the researcher should explain that cooperation is voluntary.

Rule 9.13 Administer the questionnaire at the end of the session. It is preferable to administer questionnaires at the end of a meeting or class, rather than at the beginning. If the researchers hand out the questionnaires at the beginning of a class, the problem will arise that all students will not finish at the same time, and valuable class time will be wasted as the researcher waits for the last forms to be completed. Also, the instructor will no doubt become impatient. Similarly, at a meeting, avoid handing out a questionnaire before the meeting begins; administer it at the end, or before a break. This will allow people who work at different speeds to complete the questionnaire without feeling rushed.

4. Mail Surveys

Mail surveys are popular because they provide a relatively cheap way of contacting a large number of respondents. Despite the reputation mail surveys have for producing low response rates, in fact it is possible to have the majority of questionnaires returned. Since our major concern with the mail survey is the response rate, we will consider the factors which influence whether a questionnaire will be returned. Thomas A. Heberlein and Robert Baumgartner have examined the response rates in some 98 mail questionnaire studies. Using a regression based method of analysis, they developed a ten variable model for predicting final response rate.[3] (See Figure 9.1)

There are two types of factors involved: those largely out of the control of the researcher, and those the researcher can control.

a. Factors Beyond the Control of the Researcher. These factors are of interest because they help in understanding and predicting the likely response rate to a mailed questionnaire. The *type of respondent* receiving the questionnaire is important: as Heberlein and Baumgartner have noted, students, employees, and military personnel are more inclined to return a mailed questionnaire than are members of the general public. The *type of sponsoring agency* also has an impact, with respondents favoring government-sponsored research over market research. Finally, there is the *salience* of the topic of the research to the respondent. Those subjects which are of real interest to the respondent are more likely to produce a positive response than those subjects less salient to the respondent.

b. Factors Under the Control of the Researcher. While the quality of the questionnaire does not come out as a factor identified in the Heberlein/ Baumgartner model it is to be noted that they were examining published studies which had passed various reviews before publication would have taken place, hence it would be reasonable to assume that all were highly professional. For the convenience of the respondent, include a stamped return envelope. A covering letter explaining the survey to the respondents should be included. The legitimacy of the survey is enhanced if the questionnaire is well presented, the agency sponsoring the research is identified, and the worthiness of the research is established.

Figure 9.1 Ten Variable Model Predicting Final Response Rate

Independent Variable	Coefficient	Code Values
Constant	36.3	1
Market Research Background	– 10.1	0–No, 1–Yes
Government Organization	10.2	0–No, 1–Yes
General Population	– 7.5	0–No, 1–Yes
Employee Population	11.8	0–No, 1–Yes
School or Army Population	9.9	0–No, 1–Yes
Saliency of Topic	7.3	0–Not Salient 1–Possibly Salient 2–Salient
Length–Number of Pages	– .44	Actual Number
Total Number of Contacts	7.4	Actual Number
Special Third Contact	8.6	0–No third contact 1–Regular mail 2–Special mail 3–Telephone or personal
Incentive–First Contact	6.1	0–No incentive 1–Less than $.25 2–$.25 3–$.50 4–$1.00

R^2 = .658.
Standard error of estimate = 14.2.

Source: Thomas A. Heberlein and Robert Baumgartner, "Factors Affecting Response Rates to Mailed Questionnaires," *American Sociological Review,* Vol. 43, No. 4, August, 1978, p. 456. Table 4. Reprinted by permission.

Among the variables examined, length turned out to be important. *The questionnaire must be kept short*; about one-half a percentage point in response rate is lost for every page. *Include a monetary incentive* and an increased response rate can be expected. *Follow-up contacts* in the form of letters, post card reminders, registered mail, and long distance phone calls all enhance the likelihood of a positive response. With each contact, slightly reduced effectiveness can be expected. However, registered mail and long distance phone calls seem to impress respondents with the importance of the study and of their role in it. One of the follow-up contacts should contain a replacement copy of the questionnaire in case the first one has been "misplaced." Although follow-up contacts are worthwhile, the researcher must always be careful not to harass potential respondents.

Given the many factors involved, it is not possible to estimate a response rate with precision before the survey is undertaken. However, a first-round response rate of about 50 percent should be considered average; three follow-up contacts can be expected to increase the response rate to about 75 percent.[4] Any response rate above 75 percent should be considered excellent. In Canada, Austria, and West Germany somewhat lower response rates can be expected. John Goyder has suggested that there may well be cultural factors which lower response rates to mail questionnaires in Canada. His research indicates that about a 7 percent lower response rate should be anticipated in Canadian studies compared to those done in the United States.[5]

Nonetheless, it is useful for the researcher to estimate response rates by using the formula presented in Figure 9.1. Meeting the predicted response rate should be considered an excellent response. To be within 25 percent of the predicted response rate should be viewed as acceptable.

To illustrate the use of the formula, suppose a study is designed to survey graduates of a university in terms of their job experiences since graduation. The survey is sponsored by the university. It involves a six-page questionnaire, the subject is regarded as "possibly salient," and one follow-up contact is planned. In this case, we estimate the response rate by simply plugging in the values presented in Figure 9.1. The predicted response rate would be:

Estimating a Response Rate		
Constant	36.3	
Market Research Background	0.0	(− 10.1 x 0)
Government Organization	0.0	(10.2 x 0)
General Population	0.0	(− 7.5 x 0)
Employee Population	0.0	(11.8 x 0)
School or Army Population	9.9	(9.9 x 1)
Possibly Salient	7.3	(7.3 x 1)
Length	− 2.6	(− .44 x 6)
Total Number of Contacts	7.4	(7.4 x 1)
Special Third Contact	0.0	(8.6 x 0)
Incentive-First Contact	0.0	(6.1 x 0)
Predicted Response Rate	58.3	

If it is thought that this response rate would not be adequate, then the researcher would be well advised to see what additional steps could be taken to increase the likelihood of response. The researcher might wish to consider making the questionnaire more salient for the respondents, and consider calling each one by phone. Although sending university graduates a dollar might be welcomed in times of high unemployment, some might be insulted by the gesture and so this procedure may not be advisable. However, it is to be noted that the use of incentives as small as 10 cents will increase the response rate: in one study of top corporate executives, 40 percent of those receiving no incentive responded, 54 percent of those receiving 10 cents responded, while among those who received 25 cents, 63 percent returned their questionnaires.[6]

Using the two recommended steps might boost the response rate to 91.4 percent (increased salience adds 7.3 percent, special phone contact adds 25.8 percent according to Figure 9.1).

Assuming that the questionnaire looks professional and that the appropriate covering letter is prepared, the following steps are suggested as methods for increasing the likelihood of response to a mailed questionnaire:

1. The envelope should identify the sponsoring organization's name. Identifying the sponsor is an effort to increase the perceived legitimacy of the project.

2. The respondent's name should be typed using the full name, rather than initials.

3. The mailing should be sent by first class mail, and should also use stamps rather than metered postage. The idea is to make the package seem as personal as possible. Avoid the mass produced look; do not use mailing labels.

4. Enclosed with the original material should be a stamped envelope for the return of the completed questionnaire.

5. If the questionnaires are to have identification codes placed on them, place them on the top right hand corner of the first page and indicate in the accompanying letter that the number is there to assist in following up on those respondents who have not returned the questionnaire. Do not use secret codes.

6. If an incentive is being used, use new currency, enclosed in a plastic envelope.

7. Follow-up procedures can involve sending a postcard thanking respondents if they have returned the questionnaire, and requesting that if they have not yet done so it would be greatly appreciated if they could.

8. A second follow-up, including a copy of the questionnaire, may be sent three weeks after the original has been mailed.

9. A third follow-up after six or seven weeks, using either registered mail or a phone call, is worthwhile in terms of the increased response rate. Most researchers do not go beyond the third follow-up.

Generally, returns will be fast at first and then slow down. After one week, expect to receive about 30 percent of those that will be returned, and about 85 percent within two weeks. By the end of four weeks about 96 percent of those that will be returned should have arrived.[7]

5. Phone Surveys

Phone surveys are gaining in popularity. They offer the advantages of being a relatively cheap and quick way to collect data. Since there is no travel time, phone interviewers can do many more interviews in a day than would be possible if they had to travel to each respondent's home. Moreover, phone interviewing can provide cost effective access to populations often very difficult to arrange interviews with (such as physicians), or to those scattered geographically (such as the blind).[8] In national studies, Robert M. Groves and Robert L. Kahn have estimated phone surveys to cost about 45 percent of what personal interviews cost.[9]

But there are disadvantages to phone surveys. First, they are not the best if probing is required, or if complex response categories are to be presented. Second, ownership of a phone is not always equally spread among the population. The less well-off and the mobile are less likely to have a phone or a listed phone number. However, as phones become more universally available, and as long as the researcher recognizes the possible sample distortions, there is less need to avoid phone surveys as a matter of principle. Indeed, it is possible to apply differential weightings to adjust for underrepresented categories in a survey. Finally, respondents interviewed over the phone are slightly more ill-at-ease compared to respondents being interviewed. As a result, phone interviews will generally produce slightly higher refusal rates on sensitive issues, such as income or political preference.[10]

Phone interviews also have some special problems related to assessing response rates. It is not always easy to determine how many numbers dialed are in fact active "live" phones. There will also be a fair number (generally about 20 percent) of phones attached to businesses. Furthermore, phone interviews will have higher rates of respondents failing to complete the interview and will typically not exceed 70 percent completion rates.[11]

In conducting a phone survey, the researcher will either be working with a list of potential respondents (such as a list of voters, members of a group or association), or from the names listed in the phone book. A systematic sampling procedure would then be used. The interviewer must reach the target respondent on the phone, introduce the survey, and then ask the respondent the questions. Studies based on rural populations generally have greater success in phone book based surveys since the lower level of geographic mobility means that fewer of the phones will be disconnected.

If the survey is to be done using the "heads of household" in a community, then the interviewer could again use a phone directory. When a phone is answered, the interviewer finds out who the "heads of household" are in the residence, then through some random sampling procedure (Table of Random Numbers, for example) decides which person is to be interviewed, and then asks to speak to that person; if the person is not home, a time to call back can be arranged.[12]

Another possibility is to identify the various residential phone exchanges in the area, and then use a Table of Random Numbers to determine the numbers to be dialed. Typically phone numbers are assigned in 5 digit blocks, the first three determining the exchange. The numbers might start 863-21xx. A Table of Random Numbers may be used to determine the last two digits to be dialed. If it is possible to get the information from the phone company, the researcher attempts to find out the percentage of phones in each block and then a sample is drawn to proportionally represent each block.[13]

Computer-Assisted Telephone Interviewing is becoming an important tool for polling organizations and market researchers. The computer is used to dial a sample of respondents and guides the interviewer through the data collection by presenting the questions on the screen and then, depending on the response, showing the next appropriate question. The answers are then recorded into the machine.

Rule 9.16 Begin with interesting, salient yet simple, questions. This is a tough rule to follow. Try to begin a phone interview with questions simple to answer and non-threatening, but which will nonetheless be viewed as important. Since phone respondents are a little more likely than those interviewed in person to terminate the interview, it is especially important to ease them into the discussion. While phone interviews can last up to half an hour, they should be kept as short and simple as possible.

Rule 9.17 Supply phone interviewers with rules for determining who is to be interviewed. If an equal probability sampling procedure is required, then procedures for establishing who in the household contacted by phone is to be interviewed must be provided. It is not generally acceptable to interview the person who happens to answer the phone. If this were done, the survey would, by definition, overrepresent those in the household who are most likely to answer the phone. The interviewer should not be making convenience decisions.

Rule 9.18 Simplify response categories. Phone interviews must keep the response categories simple. While it is possible to conduct lengthy interviews by telephone, keep the questions simple: often it is necessary to break a complex question into smaller simpler ones.[14] Respondents are slightly more likely to select a neutral response category and there is also a tendency to choose the last response category presented. Hence researchers frequently will vary the order of the response categories.

6. Personal Interviews

Personal interviews have the advantages of allowing an interviewer to probe in depth, deal with difficult issues, and establish a reciprocal relationship with the respondent, all of which may be necessary especially if the study is longitudinal. Among the disadvantages are that interview studies are expensive (more than double that of phone interviews)[15] and time consuming.

While it is beyond the scope of this book to discuss the selection and training of interviewers, some brief comments can be made on this subject. Research done by the National Opinion Research Center (NORC) has indicated that the quality of work done by interviewers is related to length of time working for NORC, high grade averages in high school, liking two or more science subjects, intelligence, and completion of college. In addition, people who scored high on "need achievement," high career orientation, and manipulativeness (Machiavellianism scale) will also be good interviewers. Of note is that happiness, financial need, religious behavior, perfectionism, and size of home community were not found to be related to the quality of interviewing a person does.[16]

Training for interviewing involves familiarizing potential interviewers with what social research is about and how it is conducted. Training may involve a discussion of ethical issues; a familiarization with the survey being conducted; and instruction on appropriate dress, how to introduce oneself to the respondent, gaining rapport, organizing the interview setting, how to present questions, how to react to responses, which issues are to be probed, how to probe, how to keep the respondent on topic, and how to gracefully end the interview. In addition to covering some of the above issues, research directors should also provide potential interviewers with experience in a few simulated interviews.[17]

Normally, interviewers are paid on a "per interview" basis. This method is preferred since it allows the researcher to control costs. Also it seems to be the case that many interviewers will "burn out" after six or eight weeks. Interviewing is an especially challenging task, requiring great concentration, and it is not easy to remain alert after having walked many respondents through the survey instrument. A high turnover among interviewing staff should be expected.

Rule 9.19 Spot check interviewers. It is a good idea to spot check to ensure that interviews are being done effectively. Be cautious of interviewers who are doing much more than the norm. Watch out for systematic differences in response rates to sensitive questions. If an interviewer is missing data, try to go through that part of the instrument to see if the presentation can be improved. The quality of one's research can be no better than the quality of the data collected. Monitor the process carefully.

Rule 9.20 Do not inform interviewers of hypotheses. Generally, it is not advisable to fully inform interviewers as to the hypotheses of the study: interviewer expectancy may be reduced if the hypotheses are not known.

7. On Keeping Track of Respondents in a Panel Study

On occasion, respondents will be contacted at different points in time. When the time between contacts is a year or two, and the population being studied is fairly mobile, there are special problems posed for the researcher. Those doing follow-up panel studies may find some of the following tips helpful in tracking down respondents:[18]

Tip 1. At the time of the first interview request that the name of a relative or friend who will always know how to get in touch with the respondent be provided. This information may prove invaluable later in efforts to contact individuals.

Tip 2. Try the original phone number; even though the respondent has moved, he/she may have the same phone number if still living within the same area. If the phone has been disconnected, the operator may be able to provide the new number.

Tip 3. Phone directories for both the original year and for the current one are helpful; check how the person was listed in the original directory, if the person is still in the area, chances are that the name will be listed identically.

Tip 4. Contact the employer of the respondent or contact fellow workers in an effort to locate the individual.

Tip 5. Contact neighbors.

Tip 6. Now you are desperate! Call people in the directory with the same last name, hoping to get lucky and find a relative of the person involved who might be able to give you an address or phone number.

D. EXERCISES

1. Suppose that you have census information indicating that the mean income of a population is $37 000 with a standard deviation of $21 000. You wish to draw a sample which 95% of the time will be within $2000 of the true population mean. How large a sample would be required?

2. Assuming the same population values as in the above question, determine the sample size required to produce 99% confidence that you will be within $2000 of the true mean.

3. If the most complex contingency table you wish to run in an analysis is a 2 x 2 x 2 table, what sample size would be required to yield expected frequencies of 20 in each cell (assuming breaks at the mid-point)?

NOTES

[1]See Paul L. Erdos, *Professional Mail Surveys.* Malabar, Florida: Robert E. Krieger Publishing Company, 1983, p. 146-47.

[2]Thomas A. Heberlein and Robert Baumgartner, "Factors Affecting Response Rates to Mailed Questionnaires," *American Sociological Review*, 43, 1978.

[3]*Ibid.*

[4]See Don A. Dillman *et. al.*, "Increasing Mail Questionnaire Response," *American Sociological Review*, 39, 1974. In addition, the work by Heberlein & Baumgartner (above) is crucial to understanding the factors involved in predicting response rates.

[5]See John Goyder, "Nonresponse On Surveys: A Canada-United States Comparison," *Canadian Journal of Sociology*, Vol. 10, No. 3, 1985, pp. 231-51; John C. Goyder, "Further Evidence on Factors Affecting Response Rates to Mailed Questionnaires," *American Sociological Review*, Vol. 47, August, 1982, pp. 550-53; and Klaus Eichner and Werner Habermehl, "Predicting Response Rates to Mailed Questionnaires," *American Sociological Review*, Vol. 46, pp. 361-63.

[6]Erdos, p. 97.

[7]Erdos, p. 263.

[8]Seymour Sudman, *Reducing the Cost of Surveys.* Chicago: Aldine Publishing Company, 1967, pp. 58-67.

[9]Anyone contemplating a phone survey should consult Robert M. Groves and Robert L. Kahn, *Surveys by Telephone: A National Comparison with Personal Interviews.* New York: Academic Press, 1979.

[10]*Ibid.*, p. 98.

[11]*Ibid.*, p. 75.

[12]The selection of respondents by phone is complex and if anything but the simplest sample is being drawn, the reader is encouraged to consult such excellent works as Seymour Sudman, *Applied Sampling.* New York: Academic Press, 1976.

[13]See Mark Abrahamson, *Social Research Methods.* Englewood Cliffs, N.J.: Prentice-Hall Inc., 1983, pp. 225-26.

[14]See Seymour Sudman and Norman Bradburn, *Asking Questions.* San Francisco: Jossey-Bass, Inc., Publishers, 1983.

[15]Groves and Kahn, p. 211.

[16]Seymour Sudman, "Cost and Quality of Interviewers," in *Reducing the Cost of Surveys.* Chicago: Aldine Publishing Company, 1967, pp. 100-53.

[17]See Eve Weinberg, *Community Surveys with Local Talent.* Chicago: National Opinion Research Center, 1971.

[18]Using these procedures in a project involving two interviews, spaced two years apart, following up a matched pairs sample, it was possible to locate and interview 96.0 percent of the original sample of 538. See Donald H. Clairmont and Winston Jackson "Segmentation of the Low Income Blue Collar Worker: A Canadian Test of Segmentation Theory," Halifax: Institute of Public Affairs, Dalhousie University, 1980.

PART FIVE

DATA ANALYSIS

CHAPTER TEN

STARTING THE DATA ANALYSIS

At this stage of the research, it is time to enter the results of the survey into the computer. While this process is relatively straightforward, there are a number of points to keep in mind to ensure that data entry and error checking will proceed efficiently.

A. BRIEF INTRODUCTION TO THE COMPUTER

In most cases, the contemporary researcher will be working on a terminal connected to a mainframe computer. Students need not understand much about computers in order to use them — just as one does not need to know anything about engines in order to drive a car.

This simple analogy can be used to introduce the reader to the computer: think of entering a large, strange house. It is a little frightening at first but after a while you will find that it can be fun exploring it. The first thing you will have to do is get inside. You will need a key, such as a secret password, in order to enter. Imagine that you have been provided with a password so that you can get into the house. Looking down the hall you realize that there are many rooms in this house. (The hall represents the computer's operating system with many procedures and utilities available to the user in the various rooms.) Having entered the house you now have to decide which room to explore. The first room is marked "Editor" (here you can make and modify files). The second room is marked "Storage" (you can save files here and retrieve them later). A third door is marked "SPSS" (social science data is analyzed here).

A fourth door is marked "Word Processing" (here reports are written and modified). A fifth door is marked "Line Printer" (here files are copied onto paper so that they will be available to the user). There are many other doors in the house but these need not be explored immediately by the beginning social science student.

In this house, you start off in the hall (the operating system) and from there enter a room, do something, and then re-enter the hall and from there either leave the house or go into another room to perform other tasks. The point is that it is from the operating system that you branch out to do other tasks and functions. The computer will provide a cue to inform you when it is in the operating system mode. These cues are called "prompts." Symbols such as: "$", ">", or "?" are used. So if you get lost in the house, try to get back to the operating system, back to the operating system prompt.

Before rules are given for the entry of the data into the computer, two ideas need to be explored in a little more detail. These are *files* and *editors*.

1. Files

When data, or the text of a report, are entered into a computer, they will be stored in a file. Computer files are just like those found in a filing cabinet; they contain information on some topic and are arranged so that they can be retrieved easily. Many computers use a two-word naming convention for files. The first part consists of the *file name*, the second part of the *file type*. The two parts are separated by a period, " . " Typically, one is allowed eight character spaces for the file name and three for the file type. For the data collected in a survey, one might use the name: JOAN.DAT. If Joan were involved in a number of surveys she would need to use unique names for each of her surveys. However, she would always use the same file type label for data — perhaps ".DAT". Later, we will need to know about other kinds of files and additional file types will be introduced. If a researcher is working on several surveys then the file names should refer to the subject of each survey. The following names might be used to name the raw data files for five different surveys:

    ABORTION.DAT
    ASPIRE.DAT
    CAPPUN.DAT
    ESTEEM.DAT
    PRESTIGE.DAT

2. Editors

A computer system will have one or more "Editors" available to its users. Editor programs are used to manage the entry of information into a file. Normally there will be procedures to quickly move through a file, to append information, or to make changes in the text. There will be a flashing cursor on the screen to mark the position at which the machine is ready to work.

You will need to learn how to make use of the many features available on the Editor you are using. After you have completed your work, you will need to know how to save your work permanently so that it will be available to you next time you sign on the computer. The operating system will have a simple command which will allow you to list all your files on the screen. You will learn how to call any file into the Editor so that you can look at it on the screen, perhaps make changes in it, and then print it on a line printer if you need a copy.

B. DATA ENTRY

Data entry is simply the process of transferring the information on the completed questionnaires to a computing device. It will be assumed that you have figured out how to use the Editor to create a file and you are now ready to begin data entry. The following rules provide guidelines for data entry.

Rule 10.1 Number questionnaires. Questionnaires are numbered, normally beginning with 001 (or 0001 if there are more than 1000 cases). The number is written on the front page of the questionnaire (usually top right corner). This number will be entered into the computer and provides the only link between a particular questionnaire and the data entered into the computer. If an error is found in the data, the original questionnaire can be located by using the ID number, then the information can be checked, and the error corrected. Keep the questionnaires sorted by their ID numbers.

Rule 10.2 Code any uncoded questions. If there are questions which have not been pre-coded (such as occupational codes, or open-ended opinion seeking questions) they should now be coded and the values written on the questionnaire in the margin next to the question. In the case of occupational codes, these would be looked up and a value entered onto the questionnaire.

Rule 10.3 Do a column count. Go through a blank copy of the questionnaire, and opposite each question indicate where each question will be entered on the terminal screen. Typically, screens are 80 columns wide. This means that you can enter 80 digits across the screen before you run out of space. The first three columns will be used for the ID number of the questionnaire, the fourth column will be used to identify the line number for the respondent. (This is necessary only for questionnaires requiring more than 80 columns to enter the data.) If a question can have values between 0 and 9, then one column will be required to record the data; if the values range up to 99, then two columns will be required. Up to 999 will require 3 columns. These values are recorded on the right-hand margin of the questionnaire.

The right-hand margin might look something like this:

Variable	Columns
ID	1- 3
Record	4
Sex	5
Yr. Birth	6- 7
Income	8-13
Occupation	14-15

In a short questionnaire the information for each variable will fit onto one 80 column line; each questionnaire will occupy one line of data. If more than one line is required then a second line is used with the first 3 columns being saved for a repeat of the ID number and the 4th containing a "2" meaning that it is the second line of the questionnaire. In the case of a questionnaire requiring two lines, the data might look like this:

```
0011476989232333 23222111222111 22245634564455666663339
00124534376767221122211 112229912287632145321334522
0021456338992212 21222113222112 22334110033445565443221
00222343434445857463748 4985050595211222333423334444
```

Note the first four columns. The first three contain the ID code (which has also been written on the questionnaire) and the fourth column refers to the line number. What is shown is respondent 001 1st line; then respondent 001 2nd line; followed by respondent 002, line 1 and then line 2. It is not critical that the ID numbers be in sequence but the case must be together — line 1 must be followed by line 2 for each case. The blanks in the data set are discussed below.

Rule 10.4 Enter data with the help of a partner. Inexperienced terminal operators will find that data entry will be much easier and cause fewer errors, if two people work together on entering the data. One person can read the numbers from the questionnaire, while the partner enters the values into the terminal.

Rule 10.5 Leave internal blanks to mark each page. Errors can more quickly be identified if, after the end of each page in the questionnaire, a blank is left in the data. The column of blanks must always line up when the data are printed out; if the blanks do not line up then an error has been made and must be corrected. The first 6 lines of a data set are listed below showing how the blanks line up:

```
page 1          page 2              page 3            page 4
00112435445523  211212333448976999  123232111123212  23411112
00211231231234  322213222122232212  432235333211232  34532432
00314321234443  233445324433321212  332122341122233  23323222
00413444688822  122222112232123219  234433221222321  34521211
00513335543221  223332221114124211  332111422111212  32121223
00614322345432  231143321122122121  112211222111231  22132454
```

Note that the fourth line of data contains an error; by examining the listing it becomes apparent that the error is somewhere in the data entered from page 2 of the questionnaire (there is one too many digits in the space reserved for page 2). While the introduction of blanks to mark the end of pages is helpful in error detection, if the use of these blanks forces the use of an extra line of data for each respondent, then it is probably best not to include them. The advantage of having them would be outweighed by the additional work involved in error checking an additional line of data for each respondent.

Rule 10.6 Simplify missing value codes. If respondents do not answer a question, or if the question is not applicable, a missing value code is used. These should be kept as simple and as consistent as possible. Where possible use the values "9", "99", or "999" for one, two, and three column variables respectively. Suppose a respondent is asked to indicate gender as either male or female and leaves the question blank. Instead of leaving the column blank, a "9" would be inserted into the appropriate column.

While it is possible to use alternate codes (question not answered or question not applicable) such as "8" for not answered, and "9" for not applicable, such discrimination should only be made where it is known that the information will be used later; if it is not going to be used, keep matters simple by using the single code "9" to cover both cases. In occupational codes, it may be necessary to provide special codes for "housewife" if values are not provided in the occupational code system being used. In 9-point attitudinal scales, "0" is used as the missing value code.

A code must be entered for every question even if it is not answered. The reason for this is that when instructions are given to the computer each question is identified with particular columns in the data; each question, therefore, must be in the identical position in all lines of data.

Rule 10.7 Document research decisions. When data are being entered into the terminal, a number of decisions will be required. A questionnaire may have a lot of missing data and the person entering the data might decide that it would be better to discard the questionnaire. Such decisions should be made by the research group. Cases may arise where a respondent has checked two items in a question where only one was expected. Generally these discrepancies will be rare enough so that it is appropriate to "flip a coin" to decide which of the two will be taken. (One would not systematically take the highest placed item on the list since that would systematically bias the results toward those items listed first.) When such a decision has been made, the decision should be clearly marked on the questionnaire and initialed by the person making the decision. With such documentation it is then possible for others to check through the data and understand what coding decisions were made and by whom.

Rule 10.8 Code information not on the questionnaire. Frequently there will be information not coded on the questionnaire which should be appended to the data. It is always recommended that provision be made for a code to identify who did the coding on the questionnaire, who did the data entry, and any other information that may be useful in the later data analysis or in error-checking. The reason it is helpful to indicate who did the coding is that if there are systematic differences between coders in dealing with different questions, then the cases dealt with by each coder can quickly be identified.

Rule 10.9 Practice double data entry. Where resources allow, it is recommended that data be entered twice, by different individuals. A computer program can then be used to compare the two files, flagging any differences between them. This technique is extremely helpful in reducing data entry errors.

C. STEPS IN CLEANING DATA

After the questionnaire data has been entered into the computer and saved in a file, it is time to begin the search for errors so that they can be corrected before analysis of the data can begin. This process is usually referred to as "cleaning the data."

Step 1. Sort questionnaires by ID numbers. During error correction it will be necessary to have all the questionnaires available and these should be sorted by ID number so that any particular questionnaire can be found quickly.

Step 2. Sort files by line type. When there are two or more lines of data for each case, the first step will be to SORT the data file into separate files, one for each line type. The SORT procedure, possibly called "Sort" or "SortMerge", will be available in the operating system of your computer. The objective is to create new files so that all the line 1s are together in a file, all the line 2s are in a separate file and so forth. It is also useful to sort the cases within each file by ID number to facilitate spotting errors such as repeated data lines (data entered twice) or a missed line. If there are multiple lines per case, then the following procedures will have to be repeated for each line file.

Step 3. List files on the line printer. The file(s) being checked should be listed on a line printer. The printout should be examined and any irregularities circled. Check the following:

(a) All lines must end in the same column. If there are too few or too many columns in a line it means that questions were either missed or entered twice. Mark discrepant lines so they can be checked against the original questionnaire and the error(s) located. The file must be 'rectangular" with no ragged edges.

(b) Any internal blanks must line up vertically. If end-of-page blanks have been used, one can quickly identify situations where there have been too many or too few entries made from a particular page on the questionnaire. Once again, mark any discrepancies.

(c) When there are two or more files to be checked, ensure that the file lengths are equal. If 165 questionnaires have been completed, there must be 165 lines in each of the files.

(d) Proofread ID numbers (columns 1 through 3) to ensure that there are no repeated or missing ID numbers. Again mark any errors.

(e) Finally, there must be no blank lines or partial lines left in the data set.

Step 4. Make corrections to files. After the above errors have been identified, the files should be corrected by comparing the values that should be present (those in the original questionnaire) to those present in the data file. The questionnaires can be quickly retrieved since they are in order; the ID numbers on the error lines identify which questionnaires have to be checked. A printout of the corrected files should then be made on the line printer.

Step 5. Check for out-of-range values. Many of the errors in the data will have been removed by going through the first four procedures. However, two or more errors can lead to a situation where the file may be perfectly "rectangular" yet have questions coded into the wrong columns. Furthermore, slips may have been made in entering the data where a "3" was entered when the value should have been a "2". Many such errors will show up if a frequency distribution is run on each column in the data set. For example, if, in column 5, the legitimate entries include "1" for males, "2" for females, or "9' for no response then any other value would be in error. Most computer installations will have utility programs for running such frequency distributions. The distribution should then be listed on the line printer. Once again, any discrepant values should be circled on the printout. A final alternative would be to wait until the SPSS processing begins to identify out-of-range values and, then, with SELECT IF statements, identify the ID numbers of cases with incorrect values in them.

Step 6. Make corrections to eliminate out-of-range values. Looking at the printout, you will see certain columns that have been identified as containing out-of-range values. It will be necessary to identify the line(s) containing these incorrect values. Some Editor programs will permit the searching of particular columns for specified values. If you have access to an Editor with this facility you will be able to quickly find the lines with the inappropriate values. If such a program is not available, chances are good that one of the quantitative social scientists will have a utility program for doing such searches. If all else fails, get out a ruler, place it on the printout obtained in Step 4 above, and scan the appropriate column for the out-of-range value. Mark the error. Having identified the questionnaire where the error has occurred, proofread the data and make the necessary corrections. It is useful to proofread a number of columns before and after the error to make certain that adjacent columns are correct.

Step 7. Merge data files together. Once all the files have been corrected, and the files are confirmed to have the same number of lines in each, they should be merged together and sorted, so that the cases will be in order and line 1 of case 1 will be followed by the second line of case 1. The sorting should result in a file where the first four columns are as follows:

```
0011 ...
0012 ...
0013 ...
0021 ...
0022 ...
0023 ...
0031 ...
0032 ...
0033 ...
```

In the above example, there are three lines for each case. After confirmation that the file is correctly sorted, that it contains the appropriate number of lines, and that there are no blank lines, the file should be saved and it is now ready for processing by SPSS^x.

D. INTRODUCING SPSS^x

The Statistical Package for the Social Sciences (SPSS) was developed initially in the 1960s and has gone through a series of embellishments over the years. It contains a number of statistical and data manipulation procedures. The most recent version is known as SPSS^x. In addition, a version is now available for personal computers. SPSS^x is undoubtedly the most popular and widely available statistical package used by social scientists.

1. Types of Files Used in SPSS^x

Typically, the contemporary user of SPSS^x will be working on a terminal connected to a mainframe computer. The researcher enters raw data into the terminal, and then creates files to submit instructions to SPSS^x. Five types of files will be used. A brief examination of Figure 10.1 shows how these files are related to one another.

Figure 10.1   File Types Used in SPSS^x

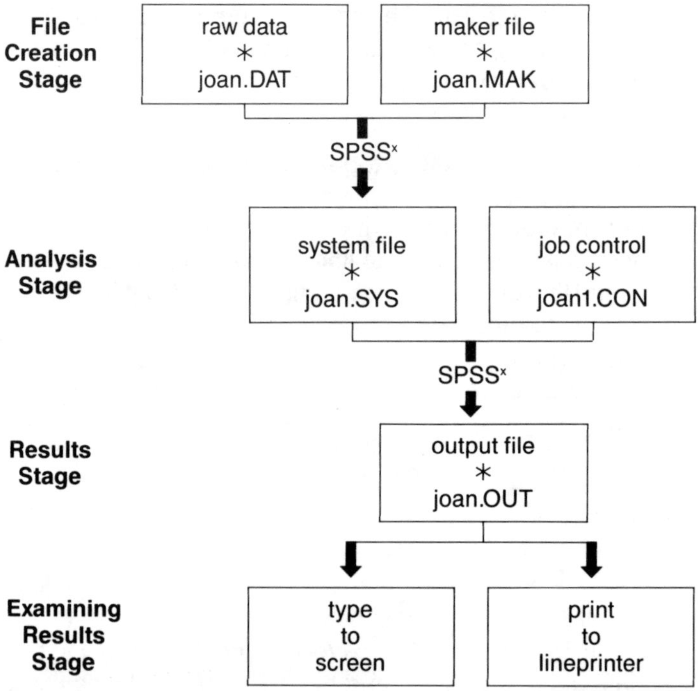

The convention is that the file types (the part following the " . ") are printed in UPPER CASE, indicating that they always remain the same. The file names preceding the " . " in lower case, are names assigned by the researcher. Each project should use distinctive file names, which will help keep the files from different projects identified. The file types are:

joan.DAT	.DAT	= raw data file
joan.MAK	.MAK	= SPSS^x system MAKER file
joan.SYS	.SYS	= SPSS^x system file
joan.OUT	.OUT	= results sent to OUTPUT file
joan1.CON	.CON	= job control file containing analysis instructions.

As discussed earlier, in many computer installations files are made up of a *file name* and a *file type* separated by a period, as in: data.DAT. The file name can be up to eight characters in length while the file type is limited to three characters. In this presentation the file name is printed in lower case, indicating that it is to be named by the researcher. For convenience, file types will always remain the same (these are in UPPER case). There is no requirement that the file names be the same for each type of file, nor that file types use the conventions given here. But whatever naming convention is chosen, it should be kept simple to avoid confusion.

a. Data Files: joan.DAT. This file contains the raw data for the survey. It will contain no blank lines, and the records will be sorted so that where there are two lines of data for each questionnaire, the file will contain the 1st line of case 1 and then the 2nd line of case 1, followed by subsequent cases. The cases must always follow the same pattern and there should be no missing lines of data. Care in the preparation and entry of data is critical because if an error occurs, incorrect data may be read. The joan.DAT file will be read into SPSS^x when the joan.MAK file is submitted to the computer.

b. SPSS System Maker Files: joan.MAK. This file type will be referred to as a *maker* file because it creates an SPSS^x system file. This file contains all the instructions about the location of the data, what the names of the variables are, how the variables are labeled, and what values have been assigned in cases where the data are missing. There will be one maker file for each project. It should be retained permanently along with the raw data file for possible future use with a different SPSS version or an entirely different system. The details for creating such a file are presented later in this chapter.

c. SPSS System Files: joan.SYS. The convention used here is that .SYS files are SPSS^x system files. These files combine all the data, and all the variable names, labels, and other information included in the .MAK file. Once created and confirmed as correct, the .SYS files are used throughout the project analysis. By always labelling such files as .SYS files they are immediately recognizable. They can only be altered by issuing commands contained in an SPSS job. .SYS files should be retained permanently, along with at least one backup copy of the file.

.SYS type files can be updated, adding new variables which have been computed. It is especially important, therefore, to retain any job control files used to create updated system files. Should errors in the raw data be discovered after analysis has started, it is then possible to make the changes in the raw data, resubmit the .MAK job, recreate the .SYS file with the new information contained in it, and then resubmit any job control files which have been used to update and modify the .SYS file. Much time will be saved if any files updating the .SYS file are retained until the project is completed. After the project is completed, however, only three files need be retained: the .DAT, .MAK, and the .SYS files. All others may be purged.

d. Job Control Files: joan1.CON. .CON files are control files indicating the procedures to be used in an analysis. For bigger jobs, or jobs which update the system file, it is a good idea to retain these files under separate names, as in: joan1.CON, joan2.CON, joan3.CON, etc. Generally these files contain just a few lines so that they will not take up too much space in the computer. They are retained so that if it becomes necessary to redo the analysis, the contents of the files will not have to be reentered. As a hint, job control files such as joan0.CON may be used for jobs which do not need to be retained (such as listing some cases, printing the dictionary or running a frequency distribution before recoding a variable). The joan0.CON contains the FILE HANDLE and GET FILE commands, and the researcher needs only to modify the procedures from run to run.

e. Output of Results Files: joan.OUT. The .OUT file is the output file which contains the results of the SPSS analysis. The researcher examines this file, determines if the run is error-free and has produced the intended analyses, and, if everything is correct, prints the file on the computer's lineprinter. It is generally advisable to use the same name for .OUT files. This makes it easier to remember the name of the file and helps to avoid a build up of unnecessary files in the directory. Remember that results to be retained should be printed before another job is run or else new results will be printed over previous ones. In cases where the lineprinter is broken, data analysis can continue, but remember that the .OUT files will have to be given different names so that they will not be destroyed. After the lineprinter is operating again, these .OUT files should be printed and then purged since they use a lot of space.

f. Backup Files: data.BAK, system.BAK, maker.BAK. A sixth type of file, not identified in Figure 10.1, is a .BAK file. These are backup files. Once again, the name assigned to them is arbitrary. It is a good idea to backup the raw data, SPSS^x system, and SPSS^x system maker files using totally different names. In case all the .DAT files should accidentally be deleted, the data would be safely stored under another name. The three critical files are the raw data, system, and system maker files. Names such as data.BAK, system.BAK, and maker.BAK may be used. These files should also be backed up on tape and removed from the computer center. That way, short of a nuclear attack, no disasters should destroy the files which have taken so much time to create.

E. CREATING AND SAVING A SIMPLE SPSSˣ SYSTEM FILE

In order to create an SPSSˣ system file, a .MAK file will be created containing all the necessary instructions. Such files should be saved permanently since they are time consuming to develop.

Figure 10.2   SPSSˣ Commands to Create a System File

```
TITLE Maker File For Survey of Graduates
FILE HANDLE (file specifications for raw data file)
FILE HANDLE (file specifications for new system file)
DATA LIST FILE =data RECORDS=2
    /1 ID 1–3, V1 TO V4 5–8, V5 9–10,
        V6 TO V22 11–45
    /2 NAME 5–33 (A)
VARIABLE LABELS ID "Identification Number"
    V1 "Sex of Respondent"
    V2 "Size of Home Community"
    V3 "Religious Affiliation"
    V4 "Ethnic Origin"
    V5 "Year of Birth"
    ...etc
    NAME "Name of School"
VALUE LABELS V1 1 "Male" 2 "Female"/
    V2 1 "Rural Area" 2 "Under 1000" 3 "1000 to 4999"
        4 "5000 to 49 999" 5 "50 000 to 99 999" 6 "Over
        100 000"/
MISSING VALUES V1, V6, V29 TO V34 (9)/
    V16, V19 (0, 98, 99)/
    V17, V18, V20 TO V22 (0)
FREQUENCIES VARIABLES = V1, V2, V17
SAVE OUTFILE = system
FINISH
```

Figure 10.2 illustrates the commands required to create an SPSSˣ system file combining raw data with instructions for how the variables are to be named and labeled. Each of the components will be discussed below. The reader should note, however, that SPSSˣ can deal with more complex data sets and one of the SPSSˣ manuals[1] should be consulted if your data does not fit into the type described below. We will assume that we have a data file of 150 observations and 25 variables. We will want to keep the raw data in a separate file which will then be combined with a set of data definition commands in order to create an SPSSˣ system file.

SPSSˣ commands are broken into two parts: a *command name*, which starts in column 1, followed by *specifications*. The continuation of a line is indented. Each of the basic commands necessary will be discussed briefly in this section. For additional information, consult an SPSSˣ manual.

1. File Definition and Control Commands

a. TITLE. The TITLE command should be included so that a label will be placed at the top of each page of output. It is a good idea to include the researcher's name in the text of the title. The text of the title can include up to 60 characters and might look like:

TITLE A Study of Sibling Rivalry, Charlie McMullin

b. FILE HANDLE. File handles provide SPSSˣ information about where raw data or system files are located. The format for these commands varies for each type of computer and operating system. Two common ones will be listed here but these may not work on your particular installation. For a DEC VAX system the following is used to identify a raw data file and a system file respectively:

FILE HANDLE data/NAME = 'joan.DAT'
FILE HANDLE system/NAME = 'joan.SYS'

The convention being followed is that lower case letters refer to those added by the researcher. (SPSSˣ works with either upper or lower case.) For an IBM/CMS system the following command lines would identify the raw data and system files:

FILE HANDLE data/NAME = 'joan.data a'
FILE HANDLE system/NAME = 'joan.sys a'

Researchers will need to consult with their computer center to find out how to do the file handles if the above commands do not work. Any file you wish to access or create in a run must be identified by a FILE HANDLE command. Normally, after the researcher has created the system file and is analyzing data, only one file handle will be required—the one that identifies the system file.

c. SET. This command sets the various output options. Two of them are particularly handy. If you require typewriter width output, rather than computer width paper, use the WIDTH = 80 option; if you wish to start a new page with each analysis, use the LENGTH = 59 option. These can be illustrated as follows:

SET WIDTH = 80
SET LENGTH = 59

d. DATA LIST. The DATA LIST command is the most complex one involved in creating a system file. Do this one carefully, and double-check it, for this is the one most likely to produce errors. A simple DATA LIST might look like this:

DATA LIST FILE = data RECORDS = 2
   /1 ID 1-3, V1 to V4 5-8, V5 9-10,
      V6 to V22 13-46, V23 48-50
   /2 NAME 5-33 (A)

The FILE= is used to identify the file where the raw data are located. This file should be fully identified in the FILE HANDLE. The RECORDS= specification indicates how many lines of data there are for each case. In the above example there are two lines, or records, per case. Variable names and the column locations of the data are then identified. The /1 identifies that what follows are the variable names and column locations for information on the first record.

The ID is the identification number of the case, and is always included; ID becomes the first *variable name* in the study. Variable names may be up to 8 characters in length and begin with an alphabetical character. For surveys involving many variables, it is best to simply use the question numbers printed on the questionnaire to name variables. In the illustration, the variables are named ID followed by V1, V2 ... V22. The advantages of using sequential numbers are that: (1) if you have a lot of variables it will be difficult to remember special variable names; (2) variables named after question numbers can be quickly identified; and (3) time can be saved because variables can be named by using the TO convention, which has the computer assign variable names, as in: V1 TO V4. Studies with just a few variables may have variable names such as "FAED, MAED, AGE, INCOME" to refer to father's education, mother's education, age of respondent, and income of respondent.

The specification following the variable name is the *column location* of the variable. The ID data are located in columns 1 through 3, indicated by "1-3". Where there are a series of variables with the same field lengths (i.e., all 1, or all 2, or all 3 columns long) then time can be saved by naming a series of variables, followed by the columns that contain the data, as in:

V1 TO V4 5-8

This series identifies four variables and the four columns where the data are found for them. It should be noted that not all columns need be read — only those that are to be used in the study.

The beginning of the second record is signalled with /2. A variable called NAME is located in columns 5-33, and is followed by an (A) in parentheses. The (A) indicates an alphabetic variable and might refer to the names of schools, names of people, or even whether responses to a set of true/false questions have been coded as T or F. Generally, however, yes/no or true/false questions are best coded numerically as it will be somewhat easier to analyze the data later.

e. VARIABLE LABELS. It is useful to label variables, since they will be printed on many of the analyses to be used in data analysis. Each label may be up to 40 characters in length. The following format is recommended:

VARIABLE LABELS ID "Identification Number"
    V1 "Sex"
    V2 "Program of Study"
    V3 "Education of Respondent's Father"

f. VALUE LABELS. Labels may be placed on the various categories within a variable. Once again, these are optional. Each label may be up to 20 characters in length. Value labels can be appended to multiple variables simultaneously by listing the variables to which the same labels should be appended. It is useful in 9-point Likert-type items to label the extremes. Note that a slash follows the labels for *each* variable. (The omission of the slash is a common error.) The labels may be illustrated as follows:

```
VALUE LABELS V1 1 "Male" 2 "Female"/
             V2 1 "Arts" 2 "Science" 3 "Business Admin."
                4 "Nursing" 5 "Physical Ed."/
             V7 to V14 1 "Strongly Disagree" 9 "Strongly Agree"/
```

g. MISSING VALUES. Most variables require a code for missing values. As discussed previously, it is best to use 9s to reflect missing values, although up to three individual values may be designated as missing values. A missing value is used when a respondent has not answered a question. SPSS^x will assign missing values where the information is not complete (for example, when new variables are created). Multiple variables can be assigned missing values by simply listing all the variables to which the same missing values apply, as in:

```
MISSING VALUES V1, V2, V7 TO V10, V21 (9)/
               V16, V19 (998, 999)/
               V3 to V6, V11 TO V15, V17, V18, V20 (0)/
```

h. FREQUENCIES. A procedure is now chosen to activate the file. Any number of procedures could be used at this point. In this case, the following command might be used:

```
FREQUENCIES VARIABLES = V1, V2
FINISH
```

2. Error Checking with SPSS^x

Having entered the above commands into a file called joan.MAK, the time has come to save the file and then to submit it to SPSS^x for processing. In DEC VAX systems, at the operating system prompt, the command is:

```
$SPSSX/OUT=joan.OUT joan.MAK
[see computer center for command]
```

Your terminal will now freeze until the job has been completed, at which point the prompt will reappear. Now you examine the results by listing joan.OUT on your terminal. If there are errors (almost a certainty the first time!), try to spot them on the screen and note them. If there are a lot of errors, print the results on the lineprinter. After you figure out what has gone wrong, put your joan.MAK file into the Editor, make the necessary corrections, and resubmit the job to SPSS^x.

When the message at the bottom of the .OUT file indicates that there are no SPSSˣ errors, you have not, however, entirely finished the error checking. A little time spent on some final checks will help eliminate data errors and ensure that when you begin analysis you will be working with a file that is substantially error-free. The following steps are recommended:

> **Step 1.** Check the printout section showing the data list command. There will be a listing of the variable names and the record number and column location of each variable. Go through the list carefully and check it against the codes on your questionnaire. For example, if question 27 is named V27 and should be located on RECORD 1, column 26-27, be certain that V27 is listed on your printout as being located in that position. (See Figure 10.3 which provides a sample listing.)

Figure 10.3   Sample Data List Output

```
1  0        TITLE GRADES FOR SOC100, Winston Jackson
2  0        FILE HANDLE SOC10013 / NAME  = 'SOC10013.DAT'
3  0        SET WIDTH=80
4  SET LENGTH=59
5  DATA LIST FILE= SOC10013  RECORDS=1/1 ID 1-6
            NAME 7-32 (A) OCT 33-34
6      SEC 36 XMAS 38-39 PAPER 41-42 TUTOR 44  FINAL 46-47
```

THE ABOVE DATA LIST STATEMENT WILL READ   1 RECORDS FROM FILE SOC10013.

VARIABLE	REC	START	END	FORMAT	WIDTH	DEC
ID	1	1	6	F	6	0
NAME	1	7	32	A	26	
OCT	1	33	34	F	2	0
SEC	1	36	36	F	1	0
XMAS	1	38	39	F	2	0
PAPER	1	41	42	F	2	0
TUTOR	1	44	44	F	1	0
FINAL	1	46	47	F	2	0

END OF DATA LIST TABLE.

```
 7  VARIABLE LABELS
 8        NAME 'STUDENT NAME'
 9        ID 'IDENTIFICATION NUMBER'
10        OCT 'OCTOBER GRADE OUT OF 33'
11        SEC 'TUTORIAL SECTION'
12        XMAS 'XMAS EXAM 100'
13        PAPER 'RESEARCH PAPER OUT OF 100'
14        TUTOR 'TUTORIAL ATTENDANCE OUT OF 5'
15        FINAL 'FINAL EXAM OUT OF 100'
```

> **Step 2.** Any errors should be corrected in the DATA LIST lines of the .MAK file. In addition, it is a good idea at this point to run a frequency

distribution on all nominal and ordinal variables and a procedure to compute the means on all ratio level variables. It is also useful to have a listing made of the names and labels placed on all variables using the DISPLAY DICTIONARY command. The following SPSSˣ commands added to the end of the .MAK file will produce the required information:

```
FREQUENCIES VARIABLES = V1 TO V6, V19, V21, V30 TO V39
CONDESCRIPTIVE V7 TO V18, V20, V22 TO V29
DISPLAY DICTIONARY
FINISH
```

Step 3. This output file will be a large one but it should be checked carefully. This is your last *easy* opportunity to correct errors. Check the frequency distributions for any out-of-range values. Make certain that the MISSING values are noted. (If the 9s, for example, have not been flagged as MISSING, note which variables have been missed so that you can make changes.) For ratio level variables, the means and minimum and maximum values are shown on the printout. Check these to make certain that the appropriate range is noted. There are two common errors that can be found now: zeros which should have been coded as MISSING; or values that are too high but not flagged as MISSING. For example, in occupational codes, "98" may have been used to identify a housewife and should be flagged as a MISSING value. (These can be switched later if necessary.) Finally, the dictionary of variables and labels should be checked carefully for completeness and for any spelling errors.

Step 4. All the changes should now be made in the .DAT file (if errors in the data have shown up) and the .MAK file, and the job should be submitted once again. The FREQUENCIES, CONDESCRIPTIVE, and DISPLAY DICTIONARY commands, however, may be removed and replaced by "contingency checking" procedures. These checks apply where branching questions have been used or where other combinations of responses are not possible. Two simple illustrations will demonstrate "contingency checks." Figure 6.5 (Chapter 6) shows a branching question asking a respondent to indicate if he/she had consumed any beer in the past seven days; those who responded with a "yes" were then asked to indicate how much had been drunk. Only those who responded "yes" should have answered the question that followed. Those who responded "no" should be consistently recorded as a "0" or as a MISSING value (9) on the amount consumed. Suppose we decided to record them all as 9s and we would like to check to make certain that the coding was done consistently. What we could do is to use the SPSSˣ procedure, CROSSTABS, to see if there is inconsistency in the data, as in:

```
CROSSTABS TABLES = V9B BY V9
```

Similar checks are commonly done with the gender variable where some questions may only apply to one sex. Suppose, for example, that the following questions should always have 9s (MISSING values) for males: V12, V23, V24, and V30. The following CROSSTABS procedure would show the relationships between gender (V3) and each of the other variables:

CROSSTABS TABLES = V12, V23, V24, V30 BY V3

The various contingency check procedures should be added to the bottom of the .MAK file and then submitted to SPSSˣ for processing.

Step 5. The results of this run should be inspected and if any inconsistencies show up, they should then be identified in the next run. Let us suppose that errors have shown up and we now need to identify the cases where the errors are found. To find these cases, the SELECT IF procedure may be used, as in:

```
TEMPORARY
SELECT IF (V9 EQ 2 AND V9B NE 9)
LIST VARIABLES = ID, V9, V9B
FREQUENCIES VARIABLES = V9
TEMPORARY
SELECT IF (V3 EQ 1 AND V24 NE 9)
LIST VARIABLES = ID, V3, V24
FREQUENCIES VARIABLES = V3
FINISH
```

These commands should be added into the .MAK file immediately before the FINISH command, and the job should be submitted to SPSSˣ.

Step 6. The results should now be inspected. They should indicate the ID numbers of inconsistent cases. The questionnaires with the errors should be pulled out and checked to see whether the problem was an error in recording gender, or in the questions to which gender as been related. The errors should be corrected in the .DAT file.

Step 7. The stage has now finally arrived when you create and save the SPSSˣ system file. The contingency check procedures should be removed from the .MAK file, and two additional commands should be added:

```
DISPLAY DICTIONARY
SAVE OUTFILE = system
FINISH
```

The .MAK file should then be submitted to SPSSˣ for processing. The results of this successful run should be printed on the lineprinter and retained as a permanent record. On the last page of the output there should be a message informing you that the system file has been saved. You are now ready to begin analyzing your data.

Should additional errors in the data become apparent during data processing, the researcher should immediately determine the ID number of the case (through SELECT IF procedure) and correct both the raw data file and the system file. The system file would be corrected and saved. Suppose we discovered during data analysis that a university student had earned $50 000 in the previous year. Through a SELECT IF we have identified that the respondent's ID is 132. We would then check the questionnaire and see if a coding error has been made. Suppose we discover that indeed an additional "0" had been recorded for V27 (income) and that it should be $5000. At this stage the system file could be updated by the following commands:

```
IF (ID EQ 132) V27 = 5000
SAVE OUTFILE = system
FINISH
```

If the corrected variable has been used in the creation of permanent indexes or variables, the runs performing those tasks would have to be resubmitted so that the error would be removed. It is a good idea to record the dates and details of such corrections for possible future reference.

NOTES

[1]See Marija J. Norusis, *SPSSx Introductory Statistics Guide.* Chicago: SPSS Inc., 1983, pp. 276. The comprehensive manual is: *SPSSx User's Guide*, second edition, 1985, pp. 988.

CHAPTER ELEVEN

ANALYZING DATA WITH SPSS^x

A. USING AN SPSS^X SYSTEM FILE

Having created an SPSS^x system file, we will now review basic procedures for using such files.[1]

a. GET FILE. System files are accessed by creating a joan0.CON file which includes commands to identify the system file, retrieve it, and list the procedures to be run, as in:

```
TITLE Analysis of Joan's Project, Joan Seymour
FILE HANDLE system/NAME = 'joan.SYS'
GET FILE system
… any analysis procedures …
FINISH
```

The first three lines retrieve the system file; these lines are followed by any number of requested procedures. The file ends with the FINISH command which tells SPSS that the run is concluded.

b. LIST. Frequently the researcher will want to list some variables for some, or all, of the cases. Anytime new variables are created, it is a good idea to list a few cases and the variables involved in the computation, so that manual checks of a few of the computations can be made to ensure that there are no errors. (Hint: if you list 12 or fewer variables, and are printing your results on computer-width paper, the output is easy to read.) The command to LIST is:

LIST VARIABLES = ID, V1, V17/ CASES = 50

The above command would list the first 50 cases for the three variables identified.

c. SORT CASES. The researcher may wish to sort cases on one or more variables. Suppose we had a list of employee names, departments, and salaries. And suppose we wish to sort them alphabetically by department, and then list the salaries. The following commands would do the task:

SORT CASES BY DEPT,NAME
LIST VARIABLES = DEPT, NAME,SALARY

The above commands would list all the cases in the file and they would be sorted alphabetically within each department.

d. SELECT IF. This procedure provides a method for selecting cases which meet designated criteria. Suppose you wished to list women earning over $50 000. The following commands would produce the list:

SELECT IF (SEX EQ 2 AND INCOME GE 50000)
LIST VARIABLES = NAME, INCOME

In the above case, the commands select and then list the names of females earning $50 000 or more. There are eight important keywords. All of them may be used in SELECT IF statements and in other similar commands to be introduced later. They are:

EQ equal to
NE not equal to
LT less than
LE less than or equal to
GT greater than
GE greater than or equal to

AND both conditions must be met
OR either condition is met

If a file is going to be saved at the end of a run, and a SELECT IF has been used, caution must be exercised since any cases not selected will disappear when the new file is saved. SPSSˣ provides a method of avoiding this problem by providing a command, called TEMPORARY, which, when placed before a SELECT IF command, will be in effect for only one procedure. The researcher must be extremely careful if a SAVE OUTFILE is used in the same run as a SELECT IF has been used. This caution reinforces the importance of always having a backup system file.

e. SAVE OUTFILE. Anytime a file has been modified, and the researcher wishes to permanently retain the changes in the system file, then the file should be updated by using the appropriate command, as in:

```
SAVE OUTFILE = system
FINISH
```

B. BASIC PROCEDURES:
PRESENTATION AND INTERPRETATION

Typically, the researcher will begin the analysis of a project with a description of the sample so that the reader of the report will understand who has been studied. Basic variables such as the age, gender, and the background of the respondents are normally presented.

1. FREQUENCIES: How Many in Each Category?

Nominal and ordinal variables are examined using the FREQUENCIES procedure. This procedure provides a count of the number of cases falling into each category. The procedure is also used to check the distribution of a variable before recoding it. Most often the researcher will just use the basic command for FREQUENCIES, as in:

```
FREQUENCIES VARIABLES = V1, V3 TO V6
```

FREQUENCIES will also produce bar charts and histograms. To automatically produce either bar charts (variables with fewer than 12 categories) or histograms (12 or more categories) use the HBAR subcommand. Various statistics are available on request. The following illustrates some of the major commands the first-time user might wish to use:

```
FREQUENCIES VARIABLES = V1, V3, V6/
             STATISTICS DEFAULT MEDIAN MODE/
             HBAR/
```

Often it is possible to present nominal/ordinal data in summary tables. Table 11.1 illustrates such a table for nominal/ordinal data (sex, rural/urban background, and religious affiliation) generated using the FREQUENCIES procedure. It is useful in summary tables to report both the numbers and the percentages. And, if there are to be any comparisons to the general population, these should also be included at this point.

Rule 11.1 FREQUENCIES are used to describe the distribution of nominal or ordinal variables. In addition, this procedure provides a variety of statistics on request, and will also provide bar charts and histograms.

Table 11.1   Sex, Background, and Religious Affiliation

Variable	Number	Percent
Gender:		
Male	97	45.6
Female	116	54.5
Total	213	100.1
Background:		
Rural	154	71.6
Urban	61	28.4
Total	215	100.0
Religious Affiliation:		
Protestant	134	61.8
Catholic	79	36.4
Jew	4	1.8
Total	217	100.0

2. CONDESCRIPTIVE: Computing the Mean

The CONDESCRIPTIVE procedure computes means and standard deviations and is appropriate for ratio level variables. Table 11.2 shows how a summary table could be constructed to show the results of a number of such analyses.

Table 11.2   Means of Selected Variables

Variable	Mean	Standard Deviation	N
Income, Full-Time Workers	$27 347	7 604	154
Age	38.4	12.7	218
Pro-Abortion Index	60.7	11.9	212
Pro-Capital Punishment Index	35.8	7.3	216

The most commonly used form of the command is simply:

CONDESCRIPTIVE V3, V6, V17

The above command would generate the means, standard deviations, and the minimum and maximum values. Usually these would be all the researcher would need. An important facility, however, is OPTIONS 3 which generates standardized values (Z scores) for the variables named. These values are stored in new variables whose names are the same as the old ones except they have a Z prefixed to them. The following would generate standardized variables:

CONDESCRIPTIVE V3, V6, V17
OPTIONS 3

The above command would result in three new variables being available on the Active file: their names would be ZV3, ZV6, and ZV17. A series of CONDESCRIPTIVES may be easily compressed into summary tables.

Rule 11.2 CONDESCRIPTIVE is used to report the means and standard deviations of equal interval/ratio variables. A variety of statistics are available and, in particular, note that the procedure may be used to generate standardized variables (Z scores).

3. CROSSTABS: Contingency Tables

With this procedure we begin to consider ways of describing relationships between variables. The reader may wish to review Figure 11.1 where appropriate analysis procedures for given levels of measurement in the independent and dependent variables are shown. In the case of CROSSTABS, information is presented so that the relationship between a nominal-level dependent variable can be related to an independent variable.

Figure 11.1 Basic SPSS^X Procedures for Different Levels of Measurement

	INDEPENDENT VARIABLE		
DEPENDENT	Nominal	Ordinal	Ratio
Nominal	CROSSTABS	CROSSTABS	CROSSTABS BREAKDOWN*
Ordinal	CROSSTABS	CROSSTABS NONPAR CORR	CROSSTABS NONPAR CORR
Ratio	BREAKDOWN	BREAKDOWN	PEARSON CORR SCATTERGRAM PARTIAL CORR REGRESSION

*In this case, one must run the independent variable as though it were the dependent variable (i.e., name it first); the interpretation of the test of significance would be standard.

Table 11.3 presents findings on the relationship between educational plans and size of home community for 360 students in rural Nova Scotia. We will examine this table in detail as it typifies the crosstabs table.

Let us now examine some of the rules for constructing and for interpreting cross-tabulation tables:

Rule 11.3 In table titles, name the dependent variable first. Tables must be numbered and given a title. In providing a title for a table, the dependent variable is named first, followed by the independent variable, followed by any control variables.

Table 11.3   Percent of Students Planning on University by Size of Home Community

University Plans?	Rural N	Rural %	Town up to 5000 N	Town up to 5000 %	Town over 5000 N	Town over 5000 %	TOTAL N	TOTAL %
Plans	69	52.3	44	48.9	102	73.9	215	59.7
No Plans	63	47.7	46	51.1	36	26.1	145	40.3
TOTAL	132	100.0	90	100.0	138	100.0	360	100.0

Chi-Square = 17.988   df = 2   Significant at .001 level.

Rule 11.4 Place the dependent variable on the vertical plane. Label the categories of the dependent variable and arrange them on the left side of the table. If the categories involve some cut-points, these should be specified.

Rule 11.5 Place the independent variable on the horizontal plane. Label the categories on the independent variable and arrange them across the top of the table. Again, if there are cut-points, be careful to specify these.

Rule 11.6 Use variable labels that are clear. Avoid the use of SPSS^x variable labels that have been designed to meet the space requirements of the program. For example, FAED may have been used to refer to the variable father's education. Use clear, easily understood labels, as in: Father's Education.

Rule 11.7 Run percentages toward the independent variable. Percentages should be computed so that each column will total 100 percent. A percentage is computed by dividing the column total into the cell frequency. In the first cell, for example, the computation involves:

$$\text{Cell percentage} = \frac{\text{Cell Total}}{\text{Column Total}} \times 100$$

$$\text{Cell percentage} = \frac{69}{132} \times 100 = 52.3$$

Rule 11.8 Report percentages to one decimal point. Percentages should be reported to one significant decimal point. If the total is 99.9 or 100.1 percent, report it as such.

Rule 11.9 Report statistical test results below the table. Any special information and the results of statistical tests should be reported below the line under the table. (Tests of significance are discussed in Chapter 8.) The preferred method for presenting the probability or significance level is to report the exact value: such as p = .0037.

Rule 11.10 Interpret the table by comparing categories of the independent variable. Since we are attempting to assess the impact of the independent variable on the dependent one (size of community on educational plans), we are interested in the percent of positive planners for each category of the independent variable. "While about one half of the rural and small town students (52.3 and 48.9 percent respectively) plan to attend university, some 73.9 percent of those from communities over 5000 have such plans." In short, compare percentages in each column. Usually it will be sufficient to use one row (in this case, just the row for those planning on university).

The SPSS^x command for CROSSTABS is:

```
CROSSTABS TABLES = depend BY independ
OPTIONS 4
STATISTICS 1
```

Rule 11.11 In SPSS^x, name the dependent variable first. In order to have SPSS^x generate a table with the dependent variable on the vertical axis and the independent one on the horizontal axis, the dependent variable is named first. Multiple tables can be generated within one command line by providing lists of dependent and/or independent variables.

Rule 11.12 In SPSS^x, use Options 4 with CROSSTABS. Options 4 will provide column percentages. These are the appropriate percentages for tables created with the dependent variable run on the vertical dimension of the table.

Rule 11.13 In SPSS^x, use Statistics 1 with CROSSTABS. If a test of significance is appropriate, the Statistics 1 option will provide a Chi-Square analysis of the data.

For analysis involving three or more variables simultaneously, the procedures are the same, with the control variable added after an additional "BY", as in:

```
CROSSTABS TABLES = depend BY independ BY control
OPTIONS 4
```

Rule 11.14 Minimize categories in control tables. Where control variables are used, it is necessary to minimize the number of categories in the independent and control variables. Generally, there should be no more than two or three categories within these variables. There are two major reasons for this limitation: first, the number of cases in each cell will become too small if there are many categories in either the independent or the control variable; second, the interpretation of the table is very difficult if simplicity is not maintained. Chapter 12 discusses interpretations of three variable contingency tables.

4. BREAKDOWN: Comparing Means

When one has an dependent variable measured at the ratio level, and either a nominal or ordinal independent variable, then it is appropriate to compute the mean values of the dependent variable for each category of the independent variable. Table 11.4 presents the kind of data appropriate for this sort of analysis. Note that the dependent variable (income) is a ratio level one, while the independent variable is nominal (gender).

Table 11.4   Mean Income by Sex

Sex	Mean Income	Number of Cases
Male	37 052	142
Female	34 706	37
COMBINED MEAN	$36 567	179

If appropriate, test of significance values entered here.

Rule 11.15 Place categories of the independent variable(s) on the vertical axis of the table. These categories should be carefully labeled. The means, standard deviations of the dependent variable, and the number of cases are normally reported in columns across the table.

A summary table may be used to report the relation between one dependent variable and a series of independent variables. A sample of such a table is presented in Table 11.5.

Table 11.5   Mean Pro-Abortion Attitude by Sex, Background, and Religion

Characteristic	Mean	Standard Deviation	N	Significance
Gender:				
Male	61.32	12.47	92	
Female	57.44	14.78	121	.0297
Background:				
Rural	59.58	13.22	152	
Urban	60.21	13.37	59	.5654
Religion:				
Protestant	63.74	13.31	128	
Catholic	56.98	11.73	76	
Jew	65.66	8.23	4	.0374

SPSS^x commands for running BREAKDOWN are as follows:

```
BREAKDOWN TABLES = income BY sex
STATISTICS 1
      Or,
BREAKDOWN TABLES = income BY sex BY control
```

Rule 11.16 In SPSS^x, the BREAKDOWN procedure requires the naming of the dependent variable first. The BREAKDOWN procedure requires that the dependent variable be named first. This will cause the program to compute the mean value for the first variable (income) for each of the categories of the independent variable (gender). In cases where there are many categories in the independent variable, these will have to be regrouped into two or three before the analysis is run (RECODE procedure). Variable lists may be used so that multiple tables may be generated with one command.

Rule 11.17 In SPSS^x, use Statistics 1 with the BREAKDOWN procedure to generate a test of significance. If a test of significance is required, use STATISTICS 1, which will generate a one-way analysis of variance for the relation between the variables.

Rule 11.18 Compare mean values. In interpreting the outcome of an analysis, the mean values should be compared. In Table 11.4, for example, the average income of the males is compared to that of the females.

5. PEARSON CORR: Correlational Analysis

Where variables are measured at the ratio level, then various correlational techniques are appropriate. As discussed in Chapter 7, a correlation, or r, measures the strength of an association between two variables. The values can range from +1.00 to -1.00. Typically, they are reported to 2 decimal places. Explained variance is the square of the correlation coefficient, or r^2.

The following is the command structure for computing a correlation using SPSS^x:

```
PEARSON CORR V17, V19, V22 TO V24
STATISTICS 1
```

The computer will automatically provide a one-tailed test of significance; if you wish a two-tailed test, include OPTIONS 3. If you wish to have the means and standard deviations reported, use STATISTICS 1.

Table 11.6 reports a summary table of correlations. It is useful in such summary tables to use an * to indicate statistically significant relations.

Table 11.6   Pearson Correlations
for Selected Characteristics

	Age	Income	Abortion Index
Income	.43		
Pro-Abortion	−.22	.27	
Pro-Capital Punishment	.13	.18	.13

6. SCATTERGRAM: The Plot Thickens

As in other procedures, the dependent variable is named first in the SCAT-TERGRAM command. This will result in a plot of the relationship between two variables, with the dependent variable on the vertical axis. Various options are available that will permit the researcher to control the intervals printed along the two dimensions and to print various statistics. A manual should be consulted if anything but a simple plot is desired. The command is:

    SCATTERGRAM depend WITH independ

7. NONPAR CORR: Spearman Correlations

Spearman Correlations are used when ordinal level measurement has been attained. They may be reported and interpreted in the same manner as Pearson Correlations. Like Pearson Correlations, they vary from -1.00 to +1.00 and measure the strength of an association. To compute them, the NONPAR CORR procedure is used:

    NONPAR CORR V16, V17, V26 TO V29

The test of significance provided will be one-tailed; if a two-tailed test is required, OPTIONS 3 should be included.

Two additional procedures will be introduced in the next chapter on testing simple causal models. These new procedures include partial correlations and regression analysis. A summary of the various introductory SPSSˣ commands is found in Appendix G.

C. CREATING NEW VARIABLES

SPSSˣ provides a number of ways to create or to change variables. We will examine three of these techniques.

1. RECODE

The RECODE procedure is used to temporarily change a variable during analysis or to create a new variable. Suppose we have three 9-point Likert-type items we wish to reverse score (ie., change the 9s into 1s, 8s into 2s, etc.) The command looks like this:

    RECODE V33, V37, V38 (9=1)(8=2)(7=3)(6=4)(5=5)(4=6)
        (3=7)(2=8)(1=9)

Suppose that we wished to regroup the values in one or more variables, and create new versions of the variables to be saved permanently. The following could be done:

```
RECODE V21, V22 (1,2,3 = 1)(4,5 = 2)(6,7,8,9 = 3) INTO V21R, V22R
VARIABLE LABELS V21R "Recoded Version V21"
    V22R "Recoded Version V22"
VALUE LABELS V21R, V22R 1 "low score"
    2 "medium score"
    3 "high score"/
... any analysis procedures here ...
SAVE OUTFILE = system
FINISH
```

This time two new variables have been created and will be saved permanently if the file is saved at the end of the run. Note that the new variable names simply have an "R" appended to the original name. It is a good idea to maintain the original name so that the researcher will know that it is a recoded version of the original variable. Variable labels may be attached as indicated.

Suppose we have a variable, MAED, indicating mother's education and we wish to divide our sample into those with low, medium, and high levels of education. We will create and save the new variable with the following commands:

```
RECODE MAED (LOWEST THRU 8 = 1)(9,10,11,12 = 2)
    (13 THRU HIGHEST = 3) INTO MAEDR
VARIABLE LABELS MAEDR "Education of Mother, Recoded"
VALUE LABELS MAEDR 1 "8 years or less" 2 "9 to 12 years"
    3 "13 or more years"/
... any analysis procedures here...
SAVE OUTFILE = system
FINISH
```

Note the use of the terms LOWEST, HIGHEST, and THRU. If there is a residual category the keyword ELSE may be used to assign values, as in:

```
RECODE MAED (13 THRU 22 = 2)(ELSE = 1)
RECODE MAED (13 THRU 22 = 13)(ELSE=COPY)
```

The ELSE=COPY command retains the original values for those not recoded in the previous statement.

RECODE is a quick way to create new variables or to regroup the values in a variable. Survey researchers have many occasions to use this procedure.

2. COMPUTE

COMPUTE allows the researcher to create new variables by performing mathematical operations on variables. The general form of a COMPUTE is:

    COMPUTE newvar = (V16 + V22) / 2

The above operation would create a new variable, newvar, which represents the addition of values in two variables divided by 2. Computations within parentheses are performed first and are used to control the order of the mathematical operations. Make certain that there are an equal number of open and closed parentheses. SPSS^x employs the following symbols to indicate basic functions:

    +   Addition
    −   Subtraction
    *   Multiplication
    /   Division
    **   Exponentiation

Many other functions are available to the researcher in SPSS^x; among three that the first-time researcher might need are:

RND(var)   rounds to whole number
SUM(var list)   sums values in variable list
MEAN(var list) mean of values

The following illustrates the use of the above procedures:

    COMPUTE wages = RND(salary)
    COMPUTE total   = SUM(V12, V13, V14, V15, V16)
    COMPUTE scale   = MEAN(V17, V18, V21)

The difference between the SUM and the MEAN functions is that the former simply adds together the values found in the designated variables (returning a SYSTEM MISSING value in cases where any of the values are missing); the latter computes the mean of the designated variables.

Whenever new variables are created, they can be given LABELS. It is also useful to document complex computations so that the researcher can return to the data set at a later date and find out how various computations were performed. An easy way to save such information is through the DOCUMENT command. The following shows the commands necessary to create and retrieve DOCUMENT statements:

    DOCUMENT The variable known as total was created in the
        following way: COMPUTE total = SUM(V12, V13, V14, V15, V16)

To retrieve DOCUMENTS in a later run include:

    DISPLAY DOCUMENTS

3. IF

A third way new variables can be created (among several available in SPSS^x) is through IF statements. The simple form of the command is as follows:

```
COMPUTE newvar = 0
IF (V15 LT 25) newvar = 1
```

Here the new variable is set to 0 initially and then whenever V15 has a value less than 25, NEWVAR is set to 1.

More complex uses of the IF statement can be illustrated by the following example. Suppose we are studying poverty in a community, have survey data on 300 people over the age of 18, and wish to create a variable identifying different types of poverty, taking into account age group and income levels. The following represents one way to go about creating the new variable:

```
COMPUTE poortype = 0
IF (age LT 25 AND income LT 12000) poortype = 1
IF (age GE 25 AND age LT 65 AND income LT 15000) poortype = 2
IF (age GE 65 AND income LT 12000) poortype = 3
VARIABLE LABELS poortype "Type of Poor"
VALUE LABELS poortype 0 "all ages, non-poor"
        1"under 25 under $12 K"
        2"25-64, under $15 K"
        3"over 64, under $12 K"/
```

The above set combines age and income levels to create a new variable called POORTYPE, which identifies the non-poor (those with incomes over $12 000 for the young and old, and over $15 000 for the middle-aged respondents) and three categories of the poor: the young, incomes under $12 000; the middle aged with incomes under $15 000; and the seniors with incomes under $12 000.

SPSS^x manuals should be consulted for other methods of creating new variables or transforming old ones. Having understood how new variables may be created and saved, it is now time to examine how scales and indexes are constructed.

D. CREATING INDEXES

Indexes combine two or more indicators to reflect complex variables such as socio-economic status, job satisfaction, or an attitude toward a social issue. Frequently, the researcher will construct *sub-indexes* which may be treated alone or combined with other sub-indexes to form a composite measure. For example, a researcher measuring attitudes toward abortion might construct a sub-index for "soft reasons" (economically inconvenient, preference for having a baby later, etc.) and "hard reasons" (pregnancy as a result of rape, severely handicapped, etc.). These sub-indexes might also be combined to form an overall index. In each case, however, the researcher will have to ensure that appropriate items are included in each sub-index.

We will next review the use of item analysis, and the RELIABILITY procedure in evaluating index items. Finally, the use of Z scores in index construction will be discussed.

1. Item Analysis

It is important that the components of an index *discriminate*. That is, various elements must discriminate between high scorers and lower scorers. To illustrate, suppose you are attempting to develop a set of multiple choice questions to measure students' knowledge of the material covered in an Introductory course, and you wish to identify those items which best measure mastery of the subject matter. Let us suppose that you have 100 questions on the test and you wish to identify the best 50 questions for a future test. The issue is to select those items which best discriminate between high and low performance on the test. Let us suppose that we have given the preliminary test to 200 Introductory students.

We could proceed by grading the test and computing the total correct responses for each student. If the "marking" was done with a computer program, we would have a matrix with students and questions on the dimensions. Each cell would identify a correct or incorrect response to each question for a particular student. Now we could arrange the students by the number of correct responses, and then choose the top and bottom quartiles. Table 11.7 shows the percent from each quartile answering each question correctly.

Table 11.7   Discrimination Ability of 100 Items: Percent Correct for Each Item, by Quartile

| | Percent Correct Each Item | |
Question #	Bottom 25%	Top 25%
1	40.0	80.0
2	5.0	95.0
3	60.0	55.0
4	80.0	80.0
5	10.0	40.0
6	20.0	60.0
...	...	...
100	30.00	20.0

The next step would be to select those items with the biggest difference in performance between the top and bottom students. The assumption here is that overall the questions do measure knowledge of the subject matter and we are simply choosing those items which best discriminate.

The first two questions discriminate well — the high scorers do considerably better on those items than the low scorers. The third question would be rejected: while 55 percent of the students in the top quartile gave the right answer, so did 60 percent of the bottom group. Similarly, question 4 would be dropped because the same proportion of top and bottom students answered correctly.

SPSSˣ may be used to produce this analysis by treating each of the 100 questions as dependent variables (scored as correct or incorrect) and by treating the top and bottom scorers as two categories of the independent variable.

Similar procedures may be used to select high discrimination items for indexes. For example, imagine that we had 15 Likert-type items for an index measuring job satisfaction, and we wished to determine which ones to include in the index. We want items which do two things: (a) validly reflect the dimension of the concept they are supposed to; and (b) discriminate between high and low scorers. What we might do is: (1) include those items which have *face validity*; (2) add them together, coming up with a total score for each individual; (3) split the sample into the top and bottom quartiles in job satisfaction scores; and (4) test each item's ability to discriminate between high and low job satisfaction. This final step would be done in a manner similar to that employed in the item selection discussed above.

2. The Use of the RELIABILITY Procedure in Selecting Items

SPSSˣ contains a procedure for evaluating potential index items. RELIABILITY examines the components of a proposed additive index providing a variety of tests for each item. The procedure does not actually compute the index, but rather provides an assessment of each item; the actual index would be constructed with a COMPUTE command.

Of particular note for the beginning survey researcher is that RELIABILITY computes item means and standard deviations, inter-item correlations, a series of item-total comparisons, and Cronbach's Alpha for index reliability.[2]

Suppose we have seven 9-point Likert-type job satisfaction items, known as SAT1, SAT2, ... SAT7. SAT3 and SAT5 are negative measures of job satisfaction. Let us go through the steps for evaluating these items. We will proceed by creating a joan.CON file to access the .SYS and do the following:

Step 1. Reverse score any items that are negative (in this case SAT3 and SAT5) using the RECODE procedure.

Step 2. Evaluate the indexes by naming all the relevant variables and then specify the one or more indexes you wish to evaluate. The command structure is as follows:

```
RELIABILITY VARIABLES = SAT1, SAT2, SAT3R, SAT4,
        SAT5R, SAT6, SAT7/
    SCALE (Jobsat1) = SAT1, SAT2, SAT3R, SAT4, SAT5R, SAT6,
        SAT7/
    SCALE (Jobsat2) = SAT2, SAT4, SAT5R, SAT6/
STATISTICS 1 2 3 4 5 6 7 8 9
```

Step 3. Examine the results. As a rule of thumb, you have an acceptable index if: (l) the correlations between the items and the index are positive; (2) the correlations are above .25; (3) the alpha is above .70. RELIABILITY computes alphas including and excluding the items. Hence, if an increase in the alpha can be achieved by eliminating the item, this can be done when the index is computed.

Step 4. If two or more items are to be removed from the final index it will be necessary to resubmit another RELIABILITY job. If one or no items need to be eliminated, then one can go immediately to Step 5.

Step 5. Having decided which items are to be included in the index, a new job should be run adding the items together using a COMPUTE command. The system file should be updated, saving the new index scores with a SAVE OUTFILE command.

It should be noted that Cronbach's Alpha varies with the average inter-item correlation, taking into account the number of items making up the index. If either the inter-item correlation increases, or the number of items increases, alpha increases. For example, with 2 items and a .4 mean inter-item correlation, the alpha value would be .572; with 8 items and a .4 mean inter-item correlation, the alpha would be .842. With .6 inter-item correlations, the alpha for 2 versus 8 items would be .750 and .924 respectively.[3]

There are many other options available within the RELIABILITY procedure. It is possible to compute split-half coefficients and various coefficents proposed by Louis Guttman.[4] Consult the *SPSSx User's Guide* for additional models and options.

3. Use of Z Scores in Index Construction

The researcher may wish to add items together to construct an index. Suppose we had two items: annual income and years of education. Given the vastly different ranges in these two variables, they should be standardized first and then added together. This may be done using the CONDESCRIPTIVE procedure's OPTIONS 3, which computes Z scores, stores them in a new variable whose name is the original one with a Z prefixed to it; "educa" becomes "Zeduca." The following job could be run to create the desired socio-economic index and save it for future runs:

```
TITLE Creating the SES index, Norm Seymour
FILE HANDLE system/NAME='norm.SYS'
GET FILE system
CONDESCRIPTIVE income, educa
OPTIONS 3
COMPUTE SES = Zincome + Zeduca
```

VARIABLE LABELS SES "Socio-economic Index"
... any analysis procedures ...
SAVE OUTFILE = system
FINISH

Items may be weighted differently by simply altering the COMPUTE statement. Suppose, for example, you wish to have income contribute two thirds and education one third of the index. The following would accomplish this weighting:

COMPUTE SES2 = (Zincome * .67) + (Zeduca * .33)
VARIABLE LABELS SES2 "Weighted Socio-economic Index"

NOTES

[1]Most beginning researchers will find that the Introductory Statistics Guide is satisfactory for listing the various options and statistics available for the major procedures. However, there will be times when other manuals would be appropriate. There are seven manuals currently available for SPSS^x. They are available in the United States from SPSS Inc., Publication Sales, 444 N. Michigan Ave., Chicago, Illinois, 60611 and in Canada, from Harcourt Brace Jovanovich, Canada, 55 Barber Greene Road, Don Mills, Ontario, M3C 2A1.

SPSS^x User's Guide, Second Edition, 988 pages, 1985.
SPSS^x Basics, 214 pages, 1983.
Marija J. Norusis, *SPSS^x Introductory Statistics Guide*, 276 pages, 1983.
Marija J. Norusis, *The SPSS^x Advanced Statistics Guide,* 505 pages, 1985.
SPSS^x Tables, 200 pages, 1985.
SPSS^x Graphics, 320 pages, 1985.

[2]See Edward G. Carmines and Richard A. Zeller, *Reliability and Validity Assessment*, Sage University Paper series on Quantitative Applications in the Social Sciences, series no. 07-017. Beverly Hills and London: Sage Publications, 1979.

[3]*Ibid.*, pp. 43-48.

[4]See Louis Guttman, "The Cornell Technique for Scale and Intensity Analysis," *Educational and Psychological Measurement*, Vol. 7, 1947. Guttman's suggestions are nicely presented by Mark Abrahamson, *Social Research Methods*. Englewood Cliffs, N.J.: Prentice-Hall Inc., 1983, pp. 156-63.

CHAPTER TWELVE

TESTING SIMPLE CAUSAL MODELS

This chapter describes procedures for evaluating causal models, such as those developed in Chapter 5. First, the type of model being dealt with must be determined: is it a source of spuriousness, an intervening variable, or a candidate variable model? Second, the appropriate statistical procedures for the analysis are determined. This determination will be based on the level of measurement involved in each of the relevant variables.[1] Simple causal models may be explored using various SPSS[x] procedures introduced in Chapter 11.

To establish a causal relationship, three conditions must be met:

    a. the variables are *associated*;
    b. they are in a plausible *causal sequence*; and,
    c. they are not *spuriously* connected.

To meet the *associated* criterion, one has to demonstrate that the two variables vary together. To argue that one variable is producing changes in another, it must be demonstrated that as one changes, so does the other. In SPSS[x], empirical association is reflected through CROSSTABS, BREAKDOWN, and various correlational techniques.

To demonstrate a plausible *causal sequence* is largely a matter either of theory or of common sense. Most commonly, however, a little thought given to the causal order will provide an answer. For example, it would be foolish to argue that the "size of your present community' influences the size of the "community in which you were born." The sequencing is wrong: the present cannot influence the past. The size of community one has chosen to live in may, of course, be influenced by the size of community in which one grew up.

To demonstrate that a relationship is not *spurious* is always a challenge; one which can never be fully met. A critic may always point to some potential source of spuriousness for the relation between the variables. The best the first-time researcher can hope to do is to deal with the more obvious potential sources of spuriousness.

This chapter shows how simple causal models are tested. Identical analyses may be used to test different models. Causal models generally attempt to explain or elaborate on some relationship known to exist or expected to be demonstrated in a research project.[2] We will use some sample data to illustrate. Suppose we have done a survey on 395 senior high school students concerning their plans for education beyond the high school level. Table 12.1 presents the results.

Table 12.1   Percent of Senior High School Students with Plans for Further Education by Socio-Economic Status (SES)

Type of Plan	Low SES Background N	Low SES Background %	High SES Background N	High SES Background %	Total N	Total %
Some Plans	144	73.1	176	88.9	320	81.0
No Plans	53	26.9	22	11.1	75	19.0
TOTAL	197	100.0	198	100.0	395	100.0

$X^2 = 16.021$ df = 1   Significant at the .001 level.

Table 12.1 is a standard contingency table, whose computations could be done with the CROSSTABS procedure. A shorter version of the table is also possible and will be used to illustrate the model testing to be presented below. The shorter version is illustrated in Table 12.2.

Table 12.2   Percent of Senior High School Students with Plans for Further Education by Socio-Economic Status (SES)

	Low SES Background	High SES Background
Percent who have plans for further education	73.1	88.9
Number of Cases	197	198

$X^2 = 16.021$ df = 1   Significant at the .001 level.

With the information provided it is possible to reconstruct the original table. Given that there are 73.1 percent of low SES students who plan on further education, and given that there are 197 low SES students, it is possible to determine the number of students who fell into the category

(.731 x 197 = 144). Similar calculations could be done to totally reconstruct Table 12.1.

The much simplified Table 12.2 is easy to read and focusses attention on the two percentage figures to be compared: while some 88.9 percent of the students with high socio-economic status backgrounds plan on some post-high school education, 73.1 percent of those with low SES backgrounds have similar plans. *Note that there is a 15.8 percentage point difference by SES categories in those planning on post-secondary education.* We will use this table in discussing the first causal model, the intervening variable model.

A. TESTING FOR INTERVENING VARIABLES

1. The Intervening Variable Model

In an *intervening variable model*, the interest is in understanding the relationship between X and Y — understanding the mechanism by which X is connected to Y. Frequently, the researcher will be testing a number of alternative explanations for how X influences Y. In the case of one intervening variable, the relationship could be diagrammed as follows:

In this diagram, I is the intervening variable, or the linking variable between X and Y. The hypothesis is that variations in X cause variations in I, which, in turn, influences Y. Typically, a number of possible intervening variables would be proposed, so the following diagram would be more appropriate:

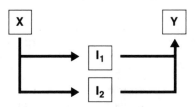

In this diagram, two alternative explanations are suggested for the connection between X and Y. The researcher would collect data measuring each of the variables involved, and then conduct the appropriate statistical tests to determine, which, if any, of the proposed alternative explanations or intervening variables explain the connection between X and Y.

Let us suppose, for example, that three alternative explanations are proposed for the relation between SES and likelihood of post-high school educational plans: (i) that high SES students associate with high SES peers who plan on post-high school training; (ii) that high SES students perceive little financial difficulty in attaining a higher education and, therefore, are more likely to plan on such training than are low SES students; and (iii) that high SES parents are more likely to pressure their children to participate in post-secondary training. How would we go about testing these three alternatives?

2. The Rationale Behind the Test

The thinking behind the test is as follows: If we have a causal relation between X and Y (SES and Plans) and we propose a link to explain how X influences Y, by holding the linking variable constant, X should not be able to exercise its influence on Y. The argument is that X influences Y through I. A plumbing analogy may be helpful. Water can only flow from X to Y through a pipe. If you turn off a valve located between X and Y, then increasing the volume of water flowing into the pipe at point X will have no influence on Y; however if we open the valve, then changes in the pressure at X will influence the flow at Y. Keeping the analogy in mind, let us now see if we can "control" for the intervening variable.

The first explanation is that high SES students tend to associate more with other high SES students, and this is the link between SES and Educational Plans. How can we analyze the data to see if the results are consistent with the model we wish to test? Using a contingency table analysis (CROSSTABS) we will run the relation between SES and plans, controlling for the intervening variable, association with high SES peers. We wish to see what happens when the control is applied; namely, does the original 15.8 percentage-point difference in the relationship between SES and Plans: (a) *increase*, (b) *stay the same*, (c) *decrease*, (d) *disappear*, or is it (e) *mixed*?

3. The Rule of Thirds

Rule 12.1 The Rule of Thirds. This rule of thumb is that if the original difference between the categories increases by one third or more, this will be interpreted as an *increase*, or a strengthening, of the original relationship; if the difference remains within one third of the original, we will interpret this as an indication that the relationship has *remained the same*; if the difference decreases between one third and two thirds, this will be interpreted as reflecting a *decrease* in the relationship; if the relationship decreases by more than two thirds of its original magnitude, then we will interpret the relationship as having *disappeared*; finally, if the relationship is markedly different in one of the control categories compared to the other one (e.g., it disappears in one, but stays the same in the other) then the result is *mixed*.

To apply the rule of thirds to the case under examination, we must first decide where the cut-points are between the thirds. To do this we take the original difference of 15.8 and divide by 3; this yields a value of 5.3. Table 12.3 presents these values and shows how the differences would be interpreted.

Table 12.3   Applying the Rule of Thirds

Sample Data Results	Interpretation
Original difference: 88.9 − 73.1 = 15.8	
Determining Thirds: 15.8 ÷ 3 = 5.3	
Outcomes:	
a. If new difference is greater than 21.1 (15.8 + 5.3 = 21.1)	*Increased*
b. If new difference is between 10.5 and 21.1 (15.8 ± 5.3)	*Stayed the Same*
c. If new difference is between 5.2 and 10.5 (15.8 − (5.3 × 2))	*Decreased*
d. If new difference is less than 5.2	*Disappeared*
e. If new differences vary markedly across categories of the control variable	*Mixed*

4. Using **CROSSTABS** to Test for an Intervening Variable

But what are our expectations? If the model being tested is correct, we would expect that the relationship between SES and Plans would *disappear* when the relationship is run, controlling for the intervening variable. If SES influences Plans through the linking variable, then if we hold the linking variable constant, there should be no relation between SES and Plans. Differences in level of planning by SES category should disappear when the control is applied. *All other outcomes are interpreted as not supportive of the model*. Table 12.4 presents summary data for five possible outcomes.

To interpret the outcomes, it is necessary to determine whether the original relationship has increased, stayed the same, decreased, disappeared, or is mixed. The beginning survey researcher should keep the interpretation of the data as simple as possible. Only when the difference disappears, do we have support for an intervening variable model. Let us look at the five outcomes and suggest an interpretation for each one.

Outcome 1. According to the rule of thirds, the relationship has disappeared. The original difference has been reduced to 1 percentage point

Table 12.4   Percent of Senior High School Students with Plans for Further Education by Socio-Economic Status (SES), Controlling for SES of Best Friend, With Five Possible Outcomes

Percent Planning Further Education	Best Friend High SES		Best Friend Low SES*	
	Low SES Background	High SES Background	Low SES Background	High SES Background
1st Outcome:	92.0	93.0	71.0	69.0
difference:		1.0		−2.0
2nd Outcome:	74.0	92.0	71.0	86.0
difference:		18.0		15.0
3rd Outcome:	85.0	92.0	68.0	76.0
difference:		7.0		8.0
4th Outcome:	74.0	96.0	61.0	82.0
difference:		22.0		21.0
5th Outcome:	90.0	92.0	60.0	82.0
difference:		2.0		22.0

*The original difference with no control for SES of Best Friend, is shown below:

	Low SES Background	High SES Background
Percent Who Have Plans for Further Education:	73.1	88.9
difference:	15.8	

in the case of those whose best friend has high SES, and to 2 percentage points for those whose best friend is classified as low SES. This is the only outcome viewed as being consistent with the intervening variable causal model.

Outcome 2. The relationship stays the same so the intervening variable model is to be rejected.

Outcome 3. The intervening variable model should be rejected. The difference weakens, but has not disappeared, so the interpretation is that the independent variable influences the dependent variable through other intervening variables.

Outcome 4. The intervening variable model should be rejected. The relationship is strengthened suggesting that the proposed alternative explanation is having an independent influence on the dependent variable.

Outcome 5. Again, the intervening variable model should be rejected. The difference disappears in one of the control categories, but increases in the other, suggesting a conditional effect — the intervening variable is probably having an independent influence but only at certain levels of the intervening variable. This is an example of a *mixed* result.

In order to run a control table with SPSS^x, two commands are necessary. The first one simply generates an analysis of the original relationship; the second introduces the control variable:

```
CROSSTABS TABLES = plan BY ses
OPTIONS 4
STATISTICS 1
CROSSTABS TABLES = plan BY ses BY peerses
OPTIONS 4
```

Note that to run a control, the control variable is simply named after the second BY command. SPSS^x will generate a table for each category of the control variable. Note as well that STATISTICS 1 is not requested. A test of significance is not relevant. We are interested, instead, in observing what happens when the original relationship is rerun, controlling for the influence of the intervening variable. In most cases, the result will produce a lower Chi-Square value simply because there are fewer cases in each of the tables. In other words, a statistically significant relationship may no longer be statistically significant within each control table even though the differences between the categories may be of the same magnitude as the original relationship. To avoid confusion, it is probably best not to run a test of significance. The issue is to determine what happens to the original relationship, not whether the relationship is, or is not, statistically significant. Finally, it should be noted that multiple intervening variables can be generated by listing these variables after the second BY in the command.

5. Using **BREAKDOWN** to Test for an Intervening Variable

The second explanation proposed for the connection between SES and Plans is that high SES students plan on post-secondary education because they know their families can afford it. We will assume that Plans are measured in terms of the number of years of post-secondary education planned on (ratio level measurement), permitting the use of the BREAKDOWN procedure.

The logic is identical to the previous procedure. We will examine the difference in the number of years planned between SES categories, we will then rerun that relationship controlling for whether students perceive financial resources adequate enough to permit them some post-secondary training. Once again, we will apply the *rule of thirds* to provide a guideline for the interpretation of the data. Table 12.5 (bottom) indicates that there is a 1.40 year difference in the number of years of post-secondary education planned by SES categories. The question is: will this difference increase, stay the same, decrease, disappear, or be mixed when the control for perceived financial support is applied?

Table 12.5   Mean Years of Further Education Planned by Socio-Economic Status (SES), Controlling for Perceived Support for Higher Education, with Five Possible Outcomes

Mean Years of Further Education Planned	No Support		Support*	
	Low SES Background	High SES Background	Low SES Background	High SES Background
1st Outcome:	1.49	3.40	3.30	5.26
difference:		1.91		1.96
2nd Outcome:	2.23	3.66	2.55	3.98
difference:		1.43		1.43
3rd Outcome:	1.56	2.27	3.42	4.10
difference:		.71		.68
4th Outcome:	2.35	2.48	3.77	3.92
difference:		.13		.15
5th Outcome:	1.64	3.13	3.89	4.01
difference:		1.49		.12

*The original difference with no control for Financial Support, is shown below:

Post High School Plans	Low SES Background	High SES Background
Mean Number of Years of Further Education Planned:	2.47	3.87
difference:	1.40	

Table 12.5 shows different outcomes. Once again, we compare the two differences in the control table between the Low and High SES students by perceived financial support, and contrast this difference with the original difference of 1.40 years.

Outcome 1. For those students who perceive no financial support being available for higher education, the data indicate a 1.91 year difference between SES categories in total years of post secondary education planned. Among those who perceive support, the difference between the categories is 1.96 years. Applying the *rule of thirds*, the difference in both SES categories has *increased* by more than one third, and we therefore argue that the relationship has been intensified: we must reject the intervening variable model. The intensification suggests that the perception of financial support has an independent, positive impact on the level of post-secondary planning.

Outcome 2. In the second outcome, in both the "No Support" and "Support" categories the difference between the Low and High SES students remains almost the same as the original difference of 1.40. We therefore reject the intervening variable model.

Outcome 3. In the third outcome, the difference has been reduced by more than one third, but less than two thirds, and we therefore conclude that while the difference has decreased, it has not disappeared. We thus reject the intervening variable model.

Outcome 4. In both the "Support" and "No Support" categories, the differences in years planned have disappeared (dropped by more than two thirds) and this outcome is the only one consistent with an intervening variable model.

Outcome 5. The final outcome suggests a mixed result. The difference disappears within the "Support" category, but remains the same within the "No Support" category. We reject the intervening variable model. The data here suggest that the financial support variable has a conditional impact on years of post-secondary education planned.

The computations for testing this model can be done in SPSS^x by using the following commands:

```
BREAKDOWN TABLES  = plan BY ses
STATISTICS 1
BREAKDOWN TABLES  = plan BY ses BY support
```

Note that no tests of significance are requested when the control variable is introduced. Table 12.6 shows SPSS output and indicates the appropriate comparisons to be made in order to test for an intervening variable. What was the original difference? What happened to the difference when the control was run? What would you conclude about the relationship tested?

Table 12.6   Sample SPSS OUTPUT *

Summaries of	SAL88				
By levels of	SEX	SEX OF RESPONDENT			
	QUAL	HIGHEST QUALIFICATION: DOCTORATE OR NOT			

Variable	Value	Label	Mean	Std Dev	Cases
For Entire Population			52089.3143	10797.3218	147
SEX	F	FEMALE	47145.4600	7987.8018	35
QUAL	0.0	NO DOCTORATE	47276.2750	7729.0449	14
QUAL	1.00	DOCTORATE	47058.2500	8343.7827	21
SEX	M	MALE	53634.2688	11121.2949	112
QUAL	0.0	NO DOCTORATE	49188.8185	12402.8448	27
QUAL	1.00	DOCTORATE	55046.3529	10366.0260	85
Total Cases = 147					

* Original gender difference = $6489 (53 634 − 47 145)
  No doctorate   = $1913 (49 189 − 47 276)
  Doctorate   = $7988 (55 046 − 47 050)

6. Using PARTIAL CORR to Test for an Intervening Variable

Partial correlations are measures of the strength of an association, but take into account one or more additional variables. They measure how closely two variables are associated when the influence of other variables is adjusted for: partials are referred to by their *order*: a *first-order* partial is one which takes into account one additional variable; a *second-order* partial takes into account two additional variables. By combining PEARSON CORR and PARTIAL CORR we can test for an intervening variable.

In this case, we wish to test whether parental influence intervenes between SES and Plans. Using correlational techniques we would first establish that there is an association between SES and Plans. If there is an association we would then proceed with the analysis to test whether the data are consistent with an intervening variable model.

What would we expect if the intervening variable model is correct?

1. That the correlation between adjacent variables will be greater than between non-adjacent categories. ($r_{XY} < r_{XI}$ or r_{IY})

2. If I is controlled through the use of a partial correlation coefficient, the relation between X and Y should disappear. ($r_{XY.I} = 0$)

The model will be tested using two correlational techniques, PEARSON CORR and PARTIAL CORR. Table 12.7 presents the Pearson Correlations between three variables: parental pressure index (I), SES score (X), and years of future education planned (Y).

Table 12.7   Pearson Correlations Between Variables in Model

Characteristics	Parental Pressure (I)	SES Score (X)	Years Education (Y)
Parental Pressure (I)	1.00		
SES Score (X)	.31	1.00	
Years of Education (Y)	.46	.22	1.00

The first test is to see if the magnitude of the correlations is consistent with the model being tested. The prediction was that adjacent correlations would be higher than non-adjacent ones. The adjacent ones are I-X and I-Y and the correlations are .31 and .46 respectively. The non-adjacent one is X-Y and the correlation is .22. So far, the data are consistent with the intervening variable model.

The next question is whether the partial correlation will be increased, stay the same, decrease, or disappear when X is controlled. For this analysis, a partial correlation would be computed. When this is done, the partial ($r_{XY.I}$) is computed[3] to be .10. Applying the *rule of thirds*, the original relation between X and Y is .22 and since the partial is about one half of the original value, we note that while the association has weakened, it has not disappeared, and therefore we reject the model.

The computations for testing this model can be done in SPSS^x by using the following commands:

```
PEARSON CORR plan, influ, ses
PARTIAL CORR plan WITH ses BY influ (1)
```

Depending on the level of measurement attained in the variables, intervening variable models can be tested using CROSSTABS, BREAKDOWN, or the PARTIAL CORR technique. In each case, the *rule of thirds* may be applied. And for each, the question is what happens to the original relationship when control variables are applied.

B. TESTING FOR SOURCES OF SPURIOUSNESS

1. The Source of Spuriousness Model

The next major type of causal model is the *source of spuriousness* model. The researcher proposes that while there is a statistically significant relation between the variables X and Y, this relationship may be a non-causal one, only existing because some third variable is influencing both X and Y. The argument is that the only reason X and Y are related to one another is because of this third factor. Having observed a statistically significant relation, the researcher will want to ensure that the relationship is not spurious and therefore will run a number of spuriousness checks. The source of spuriousness model may be diagrammed as follows:

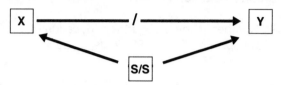

2. The Rationale Behind the Test

How do we go about testing a source of spuriousness model? The idea is this: if X and Y are spuriously associated, the reason they vary together is that a third variable (a source of spuriousness) is influencing both X and Y, and if we control for the source of spuriousness, there should no longer be any association between X and Y. This suggests that we need the same kind of analysis as we used for testing intervening variables. To test for a potential source of spuriousness, the steps are: (1) test the original relation between X and Y; if this demonstrates a robust relationship (probably statistically significant); then (2) controlling for the source of spuriousness, rerun the relation between X and Y. As in the intervening variable model, we then can apply the *rule of thirds* to determine if the relationship has increased, stayed the same, decreased, disappeared, or is mixed. *In order to conclude that the original relation is spurious, the difference between the categories must disappear.*

3. The Dilemma:
The Models Are Not Empirically Distinguishable

The difficulty is that it is possible for two researchers working with the same data, with the same three variables, to establish two different causal models: one proposing that the variables are connected in an intervening variable model, the other viewing them as possibly being spuriously associated. The researchers might then do the identical analysis but come to totally different conclusions. Let us suppose that when the control is applied, the original difference disappears: one researcher would conclude that the intervening variable model has found support in the data; the other would conclude that the relation is spurious. Both would be right.

Because the two models are not empirically distinguishable, the importance of precisely specifying models in advance becomes clear. If we develop the models after analyzing the data, the interpretation of the data is little more than a flight of fancy.

4. Using BREAKDOWN to Test for Spuriousness

To illustrate a test for spuriousness, we will use the same variables as previously. Table 12.8 presents sample data showing how the analysis turned out for the relation between SES and Plans.

Table 12.8   Number of Years of Further Education Planned by Senior High School Students, by Socio-Economic Status (SES)

Post High School Plans	Low SES Background	High SES Background
Mean Number of Years of Further Education Planned	2.47	3.87
Number of Cases	197	198

The reader should note that there is a 1.40 year difference between the Low and High SES students in the number of years of further education planned. Now suppose that we wanted to make certain that this relationship was not spuriously caused by the rural versus urban backgrounds of these students. The type of home community may be influencing the SES level achieved by the families and may also be influencing the educational plans of the students and it is, therefore, not the SES level that is influencing Plans, but rather it is the urban versus rural location that influences both the variables.

Table 12.9 reports five different outcomes for this analysis. These should be examined carefully, the *rule of thirds* applied, and a decision should be made about which outcome lends support to the spuriousness model of the relationship between the variables. To apply this rule simply divide the original difference by 3 (1.40 ÷ 3 = .47). Next, compare the difference in years of future education planned by SES categories for each of the rural and urban categories.

Outcome 1. Here the differences (2.11 and 1.93) have both grown by more than a third and we therefore reject the source of spuriousness model. Perhaps the type of background has an independent influence on the number of additional years of education planned.

Outcome 2. The original difference was 1.4 years between the number of years of education planned by Low versus High SES students. When the control for rural versus urban background is applied, the difference remains much the same and we therefore reject rural versus urban background as a source of spuriousness.

Outcome 3. The original difference in this result has been reduced to

Table 12.9 Mean Years of Further Education Planned by Socio-Economic Status (SES), Controlling for Rural and Urban Backgrounds, With Five Possible Outcomes

Mean Years of Further Education Planned	Rural Background		Urban Background*	
	Low SES Background	High SES Background	Low SES Background	High SES Background
1st Outcome:	.87	2.98	3.33	5.26
difference:		2.11		1.93
2nd Outcome:	2.27	3.67	2.58	3.96
difference:		1.40		1.38
3rd Outcome:	2.30	2.91	3.71	4.32
difference:		.61		.61
4th Outcome:	1.73	1.91	3.74	3.97
difference:		.18		.23
5th Outcome:	2.16	2.27	2.74	4.04
difference:		.11		1.30

*The original difference with no control for Urban/Rural backgrounds, is shown below:

Post High School Plans	Low SES Background	High SES Background
Mean Number of Years of Further Education Planned:	2.47	3.87
difference:	1.40	

.61 for both categories. But since the difference has not disappeared, we reject the source of spuriousness model.

Outcome 4. In this case, the original difference has been reduced to less than one third of its original value and so we cannot reject the source of spuriousness model. This is the only outcome supporting the spuriousness model.

Outcome 5. Here the result is mixed. The difference disappears among the rural students, but is only slightly reduced among the urban students. We reject the source of spuriousness model.

In order to do the analysis, we first need a table showing the difference in additional years of education planned by SES categories. Second, we will need to rerun this relationship, controlling for rural and urban backgrounds. The following commands would provide the necessary information:

```
BREAKDOWN TABLES = plan BY ses
STATISTICS 1
BREAKDOWN TABLES = plan BY ses BY rururb
```

Note that no test of significance is requested with the control table analysis. As in the intervening variable model, such an analysis would only lead to confusion and should therefore not be run. If there are a number of sources of spuriousness to run, the variable names could simply be added after the last BY in the command line.

5. Using CROSSTABS to Test for Spuriousness

To use CROSSTABS in a test for a source of spuriousness, the original relationship is run and, then rerun, controlling for the source of spuriousness. The *rule of thirds* is then applied and only if the difference disappears would the original relationship be interpreted as spurious. The commands are:

```
CROSSTABS TABLES = plan BY ses
OPTIONS 4
STATISTICS 1
CROSSTABS TABLES = plan BY ses BY control
OPTIONS 4
```

6. Using PARTIAL CORR to Test for Spuriousness

This test requires ratio level variables, and simply involves running the zero-order correlation, followed by a partial correlation controlling for the potential source of spuriousness. The analysis should be run and the data interpreted according to the *rule of thirds*. Only if the relationship disappears, do we interpret the original relation to be spurious. The SPSS[x] command structure is:

```
PEARSON CORR plan, ses, control
PARTIAL CORR plan BY ses WITH control (1)
```

C. TESTING A CANDIDATE VARIABLE MODEL

With the *candidate variable* model, the researcher is proposing that a number of independent variables may be influencing the dependent variable, Y. Such a model may be diagrammed as follows:

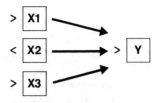

Here the variables X1, X2, and X3 are viewed as potential causes of variations in the dependent variable, Y. Ideally, these variables will be at the same "level of analysis," and will be related to the dependent variable either one at a time, or simultaneously.

The problem with simply running a series of bi-variate (two variable) relationships is that no sense of the relative importance of the independent variables or of their combined impact on the dependent variable is developed. Such relationships may, however, be run using such SPSS[x] procedures as CROSSTABS, BREAKDOWN, PEARSON CORR, or NONPAR CORR.

The major approach to examining candidate variable models is REGRESSION analysis since it simultaneously takes into account all the specified independent variables. Ideally, the variables will be measured at the ratio level. However, when indexes are constructed by combining a number of Likert-type items, they are ordinarily treated as meeting the measurement requirements. We will only consider linear models here, although alternative models are available through various transformations. The regression procedure provides standardized (*betas*), and unstandardized (*b* coefficients) values for the equation describing variations in the dependent variable. Also included is a measure of the amount of variation explained by the equation, the R^2.

1. The REGRESSION Procedure

The REGRESSION procedure is set up in the following way:

```
REGRESSION VARIABLES = depend, V12, V18, V22/
        DEPENDENT = depend/
        BACKWARD/
```

The VARIABLES specification simply lists all of the variables to be used in the analysis. The DEPENDENT specification identifies the dependent variable. The BACKWARD specification instructs SPSS[x] to include all of the independent variables, compute the various coefficients, then sequentially drop them, until only statistically significant ones remain. There are a number of different analysis models and an SPSS[x] manual should be consulted to run them.

2. Dummy Variable Analysis

There may be times when a researcher wishes to use a nominal variable within a regression analysis. This may be done by using *dummy variables*. Suppose we had three religious categories: Protestant, Catholic, and Jewish. To run religion as a variable we would create two new variables (one less than the number of categories) and enter each of these into the regression analysis. These variables are coded as 1 for presence; 0 for absence. They are best created using the RECODE procedure, as in:

```
RECODE RELIGION (1=1)(ELSE = 0) INTO PROTR
RECODE RELIGION (1=0)(2=1)(ELSE = 0) INTO CATHR
VARIABLE LABELS PROTR "Dummy Variable, Protestant"
   CATHR "Dummy Variable, Catholic"
VALUE LABELS PROTR 1 "Protestant"
   2 "non-Protestant"/
   CATHR 1 "Catholic"
   2 "non-Catholic"/
REGRESSION VARIABLES = depend, V1, V5, V10, PROTR, CATHR/
   DEPENDENT = depend/
   BACKWARD/
```

The researcher has to be cautious in interpreting the results obtained when dummy variables are used because these variables are at some disadvantage in explaining variance since they only take on two values, 0 and 1. In short, the importance of the variable religion is probably somewhat underestimated in such an analysis.

3. Some Cautions

Caution 1. Ensure variables are theoretically independent from one another. What this means is that one cannot use aspects of the dependent variable as independent variables. Ensure that you are including only meaningful potential causes of the dependent variable, not alternate measures of it.

Caution 2. Watch out for highly correlated independent variables. The weightings attached to the variables will be unstable if the independent variables are highly correlated with one another. The program will print out a warning if there is a problem in this area.

Caution 3. Interpret weightings with care. Understand that the weightings are for the particular combination of independent variables for a particular sample and these weightings may not reliably apply to other samples.

Caution 4. Monitor the number of cases carefully. Unless otherwise instructed, SPSS^x will delete a case if it has a missing value in any of the variables in the equation. Thus, if there are a lot of variables in an analysis there is a danger of losing many cases. And, as the number of cases drops close to the number of variables, the R^2 will increase dramatically. To determine the number of cases used in the analysis, add 1 to the total degrees of freedom reported in the table. If a large number of cases have been dropped, try running the analysis using PAIRWISE treatment of missing cases (a correlation is computed for each pair of variables using all cases where data is complete for the pair); and if there are still many missing try MEANS (this will substitute the mean of the variable for any missing cases). Either one of these commands can follow the DEPENDENT specification as in:

```
REGRESSION VARIABLES = depend, V1, V2/
    DEPENDENT = depend/
    MISSING = PAIRWISE/
    BACKWARD/
```

or

```
REGRESSION VARIABLES = depend, V1, V2/
    DEPENDENT = depend/
    MISSING = MEANS/
    BACKWARD/
```

An additional possibility, after an initial narrowing down of the variables has been done, is to rerun the analysis, naming only the significant variables plus perhaps two or three that were dropped in the last few steps. This will preserve those cases dropped because of missing values in variables that are not in the final equation.

4. Examining Regression Results

Table 12.10 presents a sample of a regression results table. Note that both the *b* coefficients and the *beta* weights are reported. It is possible to hand compute a rough estimate of the impact of each independent variable using the following formula:[4]

$$\% \text{ Variance Explained by Each Variable} = \frac{\beta_1 \times R^2}{\Sigma \beta s} \times 100$$

This estimate is "rough" because the betas represent the particular variables in the equation and would change if other variables were included in the equation.

The pure researcher has greater interest in the *beta* weights since these provide a basis for directly comparing the impact of the different independent variables on the dependent one. Applied researchers will be more concerned with the *b* coefficients, especially those which can be changed through alterations in policy. They provide the basis for understanding how much change in the dependent variable may be produced for each change in the independent variable. Variables may also be grouped for presentation so that the reader may more easily grasp how different types of variables are influencing the dependent variable.

Table 12.10   Multiple Regression Analysis Faculty Salaries

Variable	b Coefficient	Beta Weight	Percent Explained
Qualifications	794.	.038	3.1
Tenure Status	1326.	.065	5.3
Age in Current Year	94.	.092	7.5
Length in Rank	263.	.153	12.5
Professional Age	210.	.172	14.0
Years at Institution	264.	.250	20.4
Academic Rank	– 4570.	– .372	30.3
CONSTANT	38504.	% EXPLAINED	93.1
Multiple R	.964		
R Square	.930		

The Variables are:

Qualifications	Doctorate = 1; No Doctorate = 0
Tenure Status	Tenure = 1; No Tenure = 0
Age	Age in current year
Length in Rank	Years in Rank
Professional Age	Years since highest degree earned
Years at Institution	Years teaching at Institution
Rank	Professor = 1; Associate = 2; Assistant = 3; Lecturer = 4

This chapter has described only the minimum number of SPSS[x] instructions. The SPSS[x] package contains a broad range of options, file management, and analysis procedures. The chances are that any survey analysis you wish to do is possible within SPSS[x]. After you have mastered the basic procedures, you will be ready to begin exploring SPSS[x] in greater detail.[5]

NOTES

[1] When procedures are being selected for evaluating causal models, and where the vast majority require one type of procedure, in the interests of simplicity, one sometimes will choose to use the same procedure throughout, rather than shifting back and forth between techniques which may be confusing for your reader. Normally this will mean some underutilization of the data since the procedure selected must meet the measurement requirements of the variable with the lowest level of measurement.

[2] The classic statement concerning the interpretation of intervening, source of spuriousness, and conditional variables may be found in Paul Lazarsfeld's foreword to Herbert Hyman, *Survey Design and Analysis*. New York: The Free Press, 1955. Excellent treatments are also found in Earl Babbie, *The Practice of Social Research*. Belmont, California: Wadsworth Publishing Company, 1983; and Dennis Forcese and Stephen Richer, *Social Research Methods*. Englewood Cliffs, N.J.: Prentice-Hall Inc., 1973.

[3]Since it is easy to hand compute a first-order partial, the formula is presented here for those cases where the researcher has the zero-order correlation matrix.

$$r_{12.3} = \frac{r_{12} - (r_{13})(r_{23})}{\sqrt{1 - r_{13}^2}\ \sqrt{1 - r_{23}^2}}$$

[4]Robert L. Hamblin, "Ratio Measurement and Sociological Theory: A Critical Analysis." St. Louis: Social Sciences Institute, Washington University (mimeo), 1966.

[5]The full reference to SPSS^x procedures is found in: *SPSS^x User's Guide,* Second Edition. Chicago: SPSS Inc., 1985.

CHAPTER THIRTEEN

EXPLORING SECONDARY DATA

While this book has been directed primarily at doing a survey, much research involves the analysis of existing data. While many of the steps are identical to doing a survey, there are some differences, and these will be considered in this chapter.

A. DETERMINING THE PROBLEM

As in any project, the first step will be to state as precisely as possible the theory, hypothesis, or variables one wishes to explore. The researcher can proceed by examining theories, by deriving testable hypotheses from them, and by reviewing the literature to see what relationships and explanations have emerged in previous research. Recognize that there are many sources of data that can be used — from published government documents, to the analysis of existing material (books, TV programs, plays, etc.), through to data held in public or private data banks. Initially, at least, the researcher should not be frightened away by topics for which no data seem to be available. Probably data are available — the problem is to locate the information.

Ultimately, however, the researcher will be constrained by available data and by his or her imagination in using them. Relationships cannot be explored if indicators cannot be located. One of the major challenges in doing secondary data analysis is to come up with measures of concepts. One should not, therefore, give up prematurely if it appears that no indicator is present. Often by combining measures, or by searching carefully, one can come up with reasonable measures of the variables one needs.

B. SOURCES OF DATA

1. Government Documents

There are many government documents containing information on a great variety of subjects available in libraries. By the way the data are organized and by the way they report on similar units (census tracts, provincial, state, or national) it is possible to gather much information on a variety of topics, from one or many sources, and from one or many time periods.

Published data will ordinarily be reported on some aggregate basis (number of suicides, unemployment rates, etc. in various cities) but it may be necessary to search out a number of different sources for the required information. Sometimes data will not be available for the same year on all variables for all the units (cities, for example) and it may become necessary to estimate some variables (from previous trends). For example, if you did not have the 1920 figures for suicides in cities but all of your other data relates to 1920, and you know from previous trends that the suicide rates had been increasing by 3% per year and your latest figures are for 1918, you could simply multiply the 1918 number for each city as follows:

$$
\begin{aligned}
1920 \text{ estimate of suicides} &= ((1918 \text{ figure} * 1.03) * 1.03) \\
&= ((214 * 1.03) * 1.03) \\
&= 227
\end{aligned}
$$

Normally, one would enter the data into the computer and perform any such transformations within SPSS^x. As in:

COMPUTE suic20 = ((suic18 * 1.03) * 1.03)

When working with any documents, it is important to carefully record where the information was obtained so that if errors are found when the data are being cleaned (see Chapter 10), checking back to the original documents to identify the true value can be easily done. If at all practical, it is a good idea to make copies of the parts of the documents containing the original data.

2. Census Material

Many countries regularly do a census of their populations. Census reports provide a rich source of data for the social scientist. Ordinarily, the researcher enters the data from the census into a file which uses some aggregation as the unit of analysis. However, census tapes of the individual cases are sometimes available and normally will be a sample of the total census with some location dimensions omitted to prevent the identification of individuals.

Whenever census or other information is entered by the researcher into the computer, it is important that population totals and subtotals be included. For example, if the researcher was interested in exploring factors related to deviance in communities, deviance measures from some government documents would probably have to be combined, while census information would provide population characteristics for the communities under investigation. When the population characteristics are being entered, the researcher must be certain to enter not only the number of Catholics, people between 15 and 24, and the proportion whose mother tongue is not English, but also the number of people in each category of religion, age, and language. By including the total number, rates, ratios, proportions, and percentages may be quickly computed.

a. Computing a Proportion. To illustrate, suppose one wished to compute the proportion of people over 20 years of age who have fewer than 8 years of education. This could be done in SPSS^x with the following commands:

```
IF (AGE LE 20) LOWED = 99
TEMPORARY
SELECT IF (AGE GE 21)
COMPUTE LOWED = NED8LESS / NOVER20
VARIABLE LABELS
    LOWED 'PROPORTION OVER 20 WITH LESS THAN 8 YRS ED'
MISSING VALUES LOWED (99)
CONDESCRIPTIVE LOWED
```

In the above illustration, NED8LESS refers to a variable containing information on the number of respondents in the community with less than 8 years of education who are 21 or older; NOVER20 is the number of people 21 or over in the population. Similar procedures could be employed to compute the proportion Catholic, proportion earning less than the poverty line, or the proportion whose mother tongue is not English.

b. Computing a Rate. If there are indicators reflecting the number of suicides by age group, one can quickly convert these into *age and sex specific suicide rates* by simply computing for each age/sex grouping. To compute the suicide rate for males 16 to 20 we could do the following:

```
COMPUTE SM1620 = (NMS1624 / NM1620) * 100000
VARIABLE LABELS
    SM1620 'SUICIDE RATE MALES 16 TO 20'
```

The variable, NMS1624, refers to the number of male suicides for those 16 to 24; NM1620 refers to the total number of males in the population between 16 and 20 years of age. By multiplying the result by 100 000 the variable is converted to a rate per 100 000 in the category.

c. Computing Percentage Change. Another frequently used computation is the percent change from one period to another. Suppose we wished to compute the percent change in the burglary rate from one year to the next, assuming we already have the rate computed. We have variables BRT1 (burglary rate time one) and BRT2 (burglary rate time two) and we wish to compute the change in the burglary rate for all the communities in our SPSSx system file:

```
COMPUTE CHANGE = ((BRT2 - BRT1) / BRT1) * 100
VARIABLE LABELS CHANGE 'PERCENT CHANGE BURGLAR RATE'
```

3. Data Banks

Many universities, institutes, and faculty members maintain data banks which they make available to researchers. Once the research question has been identified, then the search for secondary data begins. Data contained in data banks ordinarily will be available on computer tapes or stored in a computer.

If the required information is available within the institution, there is a good chance that an SPSS system file will be available to the researcher. If this is the case, all the researcher will need is a "coding manual" and the name of the file. The steps involved in using such a file are:

Step 1. Transfer the file to the new account.

Step 2. Make a backup copy of the system file.

Step 3. Access the system file in order to find out what variables, variable labels, and documents are included in the file. This may be achieved with the following commands:

```
DISPLAY DICTIONARY
DISPLAY DOCUMENTS
```

Step 4. Examine the dictionary to determine which variables are of interest for the current project. Having decided which variables are to be used, access the system file once again, and use the KEEP (retains named variables) or DROP (eliminates named variables) options to define the variables which are to be saved on your working system file. When lists of variables are identified it is possible to use the TO keyword; this will include all the variables between the variables named. It is also possible to RENAME any variables during this run. The following commands may be used:

```
TITLE creating a working system file
FILE HANDLE...
GET FILE = system/
     KEEP = ID, V1 TO V10, Q12, V16 TO V29/
     RENAME = (Q12 = ESTEEM)
... any procedures ...
DISPLAY DICTIONARY
FILE HANDLE newsys/ <file specifications>
SAVE OUTFILE = newsys
FINISH
```

Step 5. A backup copy should be made before any additional runs are made on the data. It is recommended that three system files be maintained in the researcher's account: one copy of the original system file plus two copies of the new system file that will be used. It is always advisable to have backup files located on tape or floppy disks and kept in a separate location. In case of fire or some other disaster the work that has gone into creating the data set will not be lost.

If data are available from another institution, the researcher will probably have to create a .MAK file (see Chapter 11) in order to create an SPSSˣ system file. If a request is being made for data, also request a copy of the "SPSS system maker procedure file." Even though the data were probably analyzed on an earlier version of SPSS, a copy of the MAKER file can be modified to create the new SPSSˣ system file. The *SPSSˣ User's Guide* has a section in it called, "Help for Old Friends" which is extremely helpful in converting old procedure files.

PART SIX

THE FINAL REPORT

CHAPTER FOURTEEN

THE FINAL REPORT

However well designed and well executed a research project is, its final impact will depend, above all, on the quality of the written report. This chapter provides some suggestions for the organization and presentation of the final report.

A. GENERAL ORIENTATION

1. Audience

Reports are written for a variety of audiences and this should be taken into account while preparing them. If a report is intended for a professional journal, then it should be organized in a manner similar to material found in journals. On the other hand, if the audience is a non-technical one, then the report should avoid the use of technical terminology.

Most often, it is best to write for the general audience, to assume no prior knowledge of the project, and to try to convey ideas clearly. The student who is submitting a paper for a course requirement is well advised to write not for the professor, but rather to write in a manner any intelligent person would be able to follow. One hint is to write for your "Aunt Martha," not for your professor. Aunt Martha has no knowledge of your research project, she is not a social scientist, in fact she never went to university, but she is a very smart woman, and if you explain things clearly, she will understand your project. A side benefit of this is that your professor will also be able to figure it out!

Why would writing for Aunt Martha be helpful? There is a tendency in reporting on a research project to use too many computer terms, to use technical jargon, and to fail to explain the logic behind your research design or the logic behind how you have made inferences from your data. If you write for Aunt Martha you will be less likely to fall into some of these traps. And, in the process, you will probably write a better report whether it is intended for a journal, a term paper, or for the president of your company.

If you know your audience you will also know what questions will come to their minds and you will be able to address issues of concern to them. Above all, explain your points clearly and fully: do not assume specialized knowledge on the part of your reader.

2. Style

Edit your material carefully. Read it slowly, perhaps out loud, and eliminate redundant words, sentences, and paragraphs. Editing should shorten the document considerably. Do not sacrifice readability and brevity for the sake of saving a nice turn-of-phrase. Keep it short.

It is a good idea to provide headings and sub-headings to guide your reader through the material. Footnotes should be used when technical details are required but when inclusion of such details would detract from the main text. For editing purposes, it is easier to place footnotes at the end of the paper.

Tables should include sufficient information to permit the reader to read tables rather than text. It is generally best to place tables on separate sheets so retyping will not be required as the text is edited.

B. ORGANIZATION

A paper should be organized into sections. An effort should be made to cover the material discussed under each of the following headings.

1. Introduction

The introduction should tell your reader what the project is about, what the general approach to the problem is, and what the critical issues are. Generally, an effort is made to excite the reader's interest in the project. Raise interesting questions and unresolved issues which you propose to answer in your research.

2. Review of Literature

The Review of Literature section provides an overview of the "state of scientific knowledge" in your area of study. Consider reviewing the (i) appropriate theoretical models and (ii) the empirical findings which bear on the particular relationships you will be examining. If such material is not available, then some sense of what variables have been related to the major dependent variable in your study should be provided.

The review should highlight those areas where there are inconsistencies in the conclusions and the areas you intend to address. Generally, it is best not to present summaries of articles, but rather to focus on what the consensus is on the relation between particular variables and the dependent variable. For example, suppose you were examining factors related to "political conservatism." It would be useful for your reader to know whether there is any agreement in the scientific literature on whether "conservatism" is related to such variables as: age, sex, rural/urban backgrounds, and socioeconomic status. Where there are inconsistencies, have you any observations as to why they emerged? Different regions, different measurement or analytic procedures, or systematic variations in the compositions of the populations studied might all account for the variations between studies. If inconsistencies are present, these can be noted, and you can heighten your reader's interest in your project by proposing to answer some of the questions raised.

3. Hypotheses and Research Design

The Review of Literature section should lead into a section defining the hypotheses, questions, or relationships to be examined. These should be precisely stated and connected to the literature of the discipline. It is almost always best to diagram the causal models being evaluated in the research. Not only does this provide a clear presentation of the hypotheses, but the drawing in of causal arrows and "greater than"/"less than" symbols permits additional precision.

The rationale for the design selected should include the advantages the chosen design has over alternative ones. What designs have typically been used by other investigators looking at similar relationships?

4. Data Collection Procedures

Having determined the questions and the design, the next step is to describe the measurement, sample selection, and data collection procedures. In describing a questionnaire it is not necessary to discuss each question, rather, attention should be focussed on non-standard items, and, if possible, a copy of the questionnaire should be included in an Appendix to the report. Any comments on problems in data collection should also be mentioned at this point.

5. Description of the Sample

The researcher should next introduce the results of the survey by reporting some of the background characteristics of the individuals involved — sex distribution, rural/urban location, average age — all might be reported if judged to be relevant. If efforts are to be made to assure the representativeness of the sample, this is the stage in the report where such material would be appropriately introduced. If you know from census material, for example, that 54.0 percent of the region's population above 15 is female and your sample is 59.0 percent female, this fact should be noted.

6. Description of Indexes

A description and evaluation of indexes constructed and a preliminary report on the mean results should be made at this point. If you have used a previously used index, comparisons may be made between the mean results of your survey and those produced by other researchers.

7. Presenting Basic Results

The variations in the dependent variable should be explored in this section. Any basic runs leading up to an exploration of the formal hypotheses of the survey should be presented. Where possible, use summary tables to compress the results of many analyses into one table. (See Tables 11.6 and 11.7.) SPSS[x] output is not in an appropriate form for presentation. Tables included in a final report generally will need to be reformatted and should conform to those shown throughout this book or modelled after those presented in journal articles or books. While it is possible to control the SPSS[x] output format, the beginning researcher will probably find it easier to retype the tables. In some cases, if the report is being prepared with a word processor, it will be possible to read parts of the .OUT file into the report, modify it, thus saving energey in retyping the various numbers.

8. Evaluating Hypotheses and Models

The reader should now be well prepared and be anticipating the results of the hypothesis/model testing. If diagrams described the original relationships, they should be employed once again when the findings are reported. If you are testing a theory and have derived a hypothesis, then you should report the finding of the test, even if the relationship is not statistically significant.

In cases where you are investigating alternative explanations for some relationship you have initially assumed to be statistically significant, you would only continue with the tests for the alternative explanations if the relationship, in fact, turned out to be statistically significant. You would, of course, include the intervening variable model in your report. However, if no relationship has emerged, you would not proceed with an evaluation of the alternative explanations — you have no relationship to explain. All you would do is note in your report that the alternative explanations will not be explored since the original relationship was not sufficiently strong.

If the primary relationship has not turned out to be statistically significant, it is then appropriate to explore the relationship of independent variables to the dependent variable. If you are forced to this "fall back" position, and have not established the various hypotheses in advance, then you should indicate that your explorations are being conducted without the guidance of hypotheses. The reader is then alerted to the fact that you are on a hunting expedition. Hunting is fine as long as the reader is alerted.

9. Discussion

At this point an effort should be made to tie the whole project together. References should be made to the Review of Literature section once again, showing how the results of your survey fit into the general picture. Such references will also help tie the paper together, reminding the reader of the problems that the project initially raised. In what areas does your research support the general view, in what areas does it not? Where there are discrepancies, what are some of the possible explanations? This discussion should provide the reader with a sense of what has been learned, and what remains problematic.

10. Conclusion

The final section should briefly state what the central problem was and what conclusions have been identified. This section may also include suggestions about how the current project might have been improved, and what other issues the researcher identifies as worthy of further exploration.

APPENDICES

Appendix A   Areas Under the Normal Curve

Fractional parts of the total area (10,000) under the normal curve, corresponding to distances between the mean and ordinates which are Z standard-deviation units from the mean.

Z	.00	.01	.02	.03	.04	.05	.06	.07	.08	.09
0.0	0000	0040	0080	0120	0159	0199	0239	0279	0319	0359
0.1	0398	0438	0478	0517	0557	0596	0636	0675	0714	0753
0.2	0793	0832	0871	0910	0948	0987	1026	1064	1103	1141
0.3	1179	1217	1255	1293	1331	1368	1406	1443	1480	1517
0.4	1554	1591	1628	1664	1700	1736	1772	1808	1844	1879
0.5	1915	1950	1985	2019	2054	2088	2123	2157	2190	2224
0.6	2257	2291	2324	2357	2389	2422	2454	2486	2518	2549
0.7	2580	2612	2642	2673	2704	2734	2764	2794	2823	2852
0.8	2881	2910	2939	2967	2995	3023	3051	3078	3106	3133
0.9	3159	3186	3212	3238	3264	3289	3315	3340	3365	3389
1.0	3413	3438	3461	3485	3508	3531	3554	3577	3599	3621
1.1	3643	3665	3686	3718	3729	3749	3770	3790	3810	3830
1.2	3849	3869	3888	3907	3925	3944	3962	3980	3997	4015
1.3	4032	4049	4066	4083	4099	4115	4131	4147	4162	4177
1.4	4192	4207	4222	4236	4251	4265	4279	4292	4306	4319
1.5	4332	4345	4357	4370	4382	4394	4406	4418	4430	4441
1.6	4452	4463	4474	4485	4495	4505	4515	4525	4535	4545
1.7	4554	4564	4573	4582	4591	4599	4608	4616	4625	4633
1.8	4641	4649	4656	4664	4671	4678	4686	4693	4699	4706
1.9	4713	4719	4726	4732	4738	4744	4750	4758	4762	4767
2.0	4773	4778	4783	4788	4793	4798	4803	4808	4812	4817
2.1	4821	4826	4830	4834	4838	4842	4846	4850	4854	4857
2.2	4861	4865	4868	4871	4875	4878	4881	4884	4887	4890
2.3	4893	4896	4898	4901	4904	4906	4909	4911	4913	4916
2.4	4918	4920	4922	4925	4927	4929	4931	4932	4934	4936
2.5	4938	4940	4941	4943	4945	4946	4948	4949	4951	4952
2.6	4953	4955	4956	4957	4959	4960	4961	4962	4963	4964
2.7	4965	4966	4967	4968	4969	4970	4971	4972	4973	4974
2.8	4974	4975	4976	4977	4977	4978	4979	4980	4980	4981
2.9	4981	4982	4983	4984	4984	4984	4985	4985	4986	4986
3.0	4986.5	4987	4987	4988	4988	4988	4989	4989	4989	4990
3.1	4990.0	4991	4991	4991	4992	4992	4992	4992	4993	4993
3.2	4993.129									
3.3	4995.166									
3.4	4996.631									
3.5	4997.674									
3.6	4998.409									
3.7	4998.922									
3.8	4999.277									
3.9	4999.519									
4.0	4999.683									
4.5	4999.966									
5.0	4999.997133									

Source: Harold O. Rugg: *Statistical Methods Applied to Education, pp. 889-90.* Copyright © 1917, renewed 1945 by Houghton Mifflin Company, Boston, U.S.A. Used by permission.

Appendix B   Chi-Square Values

Probability

df	.99	.98	.95	.90	.80	.70	.50	.30	.20	.10	.05	.02	.01	.001
1	$.0^3157$	$.0^3628$	.00393	.0158	.0642	.148	.455	1.074	1.642	2.706	3.841	5.412	6.635	10.827
2	.0201	.0404	.103	.211	.446	.713	1.386	2.408	3.219	4.605	5.991	7.824	9.210	13.815
3	.115	.185	.352	.584	1.005	1.424	2.366	3.665	4.642	6.251	7.815	9.837	11.341	16.268
4	.297	.429	.711	1.064	1.649	2.195	3.357	4.878	5.989	7.779	9.488	11.668	13.277	18.465
5	.554	.752	1.145	1.610	2.343	3.000	4.351	6.064	7.289	9.236	11.070	13.388	15.086	20.517
6	.872	1.134	1.635	2.204	3.070	3.828	5.348	7.231	8.558	10.645	12.592	15.033	16.812	22.457
7	1.239	1.564	2.167	2.833	3.822	4.671	6.346	8.383	9.803	12.017	14.067	16.622	18.475	24.322
8	1.646	2.032	2.733	3.490	4.594	5.527	7.344	9.524	11.030	13.362	15.507	18.168	20.090	26.125
9	2.088	2.532	3.325	4.168	5.380	6.393	8.343	10.656	12.242	14.684	16.919	19.679	21.666	27.877
10	2.558	3.059	3.940	4.865	6.179	7.267	9.342	11.781	13.442	15.987	18.307	21.161	23.209	29.588
11	3.053	3.609	4.575	5.578	6.989	8.148	10.341	12.899	14.631	17.275	19.675	22.618	24.725	31.264
12	3.571	4.178	5.226	6.304	7.807	9.034	11.340	14.011	15.812	18.549	21.026	24.054	26.217	32.909
13	4.107	4.765	5.892	7.042	8.634	9.926	12.340	15.119	16.985	19.812	22.362	25.472	27.688	34.528
14	4.660	5.368	6.571	7.790	9.467	10.821	13.339	16.222	18.151	21.064	23.685	26.873	29.141	36.123
15	5.229	5.985	7.261	8.547	10.307	11.721	14.339	17.322	19.311	22.307	24.996	28.259	30.578	37.697
16	5.812	6.614	7.962	9.312	11.152	12.624	15.338	18.418	20.465	23.542	26.296	29.633	32.000	39.252
17	6.408	7.255	8.672	10.085	12.002	13.531	16.338	19.511	21.615	24.769	27.587	30.995	33.409	40.790
18	7.015	7.906	9.390	10.865	12.857	14.440	17.338	20.601	22.760	25.989	28.869	32.346	34.805	42.312
19	7.633	8.567	10.117	11.651	13.716	15.352	18.338	21.689	23.900	27.204	30.144	33.687	36.191	43.820
20	8.260	9.237	10.851	12.443	14.578	16.266	19.337	22.775	25.038	28.412	31.410	35.020	37.566	45.315
21	8.897	9.915	11.591	13.240	15.445	17.182	20.337	23.858	26.171	29.615	32.671	36.343	38.932	46.797
22	9.542	10.600	12.338	14.041	16.314	18.101	21.337	24.939	27.301	30.813	33.924	37.659	40.289	48.268
23	10.196	11.293	13.091	14.848	17.187	19.021	22.337	26.018	28.429	32.007	35.172	38.968	41.638	49.728
24	10.856	11.992	13.848	15.659	18.062	19.943	23.337	27.096	29.553	33.196	36.415	40.270	42.980	51.179
25	11.524	12.697	14.611	16.473	18.940	20.867	24.337	28.172	30.675	34.382	37.652	41.566	44.314	52.620
26	12.198	13.409	15.379	17.292	19.820	21.792	25.336	29.246	31.795	35.563	38.885	42.856	45.642	54.052
27	12.879	14.125	16.151	18.114	20.703	22.719	26.336	30.319	32.912	36.741	40.113	44.140	46.963	55.476
28	13.565	14.847	16.928	18.939	21.588	23.647	27.336	31.391	34.027	37.916	41.337	45.419	48.278	56.893
29	14.256	15.574	17.708	19.768	22.475	24.577	28.336	32.461	35.139	39.087	42.557	46.693	49.588	58.302
30	14.953	16.306	18.493	20.599	23.364	25.508	29.336	33.530	36.250	40.256	43.773	47.962	50.892	59.703

For larger values of df, the expression $\sqrt{2\chi^2} - \sqrt{2df - 1}$ may be used as a normal deviate with unit variance, remembering that the probability for χ^2 corresponds with that of a single tail of the normal curve. A slightly more complex transformation, which gives far better approximations for relatively small values of ν, is

$$Z = [\sqrt[3]{\chi^2} - \sqrt[3]{\nu}\,(1 - 2/9\nu)]/\sqrt[3]{\nu}\sqrt{2/9\nu}$$

(See A. C. Acock and G. R. Stavig: "Normal Deviate Approximations of χ^2," *Perceptual and Motor Skills*, vol. 42, p. 220, 1976.)

Source: Appendix B is taken from Table 10 of R.A. Fisher and F. Yates, *Statistical Tables for Biological, Agricultural and Medical Research*, (6th ed. 1974) published by Longman Group UK Ltd., London (previously published by Oliver and Boyd Ltd., Edinburgh) and by permission of the authors and publishers.

Appendix C   The F Distribution

$$p = .05$$

n_1 / n_2	1	2	3	4	5	6	8	12	24	∞
1	161.4	199.5	215.7	224.6	230.2	234.0	238.9	243.9	249.0	254.3
2	18.51	19.00	19.16	19.25	19.30	19.33	19.37	19.41	19.45	19.50
3	10.13	9.55	9.28	9.12	9.01	8.94	8.84	8.74	8.64	8.53
4	7.71	6.94	6.59	6.39	6.26	6.16	6.04	5.91	5.77	5.63
5	6.61	5.79	5.41	5.19	5.05	4.95	4.82	4.68	4.53	4.36
6	5.99	5.14	4.76	4.53	4.39	4.28	4.15	4.00	3.84	3.67
7	5.59	4.74	4.35	4.12	3.97	3.87	3.73	3.57	3.41	3.23
8	5.32	4.46	4.07	3.84	3.69	3.58	3.44	3.28	3.12	2.93
9	5.12	4.26	3.86	3.63	3.48	3.37	3.23	3.07	2.90	2.71
10	4.96	4.10	3.71	3.48	3.33	3.22	3.07	2.91	2.74	2.54
11	4.84	3.98	3.59	3.36	3.20	3.09	2.95	2.79	2.61	2.40
12	4.75	3.88	3.49	3.26	3.11	3.00	2.85	2.69	2.50	2.30
13	4.67	3.80	3.41	3.18	3.02	2.92	2.77	2.60	2.42	2.21
14	4.60	3.74	3.34	3.11	2.96	2.85	2.70	2.53	2.35	2.13
15	4.54	3.68	3.29	3.06	2.90	2.79	2.64	2.48	2.29	2.07
16	4.49	3.63	3.24	3.01	2.85	2.74	2.59	2.42	2.24	2.01
17	4.45	3.59	3.20	2.96	2.81	2.70	2.55	2.38	2.19	1.96
18	4.41	3.55	3.16	2.93	2.77	2.66	2.51	2.34	2.15	1.92
19	4.38	3.52	3.13	2.90	2.74	2.63	2.48	2.31	2.11	1.88
20	4.35	3.49	3.10	2.87	2.71	2.60	2.45	2.28	2.08	1.84
21	4.32	3.47	3.07	2.84	2.68	2.57	2.42	2.25	2.05	1.81
22	4.30	3.44	3.05	2.82	2.66	2.55	2.40	2.23	2.03	1.78
23	4.28	3.42	3.03	2.80	2.64	2.53	2.38	2.20	2.00	1.76
24	4.26	3.40	3.01	2.78	2.62	2.51	2.36	2.18	1.98	1.73
25	4.24	3.38	2.99	2.76	2.60	2.49	2.34	2.16	1.96	1.71
26	4.22	3.37	2.98	2.74	2.59	2.47	2.32	2.15	1.95	1.69
27	4.21	3.35	2.96	2.73	2.57	2.46	2.30	2.13	1.93	1.67
28	4.20	3.34	2.95	2.71	2.56	2.44	2.29	2.12	1.91	1.65
29	4.18	3.33	2.93	2.70	2.54	2.43	2.28	2.10	1.90	1.64
30	4.17	3.32	2.92	2.69	2.53	2.42	2.27	2.09	1.89	1.62
40	4.08	3.23	2.84	2.61	2.45	2.34	2.18	2.00	1.79	1.51
60	4.00	3.15	2.76	2.52	2.37	2.25	2.10	1.92	1.70	1.39
120	3.92	3.07	2.68	2.45	2.29	2.17	2.02	1.83	1.61	1.25
∞	3.84	2.99	2.60	2.37	2.21	2.09	1.94	1.75	1.52	1.00

Values of n_1 and n_2 represent the degrees of freedom associated with the larger and smaller estimates of variance respectively.

Source: Appendix C is taken from Table V of R.A. Fisher and F. Yates, *Statistical Tables for Biological, Agricultural and Medical Research*, (6th ed. 1974) published by Longman Group UK Ltd., London (previously published by Oliver and Boyd Ltd., Edinburgh) and by permission of the authors and publishers.

Appendix C   continued

$$p = .01$$

n_1 / n_2	1	2	3	4	5	6	8	12	24	∞
1	4052	4999	5403	5625	5764	5859	5981	6106	6234	6366
2	98.49	99.01	99.17	99.25	99.30	99.33	99.36	99.42	99.46	99.50
3	34.12	30.81	29.46	28.71	28.24	27.91	27.49	27.05	26.60	26.12
4	21.20	18.00	16.69	15.98	15.52	15.21	14.80	14.37	13.93	13.46
5	16.26	13.27	12.06	11.39	10.97	10.67	10.27	9.89	9.47	9.02
6	13.74	10.92	9.78	9.15	8.75	8.47	8.10	7.72	7.31	6.88
7	12.25	9.55	8.45	7.85	7.46	7.19	6.84	6.47	6.07	5.65
8	11.26	8.65	7.59	7.01	6.63	6.37	6.03	5.67	5.28	4.86
9	10.56	8.02	6.99	6.42	6.06	5.80	5.47	5.11	4.73	4.31
10	10.04	7.56	6.55	5.99	5.64	5.39	5.06	4.71	4.33	3.91
11	9.65	7.20	6.22	5.67	5.32	5.07	4.74	4.40	4.02	3.60
12	9.33	6.93	5.95	5.41	5.06	4.82	4.50	4.16	3.78	3.36
13	9.07	6.70	5.74	5.20	4.86	4.62	4.30	3.96	3.59	3.16
14	8.86	6.51	5.56	5.03	4.69	4.46	4.14	3.80	3.43	3.00
15	8.68	6.36	5.42	4.89	4.56	4.32	4.00	3.67	3.29	2.87
16	8.53	6.23	5.29	4.77	4.44	4.20	3.89	3.55	3.18	2.75
17	8.40	6.11	5.18	4.67	4.34	4.10	3.79	3.45	3.08	2.65
18	8.28	6.01	5.09	4.58	4.25	4.01	3.71	3.37	3.00	2.57
19	8.18	5.93	5.01	4.50	4.17	3.94	3.63	3.30	2.92	2.49
20	8.10	5.85	4.94	4.43	4.10	3.87	3.56	3.23	2.86	2.42
21	8.02	5.78	4.87	4.37	4.04	3.81	3.51	3.17	2.80	2.36
22	7.94	5.72	4.82	4.31	3.99	3.76	3.45	3.12	2.75	2.31
23	7.88	5.66	4.76	4.26	3.94	3.71	3.41	3.07	2.70	2.26
24	7.82	5.61	4.72	4.22	3.90	3.67	3.36	3.03	2.66	2.21
25	7.77	5.57	4.68	4.18	3.86	3.63	3.32	2.99	2.62	2.17
26	7.72	5.53	4.64	4.14	3.82	3.59	3.29	2.96	2.58	2.13
27	7.68	5.49	4.60	4.11	3.78	3.56	3.26	2.93	2.55	2.10
28	7.64	5.45	4.57	4.07	3.75	3.53	3.23	2.90	2.52	2.06
29	7.60	5.42	4.54	4.04	3.73	3.50	3.20	2.87	2.49	2.03
30	7.56	5.39	4.51	4.02	3.70	3.47	3.17	2.84	2.47	2.01
40	7.31	5.18	4.31	3.83	3.51	3.29	2.99	2.66	2.29	1.80
60	7.08	4.98	4.13	3.65	3.34	3.12	2.82	2.50	2.12	1.60
120	6.85	4.79	3.95	3.48	3.17	2.96	2.66	2.34	1.95	1.38
∞	6.64	4.60	3.78	3.32	3.02	2.80	2.51	2.18	1.79	1.00

Values of n_1 and n_2 represent the degrees of freedom associated with the larger and smaller estimates of variance respectively.

Appendix C   continued

$$p = .001$$

n_1 \ n_2	1	2	3	4	5	6	8	12	24	∞
1	405284	500000	540379	562500	576405	585937	598144	610667	623497	636619
2	998.5	999.0	999.2	999.2	999 3	999.3	999.4	999.4	999.5	999.5
3	167.5	148.5	141.1	137.1	134.6	132.8	130.6	128.3	125.9	123.5
4	74.14	61.25	56.18	53.44	51.71	50.53	49.00	47.41	45.77	44.05
5	47.04	36.61	33.20	31.09	29.75	28.84	27.64	26.42	25.14	23.78
6	35.51	27.00	23.70	21.90	20.81	20.03	19.03	17.99	16.89	15.75
7	29.22	21.69	18.77	17.19	16.21	15.52	14.63	13.71	12.73	11.69
8	25.42	18.49	15.83	14.39	13.49	12.86	12.04	11.19	10.30	9.34
9	22.86	16.39	13.90	12.56	11.71	11.13	10.37	9.57	8.72	7.81
10	21.04	14.91	12.55	11.28	10.48	9.92	9.20	8.45	7.64	6.76
11	19.69	13.81	11.56	10.35	9.58	9.05	8.35	7.63	6.85	6.00
12	18.64	12.97	10.80	9.63	8.89	8.38	7 71	7.00	6.25	5.42
13	17.81	12.31	10.21	9.07	8.35	7.86	7.21	6.52	5.78	4.97
14	17.14	11.78	9 73	8.62	7.92	7.43	6.80	6.13	5.41	4.60
15	16.59	11.34	9.34	8.25	7.57	7.09	6.47	5.81	5.10	4.31
16	16.12	10.97	9.00	7.94	7.27	6.81	6.19	5.55	4.85	4.06
17	15.72	10.66	8.73	7.68	7.02	6.56	5.96	5.32	4.63	3.85
18	15.38	10.39	8.49	7.46	6.81	6.35	5.76	5.13	4.45	3.67
19	15.08	10.16	8.28	7.26	6.61	6.18	5.59	4.97	4.29	3.52
20	14.82	9.95	8.10	7.10	6.46	6.02	5.44	4.82	4.15	3.38
21	14.59	9.77	7.94	6.95	6.32	5.88	5.31	4.70	4.03	3.26
22	14.38	9.61	7.80	6.81	6.19	5.76	5.19	4.58	3.92	3.15
23	14.19	9.47	7.67	6.69	6.08	5.65	5.09	4.48	3.82	3.05
24	14.03	9.34	7.55	6.59	5 98	5.55	4.99	4.39	3.74	2.97
25	13.88	9.22	7.45	6.49	5.88	5.46	4.91	4.31	3.66	2.89
26	13.74	9.12	7.36	6.41	5.80	5.38	4.83	4.24	3.59	2.82
27	13.61	9.02	7.27	6.33	5.73	5.31	4.76	4.17	3.52	2.75
28	13.50	8.93	7.19	6.25	5 66	5.24	4.69	4.11	3.46	2.70
29	13.39	8.85	7.12	6.19	5.59	5.18	4.64	4.05	3.41	2.64
30	13.29	8.77	7.05	6.12	5.53	5.12	4.58	4.00	3.36	2.59
40	12.61	8.25	6.60	5.70	5.13	4.73	4.21	3.64	3.01	2.23
60	11.97	7.76	6.17	5.31	4.76	4.37	3.87	3.31	2.69	1.90
120	11.38	7.31	5.79	4.95	4.42	4.04	3.55	3.02	2.40	1.56
∞	10.83	6.91	5.42	4.62	4.10	3.74	3.27	2.74	2.13	1.00

Values of n_1 and n_2 represent the degrees of freedom associated with the larger and smaller estimates of variance respectively.

Appendix D   Table of Random Numbers

```
10 09 73 25 33   76 52 01 35 86   34 67 35 48 76   80 95 90 91 17   39 29 27 49 45
37 54 20 48 05   64 89 47 42 96   24 80 52 40 37   20 63 61 04 02   00 82 29 16 65
08 42 26 89 53   19 64 50 93 03   23 20 90 25 60   15 95 33 47 64   35 08 03 36 06
99 01 90 25 29   09 37 67 07 15   38 31 13 11 65   88 67 67 43 97   04 43 62 76 59
12 80 79 99 70   80 15 73 61 47   64 03 23 66 53   98 95 11 68 77   12 17 17 68 33

66 06 57 47 17   34 07 27 68 50   36 69 73 61 70   65 81 33 98 85   11 19 92 91 70
31 06 01 08 05   45 57 18 24 06   35 30 34 26 14   86 79 90 74 39   23 40 30 97 32
85 26 97 76 02   02 05 16 56 92   68 66 57 48 18   73 05 38 52 47   18 62 38 85 79
63 57 33 21 35   05 32 54 70 48   90 55 35 75 48   28 46 82 87 09   83 49 12 56 24
73 79 64 57 53   03 52 96 47 78   35 80 83 42 82   60 93 52 03 44   35 27 38 84 35

98 52 01 77 67   14 90 56 86 07   22 10 94 05 58   60 97 09 34 33   50 50 07 39 98
11 80 50 54 31   39 80 82 77 32   50 72 56 82 48   29 40 52 42 01   52 77 56 78 51
83 45 29 96 34   06 28 89 80 83   13 74 67 00 78   18 47 54 06 10   68 71 17 78 17
88 68 54 02 00   86 50 75 84 01   36 76 66 79 51   90 36 47 64 93   29 60 91 10 62
99 59 46 73 48   87 51 76 49 69   91 82 60 89 28   93 78 56 13 68   23 47 83 41 13

65 48 11 76 74   17 46 85 09 50   58 04 77 69 74   73 03 95 71 86   40 21 81 65 44
80 12 43 56 35   17 72 70 80 15   45 31 82 23 74   21 11 57 82 53   14 38 55 37 63
74 35 09 98 17   77 40 27 72 14   43 23 60 02 10   45 52 16 42 37   96 28 60 26 55
69 91 62 68 03   66 25 22 91 48   36 93 68 72 03   76 62 11 39 90   94 40 05 64 18
09 89 32 05 05   14 22 56 85 14   46 42 75 67 88   96 29 77 88 22   54 38 21 45 98

91 49 91 45 23   68 47 92 76 86   46 16 28 35 54   94 75 08 99 23   37 08 92 00 48
80 33 69 45 98   26 94 03 68 58   70 29 73 41 35   53 14 03 33 40   42 05 08 23 41
44 10 48 19 49   85 15 74 79 54   32 97 92 65 75   57 60 04 08 81   22 22 20 64 13
12 55 07 37 42   11 10 00 20 40   12 86 07 46 97   96 64 48 94 39   28 70 72 58 15
63 60 64 93 29   16 50 53 44 84   40 21 95 25 63   43 65 17 70 82   07 20 73 17 90

61 19 69 04 46   26 45 74 77 74   51 92 43 37 29   65 39 45 95 93   42 58 26 05 27
15 47 44 52 66   95 27 07 99 53   59 36 78 38 48   82 39 61 01 18   33 21 15 94 66
94 55 72 85 73   67 89 75 43 87   54 62 24 44 31   91 19 04 25 92   92 92 74 59 73
42 48 11 62 13   97 34 40 87 21   16 86 84 87 67   03 07 11 20 59   25 70 14 66 70
23 52 37 83 17   73 20 88 98 37   68 93 59 14 16   26 25 22 96 63   05 52 28 25 62

04 49 35 24 94   75 24 63 38 24   45 86 25 10 25   61 96 27 93 35   65 33 71 24 72
00 54 99 76 54   64 05 18 81 59   96 11 96 38 96   54 69 28 23 91   23 28 72 95 29
35 96 31 53 07   26 89 80 93 54   33 35 13 54 62   77 97 45 00 24   90 10 33 93 33
59 80 80 83 91   45 42 72 68 42   83 60 94 97 00   13 02 12 48 92   78 56 52 01 06
46 05 88 52 36   01 39 09 22 86   77 28 14 40 77   93 91 08 36 47   70 61 74 29 41

32 17 90 05 97   87 37 92 52 41   05 56 70 70 07   86 74 31 71 57   85 39 41 18 38
69 23 46 14 06   20 11 74 52 04   15 95 66 00 00   18 74 39 24 23   97 11 89 63 38
19 56 54 14 30   01 75 87 53 79   40 41 92 15 85   66 67 43 68 06   84 96 28 52 07
45 15 51 49 38   19 47 60 72 46   43 66 79 45 43   59 04 79 00 33   20 82 66 95 41
94 86 43 19 94   36 16 81 08 51   34 88 88 15 53   01 54 03 54 56   05 01 45 11 76
```

Source: Reprinted from pages 1-3 of *A Million Random Digits with 100,000 Normal Deviates* by RAND Corporation (New York: The Free Press, 1955). Copyright 1955 and 1983 by the RAND Corporation. Used by permission.

Appendix D   continued

```
98 08 62 48 26   45 24 02 84 04   44 99 90 88 96   39 09 47 34 07   35 44 13 18 80
33 18 51 62 32   41 94 15 09 49   89 43 54 85 81   88 69 54 19 94   37 54 87 30 43
80 95 10 04 06   96 38 27 07 74   20 15 12 33 87   25 01 62 52 98   94 62 46 11 71
79 75 24 91 40   71 96 12 82 96   69 86 10 25 91   74 85 22 05 39   00 38 75 95 79
18 63 33 25 37   98 14 50 65 71   31 01 02 46 74   05 45 56 14 27   77 93 89 19 36

74 02 94 39 02   77 55 73 22 70   97 79 01 71 19   52 52 75 80 21   80 81 45 17 48
54 17 84 56 11   80 99 33 71 43   05 33 51 29 69   56 12 71 92 55   36 04 09 03 24
11 66 44 98 83   52 07 98 48 27   59 38 17 15 39   09 97 33 34 40   88 46 12 33 56
48 32 47 79 28   31 24 96 47 10   02 29 53 68 70   32 30 75 75 46   15 02 00 99 94
69 07 49 41 38   87 63 79 19 76   35 58 40 44 01   10 51 82 16 15   01 84 87 69 38

09 18 82 00 97   32 82 53 95 27   04 22 08 63 04   83 38 98 73 74   64 27 85 80 44
90 04 58 54 97   51 98 15 06 54   94 93 88 19 97   91 87 07 61 50   68 47 66 46 59
73 18 95 02 07   47 67 72 52 69   62 29 06 44 64   27 12 46 70 18   41 36 18 27 60
75 76 87 64 90   20 97 18 17 49   90 42 91 22 72   95 37 50 58 71   93 82 34 31 78
54 01 64 40 56   66 28 13 10 03   00 68 22 73 98   20 71 45 32 95   07 70 61 78 13

08 35 86 99 10   78 54 24 27 85   13 66 15 88 73   04 61 89 75 53   31 22 30 84 20
28 30 60 32 64   81 33 31 05 91   40 51 00 78 93   32 60 46 04 75   94 11 90 18 40
53 84 08 62 33   81 59 41 36 28   51 21 59 02 90   28 46 66 87 95   77 76 22 07 91
91 75 75 37 41   61 61 36 22 69   50 26 39 02 12   55 78 17 65 14   83 48 34 70 55
89 41 59 26 94   00 39 75 83 91   12 60 71 76 46   48 94 97 23 06   94 54 13 74 08

77 51 30 38 20   86 83 42 99 01   68 41 48 27 74   51 90 81 39 80   72 89 35 55 07
19 50 23 71 74   69 97 92 02 88   55 21 02 97 73   74 28 77 52 51   65 34 46 74 15
21 81 85 93 13   93 27 88 17 57   05 68 67 31 56   07 08 28 50 46   31 85 33 84 52
51 47 46 64 99   68 10 72 36 21   94 04 99 13 45   42 83 60 91 91   08 00 74 54 49
99 55 96 83 31   62 53 52 41 70   69 77 71 28 30   74 81 97 81 42   43 86 07 28 34

33 71 34 80 07   93 58 47 28 69   51 92 66 47 21   58 30 32 98 22   93 17 49 39 72
85 27 48 68 93   11 30 32 92 70   28 83 43 41 37   73 51 59 04 00   71 14 84 36 43
84 13 38 96 40   44 03 55 21 66   73 85 27 00 91   61 22 26 05 61   62 32 71 84 23
56 73 21 62 34   17 39 59 61 31   10 12 39 16 22   85 49 65 75 60   81 60 41 88 80
65 13 85 68 06   87 64 88 52 61   34 31 36 58 61   45 87 52 10 69   85 64 44 72 77

38 00 10 21 76   81 71 91 17 11   71 60 29 29 37   74 21 96 40 49   65 58 44 96 98
37 40 29 63 97   01 30 47 75 86   56 27 11 00 86   47 32 46 26 05   40 03 03 74 38
97 12 54 03 48   87 08 33 14 17   21 81 53 92 50   75 23 76 20 47   15 50 12 95 78
21 82 64 11 34   47 14 33 40 72   64 63 88 59 02   49 13 90 64 41   03 85 65 45 52
73 13 54 27 42   95 71 90 90 35   85 79 47 42 96   08 78 98 81 56   64 69 11 92 02

07 63 87 79 29   03 06 11 80 72   96 20 74 41 56   23 82 19 95 38   04 71 36 69 94
60 52 88 34 41   07 95 41 98 14   59 17 52 06 95   05 53 35 21 39   61 21 20 64 55
83 59 63 56 55   06 95 89 29 83   05 12 80 97 19   77 43 35 37 83   92 30 15 04 98
10 85 06 27 46   99 59 91 05 07   13 49 90 63 19   53 07 57 18 39   06 41 01 93 62
39 82 09 89 52   43 62 26 31 47   64 42 18 08 14   43 80 00 93 51   31 02 47 31 67
```

Appendix D   continued

```
59 58 00 64 78    75 56 97 88 00    88 83 55 44 86    23 76 80 61 56    04 11 10 84 08
38 50 80 73 41    23 79 34 87 63    90 82 29 70 22    17 71 90 42 07    95 95 44 99 53
30 69 27 06 68    94 68 81 61 27    56 19 68 00 91    82 06 76 34 00    05 46 26 92 00
65 44 39 56 59    18 28 82 74 37    49 63 22 40 41    08 33 76 56 76    96 29 99 08 36
27 26 75 02 64    13 19 27 22 94    07 47 74 46 06    17 98 54 89 11    97 34 13 03 58

91 30 70 69 91    19 07 22 42 10    36 69 95 37 28    28 82 53 57 93    28 97 66 62 52
68 43 49 46 88    84 47 31 36 22    62 12 69 84 08    12 84 38 25 90    09 81 59 31 46
48 90 81 58 77    54 74 52 45 91    35 70 00 47 54    83 82 45 26 92    54 13 05 51 60
06 91 34 51 97    42 67 27 86 01    11 88 30 95 28    63 01 19 89 01    14 97 44 03 44
10 45 51 60 19    14 21 03 37 12    91 34 23 78 21    88 32 58 08 51    43 66 77 08 83

12 88 39 73 43    65 02 76 11 84    04 28 50 13 92    17 97 41 50 77    90 71 22 67 69
21 77 83 09 76    38 80 73 69 61    31 64 94 20 96    63 28 10 20 23    08 81 64 74 49
19 52 35 95 15    65 12 25 96 59    86 28 36 82 58    69 57 21 37 98    16 43 59 15 29
67 24 55 26 70    35 58 31 65 63    79 24 68 66 86    76 46 33 42 22    26 65 59 08 02
60 58 44 73 77    07 50 03 79 92    45 13 42 65 29    26 76 08 36 37    41 32 64 43 44

53 85 34 13 77    36 06 69 48 50    58 83 87 38 59    49 36 47 33 31    96 24 04 36 42
24 63 73 87 36    74 38 48 93 42    52 62 30 79 92    12 36 91 86 01    03 74 28 38 73
83 08 01 24 51    38 99 22 28 15    07 75 95 17 77    97 37 72 75 85    51 97 23 78 67
16 44 42 43 34    36 15 19 90 73    27 49 37 09 39    85 13 03 25 52    54 84 65 47 59
60 79 01 81 57    57 17 86 57 62    11 16 17 85 76    45 81 95 29 79    65 13 00 48 60

03 99 11 04 61    93 71 61 68 94    66 08 32 46 53    84 60 95 82 32    88 61 81 91 61
38 55 59 55 54    32 88 65 97 80    08 35 56 08 60    29 73 54 77 62    71 29 92 38 53
17 54 67 37 04    92 05 24 62 15    55 12 12 92 81    59 07 60 79 36    27 95 45 89 09
32 64 35 28 61    95 81 90 68 31    00 91 19 89 36    76 35 59 37 79    80 86 30 05 14
69 57 26 87 77    39 51 03 59 05    14 06 04 06 19    29 54 96 96 16    33 56 46 07 80

24 12 26 65 91    27 69 90 64 94    14 84 54 66 72    61 95 87 71 00    90 89 97 57 54
61 19 63 02 31    92 96 26 17 73    41 83 95 53 82    17 26 77 09 43    78 03 87 02 67
30 53 22 17 04    10 27 41 22 02    39 68 52 33 09    10 06 16 88 29    55 98 66 64 85
03 78 89 75 99    75 86 72 07 17    74 41 65 31 66    35 20 83 33 74    87 53 90 88 23
48 22 86 33 79    85 78 34 76 19    53 15 26 74 33    35 66 35 29 72    16 81 86 03 11

60 36 59 46 53    35 07 53 39 49    42 61 42 92 97    01 91 82 83 16    98 95 37 32 31
83 79 94 24 02    56 62 33 44 42    34 99 44 13 74    70 07 11 47 36    09 95 81 80 65
32 96 00 74 05    36 40 98 32 32    99 38 54 16 00    11 13 30 75 86    15 91 70 62 53
19 32 25 38 45    57 62 05 26 06    66 49 76 86 46    78 13 86 65 59    19 64 09 94 13
11 22 09 47 47    07 39 93 74 08    48 50 92 39 29    27 48 24 54 76    85 24 43 51 59

31 75 15 72 60    68 98 00 53 39    15 47 04 83 55    88 65 12 25 96    03 15 21 92 21
88 49 29 93 82    14 45 40 45 04    20 09 49 89 77    74 84 39 34 13    22 10 97 85 08
30 93 44 77 44    07 48 18 38 28    73 78 80 65 33    28 59 72 04 05    94 20 52 03 80
22 88 84 88 93    27 49 99 87 48    60 53 04 51 28    74 02 28 46 17    82 03 71 02 68
78 21 21 69 93    35 90 29 13 86    44 37 21 54 86    65 74 11 40 14    87 48 13 72 20
```

Appendix D   continued

```
41 84 98 45 47   46 85 05 23 26   34 67 75 83 00   74 91 06 43 45   19 32 58 15 49
46 35 23 30 49   69 24 89 34 60   45 30 50 75 21   61 31 83 18 55   14 41 37 09 51
11 08 79 62 94   14 01 33 17 92   59 74 76 72 77   76 50 33 45 13   39 66 37 75 44
52 70 10 83 37   56 30 38 73 15   16 52 06 96 76   11 65 49 98 93   02 18 16 81 61
57 27 53 68 98   81 30 44 85 85   68 65 22 73 76   92 85 25 58 66   88 44 80 35 84

20 85 77 31 56   70 28 42 43 26   79 37 59 52 20   01 15 96 32 67   10 62 24 83 91
15 63 38 49 24   90 41 59 36 14   33 52 12 66 65   55 82 34 76 41   86 22 53 17 04
92 69 44 82 97   39 90 40 21 15   59 58 94 90 67   66 82 14 15 75   49 76 70 40 37
77 61 31 90 19   88 15 20 00 80   20 55 49 14 09   96 27 74 82 57   50 81 69 76 16
38 68 83 24 86   45 13 46 35 45   59 40 47 20 59   43 94 75 16 80   43 85 25 96 93

25 16 30 18 89   70 01 41 50 21   41 29 06 73 12   71 85 71 59 57   68 97 11 14 03
65 25 10 76 29   37 23 93 32 95   05 87 00 11 19   92 78 42 63 40   18 47 76 56 22
36 81 54 36 25   18 63 73 75 09   82 44 49 90 05   04 92 17 37 01   14 70 79 39 97
64 39 71 16 92   05 32 78 21 62   20 24 78 17 59   45 19 72 53 32   83 74 52 25 67
04 51 52 56 24   95 09 66 79 46   48 46 08 55 58   15 19 11 87 82   16 93 03 33 61

83 76 16 08 73   43 25 38 41 45   60 83 32 59 83   01 29 14 13 49   20 36 80 71 26
14 38 70 63 45   80 85 40 92 79   43 52 90 63 18   38 38 47 47 61   41 19 63 74 80
51 32 19 22 46   80 08 87 70 74   88 72 25 67 36   66 16 44 94 31   66 91 93 16 78
72 47 20 00 08   80 89 01 80 02   94 81 33 19 00   54 15 58 34 36   35 35 25 41 31
05 46 65 53 06   93 12 81 84 64   74 45 79 05 61   72 84 81 18 34   79 98 26 84 16

39 52 87 24 84   82 47 42 55 93   48 54 53 52 47   18 61 91 36 74   18 61 11 92 41
81 61 61 87 11   53 34 24 42 76   75 12 21 17 24   74 62 77 37 07   58 31 91 59 97
07 58 61 61 20   82 64 12 28 20   92 90 41 31 41   32 39 21 97 63   61 19 96 79 40
90 76 70 42 35   13 57 41 72 00   69 90 26 37 42   78 46 42 25 01   18 62 79 08 72
40 18 82 81 93   29 59 38 86 27   94 97 21 15 98   62 09 53 67 87   00 44 15 89 97

34 41 48 21 57   86 88 75 50 87   19 15 20 00 23   12 30 28 07 83   32 62 46 86 91
63 43 97 53 63   44 98 91 68 22   36 02 40 09 67   76 37 84 16 05   65 96 17 34 88
67 04 90 90 70   93 39 94 55 47   94 45 87 42 84   05 04 14 98 07   20 28 83 40 60
79 49 50 41 46   52 16 29 02 86   54 15 83 42 43   46 97 83 54 82   59 36 29 59 38
91 70 43 05 52   04 73 72 10 31   75 05 19 30 29   47 66 56 43 82   99 78 29 34 78
```

Appendix E   Ethical Guidelines, Canadian Sociology and Anthropology Association

NOTE
La version française sera disponible au bureau de Montréal au début de 1986.

Preamble:
The following statement, passed at the 1985 Annual General Meeting, outlines a code of professional ethics for anthropologists and sociologists in Canada. This Code attempts to articulate in general terms those issues and principles that appear to be salient in the profession at this time. It is not intended to prescribe professional behaviour in detail. It is expected to require amendment and refinement as the Association gains experience with it and as members become sensitized to other issues. The Committee will be mainly concerned with the adjudicaton of cases submitted to it. While members may seek clarification or guidance from the Committee, the assumption is that individual professionals will interpret the Code for themselves and consult their colleagues in cases of doubt. It is understood that Committee members will respect the confidentiality of all information submitted to them. Throughout this report, "The Committee" refers to the Committee on Professional Ethics and Employment Cases (COPEEC).

1. General Principles
The development of sociology and anthropology as social sciences is dependent upon open enquiry. The sociologist and anthropologist must be responsive, first and foremost, to the integrity of social scientific investigation and attempt to ensure unencumbered dissemination of results.

The search for knowledge about society must itself operate within standards. Its limitations arise when enquiry infringes on the rights of individuals to be treated as persons, to be considered as ends, not means. Sociologists and anthropologists must not manipulate persons to service their quest for knowledge. The study of society imposes the responsibility of respecting the rights, dignity and autonomy of individuals and groups. The inseparability of knowledge and action must lead to accountability.

1.1 Conduct of Research

1.1.1 Sociological and anthropological research involves persons, organizations, societies and cultures. Sociologists and anthropologists have an obligation to respect the basic rights of individual's, and communities, and to be particularly sensitive to those in dependent and/or vulnerable situations. This includes providing information regarding the nature and objectives of the study; obtaining free consent to participate; according privacy and dignity of treatment; maintaining anonymity of person and confidentiality of information; and providing information about known and anticipated consequences, including risks and repercussions such as false expectations which may arise from the research. Sociologists and anthropologists should not engage in research that leads to a violation of human rights, although this should not be interpreted as an exclusion of legitimate criticism.

1.1.2 The research aims, procedures, sources of funding and possible future use of findings should be explained to the participants as fully as possible in view of the research objectives and methodology.

1.1.3 Guarantees of anonymity and confidentiality should not be made unless they can be fulfilled both in the conduct of the research and in the publication of results.

1.1.4 Researchers should disseminate their findings as widely as possible. Where feasible, research subjects should be allowed reasonable access to the results of the study in which they participated.

Source: Code of Professional Ethics (subject to revisions by the Committee and the membership), The Canadian Sociology & Anthropology Association. Used by permission.

Appendix E   continued

1.1.5 The researcher should not falsify or distort his or her findings or omit data which might significantly alter the conclusions. He or she should attempt to make explicit the methodological and theoretical bases of the study, including stating the limitations of the data and subsequent qualifications of the generalizations.

1.1.6 Researchers are responsible for the content of their professional opinions and also for explaining those opinions and the bases on which they have been developed.

1.1.7 In any public presentation of findings, researchers must acknowledge the contributions or assistance of all who collaborated in the research.

1.1.8 The researcher should attempt to conduct research in such a way that his or her personal and professional behaviour will not jeopardize further research by self or others.

1.2 Conduct of Relations

a) With Students

1.2.1 Students have a responsibility for their own ethical conduct as professionals in training.

1.2.2 A professor has the responsibility to train students to conduct themselves professionally before they carry out research.

1.2.3 When students are asked to be research subjects as part of a course, they should enjoy the same rights as other research participants.

1.2.4 The relationship of sociologists or anthropologists to students should be a non-exploitative one. This applies both to compensation for work and to credit for students' work on or collaboration in research projects, in accordance with the amount, nature, and significance of their contributions.

b) With Employers and Sponsoring Agencies

1.2.5 When a project has severe methodological limitations or unrealistic constraints with respect to time and funds, the researcher has a responsibility to alert the employer or project sponsor to these inadequacies and to the adjustments needed.

1.2.6 The sociologist or anthropologist should be honest about his or her qualifications and aims when seeking employment, research funds, or permission to carry out research.

1.2.7 Researchers have the responsibility to make all ethical decisions in their research and its use.

1.2.8 Researchers are obliged to try to clarify any significant distortion made by a sponsor or client of the findings of a research project in which he or she has participated.

1.2.9 The researcher should acknowledge all sources of financial support for his or her research and any special relationship to the sponsor which might affect the interpretations of the findings.

c) With Colleagues

1.2.10 Sociologists and anthropologists have a professional responsibility to provide promptly references requested by colleagues and students regarding their professional activities, grant applications or career decisions.

1.2.11 The evaluation of colleagues should be based on criteria of professional qualifications.

1.2.12 Evaluations should be in writing, with reasons for judgements provided and hearsay evidence, if considered appropriate, clearly identified as such.

1.2.13 Negative evaluations, when appropriate, are part of professional responsibility, but irrelevant negative information should be avoided.

1.2.14 When unsolicited negative evaluation is considered appropriate, it should be presented in writing, understood to be public, and made available to the person(s) evaluated.

1.2.15 The content of all evaluations should be available to the individual evaluated, and the individual's right of reply or defence ensured.

Appendix E   continued

1.2.16 Team research among colleagues is subject to the same considerations stipulated in 1.2.4 – viz., that relationships should be non-exploitative, with full credit given in accordance with each person's contribution.

1.3   Cooperation with Other Organizations

1.3.1 The sociologists and anthropologists endorse the CAUT Code of Ethics in respect of teaching.

1.3.2 The CSAA has agreed to involve itself to a limited extent in employment-related cases; a separate set of guidelines apply to these cases.

1.4   Sexual Harassment

Sociologists and anthropologists shall not engage in the sexual harassment of students, colleagues, support or administrative staff, research assistants or subjects of research. Following the CAUT guidelines on sexual harassment, the term is defined as sexual advances, requests for sexual favours and other verbal or physical conduct of a sexual nature when:

a) submission to such conduct is made explicitly or implicitly a term or condition of an individual's employment, academic status, academic accreditation or involvement in research

b) submission to or rejection of such conduct by an individual is used as the basis for employment, academic status, academic accreditation or research involvement decisions affecting such an individual, or

c) such conduct has the purpose or effect of unreasonably interfering with an individual's work or academic performance or creating an intimidating, hostile or offensive working, academic or research environment.

These principles are not intended to inhibit normal social relationships or freedom of expression which are in accord with professional ethics. Sexual interaction between consenting adults is a basic human right. However, an individual involved in or entering into a sexual relationship with a consenting adult who is or who is about to be subject to him or her for the purpose of evaluation or supervision is advised to terminate or to decline his or her supervisory or evaluation role.

Appendix F Code of Ethics, American Sociological Association

PREAMBLE

Along with those in other scholarly and scientific disciplines, sociologists subscribe to the general tenets of science and scholarship. Teaching sociologists are also guided by ethical and professional principles that govern that activity. In addition, because of its specific subject matters, sociologists are especially sensitive to the potential for harm to individuals, groups, organizations, communities and societies that may arise out of the misuse of sociological work and knowledge.

As a discipline committed to the free and open access to knowledge and to self regulation through peer review and appraisal, sociology shares with other disciplines the commitment to the pursuit of accurate and precise knowledge and to public disclosure of findings. However, because sociology necessarily entails study of individuals, groups, organzations and societies, these principles may occasionally conflict with more general ethical concerns for the rights of subjects to privacy and for the treatment of subjects with due regard for their integrity, dignity and autonomy. This potential conflict provides one of the justifications for a code of ethics.

The styles of sociological work are diverse and changing. So also are the contexts within which sociologists find employment. These diversities of procedures and context have led to ambiguities concerning appropriate professional behavior. These ambiguities provide another justification for this code.

Finally, this code also attempts to meet the expressed needs of sociologists who have asked for guidance in how best to proceed in a variety of situations involving subjects of investigation, relations with colleagues, and public authorities.

This code establishes feasible requirements for ethical behavior. These requirements cover many-but not all-of the potential sources of ethical conflict that may arise in scholarship, research, teaching and practice. Most represent prima facie obligations that may admit of exceptions but which should generally stand as principles for guiding conduct. The code states an associational consensus about ethical behavior upon which the Committee on Professional Ethics will base its judgments when it must decide whether individual members of the Association have acted unethically in specific instances. More than this, however, the code is meant to sensitize all sociologists to the ethical issues that may arise in their work, and to encourage sociologists to educate themselves and their colleagues to behave ethically. To fulfill these purposes, we, the members of the American Sociological Association, affirm and support the following Code of Ethics:

I. SOCIOLOGICAL RESEARCH AND PRACTICE

A. *Objectivity and Integrity*
   Sociologists should strive to maintain objectivity and integrity in the conduct of sociological and research practice.

   1. Sociologists should adhere to the highest possible technical standards in their research . When findings may have direct implications for public policy or for the well-being of subjects, research should not be undertaken unless the requisite skills and resources are available to accomplish the research adequately.
   2. Since individual sociologists vary in their research modes, skills and experience, sociologists should always set forth *ex ante* the disciplinary and personal limitations that condition whether or not a research project can be successfully completed and condition the validity of findings.

Appendix F   continued

3. Regardless of work settings, sociologists are obligated to report findings fully and without omission of significant data. Sociologists should also disclose details of their theories, methods and research designs that might bear upon interpretation of research findings.
4. Sociologists must report fully all sources of financial support in their publications and must note any special relations to any sponsor.
5. Sociologists should not make any guarantees to subjects-individuals, groups or organizations-unless there is full intention and ability to honor such commitments. All such guarantees, once made, must be honored unless there is a clear, compelling and overriding reason not to do so.
6. Consistent with the spirit of full disclosure of method and analysis, sociologists should make their data available to other qualified social scientists, at reasonable cost, after they have completed their own analyses, except in cases where confidentiality or the claims of a fieldworker to the privacy of personal notes necessarily would be violated in doing so. The timeliness of this obligation is especially critical where the research is perceived to have policy implications.
7. Sociologists must not accept grants, contracts or research assignments that appear likely to require violation of the principles above, and should dissociate themselves from research when they discover a violation and are unable to achieve its correction.
8. When financial support for a project has been accepted, sociologists must make every reasonable effort to complete the proposed work, including reports to the funding source.
9. When several sociologists, including students, are involved in joint projects, there should be mutually accepted explicit agreements, preferably written, at the outset with respect to division of work, compensation, access to data, rights of authorship, and other rights and responsibilities. Of course, such agreements may need to be modified as the project evolves.
10. When it is likely that research findings will bear on public policy or debate, sociologists should take particular care to state all significant qualifications on the findings and interpretations of their research.

B. *Sociologists must not knowingly use their disciplinary roles as covers to obtain information for other than disciplinary purposes.*

C. *Cross-national Research*
Research conducted in foreign countries raises special ethical issues for the investigator and the professional. Disparities in wealth, power, and political systems between the researcher's country and the host country may create problems of equity in research collaboration and conflicts of interest for the visiting scholar. Also, to follow the precepts of the scientific method-such as those requiring full disclosure-may entail adverse consequences or personal risks for individuals and groups in the host country. Finally, irresponsible actions by a single researcher or research team can eliminate or reduce future access to a country by the entire profession and its allied fields.

1. Sociologists should not use their research or consulting roles as covers to gather intelligence for any government.
2. Sociologists should not act as agents for any organization or government without disclosing that role.
3. Research should take culturally appropriate steps to secure informed consent and to avoid invasions of privacy. Special actions may be necessary where the individuals studied are illiterate, of very low social status, and/or unfamiliar with social research.

Appendix F   continued

4. While generally adhering to the norm of acknowledging the contributions of all collaborators, sociologists working in foreign areas should be sensitive to harm that may arise from disclosure, and respect a collaborator's wish/or need for anonymity. Full disclosure may be made later if circumstances permit.
5. All research findings, except those likely to cause harm to collaborators and participants, should be made available in the host country, ideally in the language of that country. Where feasible, raw data stripped of identifiers should also be made available. With repressive governments and in situations of armed conflict, researchers should take particular care to avoid inflicting harm.
6. Because research and/or findings may have important political repercussions, sociologists must weigh carefully the political effects of conducting research or disclosure of findings on international tensions or domestic conflicts. It can be anticipated that there are some circumstances where disclosure would be desirable despite possible adverse effects; however, ordinarily research should not be undertaken or findings released when they can be expected to exacerbate international tensions or domestic conflicts.

D. *Work Outside of Academic Settings*
Sociologists who work in organizations providing a lesser degree of autonomy than academic settings may face special problems. In satisfying their obligations to employers, sociologists in such settings must make every effort to adhere to the professional obligations contained in the code. Those accepting employment as sociologists in business, government, and other non-academic settings should be aware of possible constraints on research and publication in those settings and should negotiate clear understandings about such conditions accompanying their research and scholarly activity.

E. *Respect for the Rights of Research Populations*
1. Individuals, families, households, kin and friendship groups that are subjects of research are entitled to rights of biographical anonymity. Organizations, large collectivities such as neighborhoods, ethnic groups, or religious denominations, corporations, governments, public agencies, public officials, persons in the public eye, are not entitled automatically to privacy and need not be extended routinely guarantees of privacy and confidentiality. However, if any guarantees are made, they must be honored unless there are clear and compelling reasons not to do so.
2. Information about persons obtained from records that are open to public scrutiny cannot be protected by guarantees of privacy or confidentiality.
3. The process of conducting sociological research must not expose subjects to substantial risk of personal harm. Where modest risk or harm is anticipated, informed consent must be obtained.
4. To the extent possible in a given study, researchers should anticipate potential threats to confidentiality. Such means as the removal of identifiers, the use of randomized responses, and other statistical solutions to problems of privacy should be used where appropriate.
5. Confidential information provided by research participants must be treated as such by sociologists, even when this information enjoys no legal protection or privilege and legal force is applied. The obligation to respect confidentiality also applies to members of research organizations (interviewers, coders, clerical staff, etc.) who have access to the information. It is the responsibility of the chief investigator to instruct staff members on this point.

Appendix F   continued

II. PUBLICATIONS AND REVIEW PROCESS

A. *Questions of Authorship and Acknowledgment*

1. Sociologists must acknowledge all persons who contributed significantly to the research and publication processes.
2. Claims and ordering of authorship must accurately reflect the contributions of all main participants in the research and writing process, including students.
3. Material taken verbatim from another person's published or unpublished work must be explicitly identified and referenced to its author. Borrowed ideas or data, even if not quoted, must be explicitly acknowledged.

B. *In submission for publication, authors, editors and referees share coordinate responsibilities.*

1. Journal editors must provide prompt decisions to authors of submitted manuscripts. They must monitor the work of associate editors and other referees so that delays are few and reviews are conscientious.
2. An editor's commitment to publish an essay must be binding on the journal.
3. Editors receiving reviews of manuscripts from persons who have previously reviewed those manuscripts for another journal should ordinarily seek additional reviews.
4. Submission of a manuscript to a professional journal clearly grants that journal first claim to publish, provided a decision on the submitted paper is rendered with reasonable promptness. Except where journal policies explicitly allow multiple submissions, a paper submitted to one English language journal may not be submitted to another journal published in English until after an offical decision has been received from the first journal, although, of course, the article can be withdrawn from all consideration to publish.

C. *Participation in Review Processes*
Sociologists are frequently asked to provide evaluations of manuscripts, research proposals, or other work of professional colleagues. In such work, sociologists should hold themselves to high standards of performance, in several specific ways:

1. Sociologists should decline requests for reviews of work of others where strong conflicts of interest are involved, such as may occur when a person is asked to review work by teachers, friends, or colleagues for whom he or she feels an overriding sense of personal obligation, competition, or enmity, or when such requests cannot be fulfilled on time.
2. Materials sent for review should be read in their entirety and considered carefully. Evaluations should be justified with explicit reasons.
3. Sociologists who are asked to review manuscripts and books they have previously reviewed should make this fact known to the editor requesting the review.

III. TEACHING AND SUPERVISION

The routine conduct of faculty responsibilities is treated at length in the faculty codes and AAUP rules accepted as governing procedures by the various institutions of higher learning. Sociologists in teaching roles should be familiar with the content of the codes in force at their institutions and should perform their responsibilities within such guidelines.

Appendix F   continued

A. *Sociologists are obligated to protect the rights of students to fair treatment.*

   1. Sociologists should provide students with a fair and honest statement of the scope and perspective of their courses, clear expectations for student performance and fair evaluations of their work.
   2. Departments of Sociology must provide graduate students with explicit policies and criteria about recruitment, admission, courses and examination requirements, financial support, and conditions of possible dismissal.
   3. Sociology Departments should help to locate employment for their graduates.
   4. Sociologists must refrain from disclosure of personal information concerning students where such information is not directly relevant to issues of professional competence.

B. *Sociologists must refrain from exploiting students.*

   1. Sociologists must not coerce or deceive students into serving as research subjects.
   2. Sociologists must not represent the work of students as their own.

C. *Sociologists must not use their professional positions or rank to coerce personal or sexual favors or economic or professional advantages from students, research assistants, clerical staff or colleagues.*

D. *Sociologists may not permit personal animosities or intellectual differences vis-a-vis colleagues to foreclose student access to those colleagues.*

Appendix G   Two Student Designed Questionnaires

The following questionnaire has been prepared by Sociology 300 students from St. Francis Xavier University to compare the future plans of high school students. Your cooperation in completing this study by responding to the following questions would be greatly appreciated.

GENERAL INFORMATION:

1. Sex: I am a:

                    Male-------------1( )
                    Female-----------2( )

2. The population of the area in which I spent most of my childhood is:

          Rural area under 1,000-------------1( )
           1,000 -   4,999-----------------2( )
           5,000 -   9,999-----------------3( )
          10,000 - 19,999-----------------4( )
          20,000 - 29,999-----------------5( )
          30,000 - 39,999-----------------6( )
          40,000 - 49,999-----------------7( )
          Over 50,000----------------------8( )

3. The population of the area in which I presently live is:

          Rural area under 1,000----------------1( )
           1,000 -   4,999--------------------2( )
           5,000 -   9,999--------------------3( )
          10,000 - 19,999--------------------4( )
          20,000 - 29,999--------------------5( )
          30,000 - 39,999--------------------6( )
          40,000 - 49,999--------------------7( )
          Over 50,000------------------------8( )

4. What is the highest education completed by your father and mother?

                                        Father   Mother
          Grades 0 - 6--------------------1( )-------1( )
          Grades 7 - 9--------------------2( )-------2( )
          Grades 10 - 12--------------------3( )-------3( )
          Some post secondary---------------4( )-------4( )
          University graduate---------------5( )-------5( )

5. My father is/was:

                    employed, full-time------------1( )
                    employed, part-time------------2( )
                    unemployed--------------------3( )

Appendix G   continued

6. What is (or was) your father's occupation? (e.g., foreman for CNR)

    Job position_____

    Brief job description_____

    _____

7. My mother is/was:

                employed, full-time----------------1( )
                employed, part-time----------------2( )
                a housewife-----------------------3( )
                unemployed------------------------4( )

8. What is (or was) your mother's occupation? (e.g., registered nurse)

    Job position_____

    Brief job description_____

    _____

9. How many brothers do you have?_____

10. How many sisters do you have? _____

11. I was the _____ child born in my family.
              1st., 2nd., 3rd., etc.

12. Do you have a brother or sister who is 24 years or older?

        Yes------------1( )
        No------------2( )

        12a. If yes, what is the highest level of education attained by any
              of your older brothers or sisters?

                Grades 0 - 6----------------------1( )
                Grades 7 - 9----------------------2( )
                Grades 10 - 12----------------------3( )
                Some post secondary-----------------4( )
                University graduate-----------------5( )

What are the initials of your two closest friends? _____ and _____

EDUCATION PLANS

13. What was your average at Christmas this year? _____

14. Do you plan to continue your education after high school?

        Yes--------------------1( )
        No--------------------2( )
        Undecided-------------3( )

Appendix G   continued

15. My father/mother/teachers have:

	Father	Mother	Teachers
Strongly encouraged me to continue my education after high school	1( )	1( )	1( )
Given some encouragement	2( )	2( )	2( )
Encouraged me to work after high school	3( )	3( )	3( )
Encouraged me to quit high school and work	4( )	4( )	4( )
Not voiced his/her opinion	5( )	5( )	5( )

16. Who is (or was) the most influential in determining your future education plans?

```
Father---------------------1( )
Mother---------------------2( )
Brothers/sisters-----------3( )
Friends--------------------4( )
Teachers-------------------5( )
Guidance counsellors-------6( )
Other----------------------7( )
```

17. If you were _free_ to choose, how much education would you like to complete?

```
Would not complete high school-------------------------------1( )
Would complete high school-----------------------------------2( )
Would complete vocational or trade school--------------------3( )
Would complete teacher's or business college-----------------4( )
Would complete agricultural or nurse's training--------------5( )
Would graduate from university-------------------------------6( )
Would graduate from university and continue professional
   training (i.e., doctor, lawyer)---------------------------7( )
Undecided----------------------------------------------------8( )
```

18. How much education do you _actually expect_ to complete?

```
Will not complete high school--------------------------------1( )
Will complete high school------------------------------------2( )
Will complete vocational or trade school---------------------3( )
Will complete teacher's or business college------------------4( )
Will complete agricultural or nurse's training---------------5( )
Will graduate from university--------------------------------6( )
Will graduate from university and continue professional
   training (i.e., doctor, lawyer)---------------------------7( )
Undecided----------------------------------------------------8( )
```

19. If you plan to continue after completing high school, will your parents help to pay for your education?

```
Yes-------------------1( )
No--------------------2( )
```

19a. If yes, approximately, what percentage? _____ %

Appendix G   continued

20. Recalling the initials of the two friends mentioned earlier, what are the
     education plans of these two persons?

                                                    Initials:_____and _____

Does not plan to complete high school---------------------------1( )------1( )

Plans to complete high school-----------------------------------2( )------2( )

Plans to complete vocational or trade school--------------------3( )------3( )

Plans to complete teacher's or business college-----------------4( )------4( )

Plans to complete agricultural or nurse's training--------------5( )------5( )

Plans to graduate from university-------------------------------6( )------6( )

Plans to graduate from university and continue professional
  training (i.e., doctor, lawyer)------------------------------7( )------7( )
Undecided---8( )------8( )

21. What are the three most important things you expect of the job you
     want to make your life's work? (Place a 1 beside the most important
     one; a 2 beside the next most important one; and a 3 beside the next
     important one).

              Money-----------------------_____
              Security---------------------_____
              Continued Interest-----------_____
              Power-----------------------_____
              Prestige---------------------_____
              Freedom of Behaviour---------_____
              Excitement-------------------_____

22. What type of work do you think you would like best?

              Work with people----------1( )
              Work with ideas-----------2( )
              Work with things----------3( )
              Other--------------------4( ) Please specify_____

23. Referring to my future job plans:

              I have given the subject a lot of thought---------1( )
              I have given the subject some thought-------------2( )
              I have given the subject little thought-----------3( )
              I have given the subject no thought---------------4( )

24. If you were completely free to choose, what job would you pick to be
     your life's work?
                          _____

25. What are the chances you actually will do this?

              Certainly will--------------------------1( )
              Probably will---------------------------2( )
              Chances are 50%-50%---------------------3( )
              Probably will not-----------------------4( )
              Certainly won't-------------------------5( )
              Don't know------------------------------6( )

Appendix G   continued

26. What is the job you realistically see yourself doing as your life's work?
    _____

27. What are the chances you will actually do this?

    Certainly will-----------------1( )
    Probably will------------------2( )
    Chances are 50%-50%------------3( )
    Probably will not--------------4( )
    Certainly won't----------------5( )
    Don't know---------------------6( )

28. What is the most important reason which led you to choose this occupation?

    Family tradition--1( )
    Friends---2( )
    Teachers--3( )
    The occupation of someone I respect----------------------4( )
    Suggested by a vocational counsellor---------------------5( )
    Interest comes from a personal experience in this field---6( )
    Most profitable financially------------------------------7( )
    Prestige--8( )
    Don't really know---9( )

29. To what extent have you discussed your vocational plans with your: (Mark 1 check mark below parents; one below peers, etc.

	Parents	Peers	Teachers	Vocational Counsellor
Very much	1( )	1( )	1( )	1( )
A lot	2( )	2( )	2( )	2( )
Some	3( )	3( )	3( )	3( )
Very little	4( )	4( )	4( )	4( )
Not at all	5( )	5( )	5( )	5( )

30. How much did your parents, peers, teachers and vocational counsellors influence your occupational plans? (Mark 1 check mark below parents, one check mark below peers, etc.)

	Parents	Peers	Teachers	Vocational Counsellor
Very much	1( )	1( )	1( )	1( )
A lot	2( )	2( )	2( )	2( )
Some	3( )	3( )	3( )	3( )
Very little	4( )	4( )	4( )	4( )
Not at all	5( )	5( )	5( )	5( )

31. How many jobs (approximately) have you had in your life?

    How many part-time jobs----------------------_____
    How many summer time jobs-------------------_____
    How many full-time jobs---------------------_____

Appendix G   continued

32. What source of information was the most helpful in finding your most recent job?

```
Register through Manpower--------------------------------------01( )
Ask friends or relatives to help you find the job---------------02( )
Answered ads---------------------------------------------------03( )
Placed ads-----------------------------------------------------04( )
Asked for a job in person, at employer's business, or by phone--05( )
Wrote a letter to employer-------------------------------------06( )
Responded to job posted in place of work-----------------------07( )
Was approached by someone--------------------------------------08( )
Suggested by radio, film, or T.V.------------------------------09( )
Checked with school placement office---------------------------10( )
Other----------------------------------------------------------11( )
Don't know for sure--------------------------------------------12( )
```

33. Do you hold a part-time job?

```
Yes-----------------1( )
No------------------2( )
```

33a. If so, what type of job is it?

_____

_____

****

THANK YOU

Appendix G   continued

Questionnaire

Please check or specify the response which best answers the
following:

GENERAL INFORMATION

		Variable Names	Cols

In 1977, I received the following degree: V1   5-6

        Bachelor of Science---------------------------01( )
        Bachelor of Science in Home Economics---------02( )
        Bachelor of Science in Physical Education-----03( )
        Engineering Diploma---------------------------04( )
        Bachelor of Arts------------------------------05( )
        Bachelor of Arts in Music---------------------06( )
        Bachelor of Secretarial Arts------------------07( )
        Bachelor of Business Administration-----------08( )
        Bachelor of Science in Nursing----------------09( )
        Other---10( )
        If other, please specify_____

I was in a:

                two-year program--------------------1( )   V2   7
                three-year program------------------2( )
                four-year program-------------------3( )
                five-year program-------------------4( )

Type of program:

                Honours------------------1( )   V3   8
                Major--------------------2( )
                General------------------3( )

Main Subject (please specify)   V4   9-10

Sex: I am a:

        male-----------1( )   V5   11
        female---------2( )

What is your marital status?

                single----------------1( )   V6   12
                married---------------2( )
                divorced (separated)---3( )
                widowed---------------4( )

How many children, if any, do you have?   V7   13

What is your religious affiliation?   V8   14

        Catholic------------1( )
        Anglican------------2( )
        United--------------3( )
        Baptist-------------4( )
        Jewish--------------5( )
        Other--------------6( )   Specify _____
   None---------------7( )

Appendix G   continued

How often did you attend church services while at university?

```
                More than once in a week------1( )        V9    15
                Once every week---------------2( )
                2 to 3 times every month------3( )
                Once in a month--------------4( )
                7 to 11 times in a year-------5( )
                2 to 6 times in a year--------6( )
                Once in a year---------------7( )
                Never------------------------8( )
```

What is your height? _____[coded in inches]   V10   16-17

What is your weight? _____[coded in pounds]   V11   18-20

From which region did you come prior to attending university?

```
        Cape Breton Island----------------01( )           V12    21-22
        Mainland Nova Scotia--------------02( )
        Prince Edward Island--------------03( )
        New Brunswick---------------------04( )
        Newfoundland----------------------05( )
        Labrador--------------------------06( )
        Quebec----------------------------07( )
        Ontario---------------------------08( )
        Manitoba--------------------------09( )
        Saskatchewan----------------------10( )
        Alberta---------------------------11( )
        British Columbia------------------12( )
        Yukon-----------------------------13( )
        North West Territories------------14( )
        Other, non-Canadian---------------15( )
            If other, please specify_____
```

EDUCATIONAL BACKGROUND

What is the highest education completed by your father?   V13   23

```
                Grades 0-6-----------------1( )
                Grades 7-9-----------------2( )
                Grades 10-12--------------3( )
                Some post secondary--------4( )
                University graduate--------5( )
```

If your father has obtained post secondary education,
was it from this university?
```
                        Yes------------1( )              V14    24
                        No-------------2( )
```

What is the highest education completed by your mother?   V15   25

```
                Grades 0-6-----------------1( )
                Grades 7-9-----------------2( )
                Grades 10-12--------------3( )
                Some post secondary--------4( )
                University graduate--------5( )
```

If your mother has obtained post secondary education,
was it from this university?
```
                        Yes------------1( )              V16    26
                        No------------2( )
```

Appendix G   continued

What is (or was) your father's occupation?
(e.g., office manager for CNR)   V17   27-28

Job position_____
                        [Occupational prestige score]

Brief job description_____

_____

What is (or was) your mother's occupation?
                                                           V18   29-30
Job position _____
                        [Occupational prestige score]

Brief job description [homemaker = 98]

_____

Did your mother work during your years at university?   V19   31

                    Yes------------1( )
                    No------------2( )

Did your parents help pay your way through university?
                                                           V20   32

                        Yes-----------1( )
                        No------------2( )

If yes, what percentage?_____%   V21   33-34

For how many years did you receive a student loan?   V22   35

    None--------------1( )
    1-----------------2( )
    2-----------------3( )
    3-----------------4( )
    4-----------------5( )
    More-------------6( )

How many brothers do you have?_____   V23   36

How many sisters do you have?_____
                        [coded as total children]   V24   37-38

I was the____(e.g., 1st, 2nd, 3rd, etc.) born child   V25   39
in a family of_____children.   V26   40

Coding for V25 as follows: Coding for V26:
        Only child ---1   only male in family ----1
        First child --2   male (with no brothers--2
        Middle child -3   male with brothers------3
        Last born ----4   only female in family---4
                                 female (no sisters)-----5
                                 female with sisters-----6

I speak: (check as many as appropriate)   V27   41
                    Yes No
    English-------   coding: 1 - English only
    French--------   2 - English/French
    Other---------   3 - Eng/Fr/Other
      Specify

Appendix G   continued

I write:
```
                    Yes  No                              V28    42
     English-------              coding:  1 - English only
     French--------                       2 - English/French
     Other---------                       3 - Eng/Fr/Other
       Specify
```

Approximately, what was the population of your hometown
or city before coming to university?

```
                Under 4,999------------------1( )         V29    43
                5000-9,999------------------2( )
                10,000-19,999---------------3( )
                20,000-29,999---------------4( )
                30,999-39,999---------------5( )
                40,000-49,999---------------6( )
                Over 50,000-----------------7( )
```

Approximately, what is the population of the town or
city you are presently living in?   V30   44

```
                Under 4,999------------------1( )
                5000-9,999------------------2( )
                10,000-19,999---------------3( )
                20,000-29,999---------------4( )
                30,999-39,999---------------5( )
                40,000-49,999---------------6( )
                Over 50,000-----------------7( )
```

Do you presently live in the same town or community as
you did prior to attending university?

```
     Yes--------------1( )                                V31    45
     No--------------2( )
```

Presently, I live in the following region:

```
                Cape Breton Island----------------01( )   V32   46-47
                Mainland Nova Scotia--------------02( )
                Prince Edward Island-------------03( )
                New Brunswick--------------------04( )
                Newfoundland---------------------05( )
                Labrador-------------------------06( )
                Quebec---------------------------07( )
                Ontario--------------------------08( )
                Manitoba-------------------------09( )
                Saskatchewan---------------------10( )
                Alberta--------------------------11( )
                British Columbia-----------------12( )
                Yukon----------------------------13( )
                North West Territories-----------14( )
                Other, non-Canadian--------------15( )
```

Approximately, what was your average in your final year
high school?_____ _____%   V33   48-49

Approximately, what was your average in your final year
at university?_____ _____ %   V34
50-51

If you could do it over again, would you choose the
degree you have obtained?

```
                Yes-------------1( )                       V35    52
                No-------------2( )
```

Appendix G   continued

If you could do it over again, would you choose to
attend the same university?

      Yes-------------1( )   V36   53
      No--------------2( )

Please rate the following:

While I was at university I would rate the sports facilities as:
     POOR 1 2 3 4 5 6 7 8 9 EXCELLENT   V37   54

While I was at university I would rate the teaching staff as
     POOR 1 2 3 4 5 6 7 8 9 EXCELLENT   V38   55

While I was at university I would rate the academic facilities as:
     POOR 1 2 3 4 5 6 7 8 9 EXCELLENT   V39   56

While I was at university I would rate the residences as:
     POOR 1 2 3 4 5 6 7 8 9 EXCELLENT   V40   57

While I was at university I would rate the food as:
     POOR 1 2 3 4 5 6 7 8 9 EXCELLENT   V41   58

What is the one thing you would change at the university
if you had the chance? (No restriction on what
you choose)   V42   59-60

In your opinion, what was the single best thing about
attending university?   V43   61-62

                                     new record starts here
                                       ID 1-3

PAST JOB INFORMATION   RECORD 4 (2)

Have you furthered your education after under-
graduate studies?   V44   5
                        Yes---------------1( )
                        No----------------2( )

If yes, please indicate the subject and program studied:

Subject_____   V45   6-7

Program_____

How long did you look for employment before obtaining your
first full-time job after graduating?

_____week(s)   V46   8-9

Total number of week(s) unemployed since leaving university.
(when available for work)?

_____week(s)   V47   10-12

Appendix G   continued

How many full-time jobs have you had, with different
employers, since completing your first degree?
(CIRCLE NUMBER)

                1 2 3 4 5 6 7 8 9   V48   13

What was the starting gross wage of your first full-time
job since leaving university? (Please specify if $ per hr.,
$ per wk., $ per month.)

Job position_____   V49   14-15
                    [Occupational Prestige]

Wage $ _____/per_____[coded $ per year]   V50   16-20

Brief job description _____

_____

PRESENT JOB INFORMATION

We would like to know how you got your present job.

When you were looking, did you do any of the things listed
below? Please place a check beside those items which you did.

                                            Yes   No
                                            (1)   (0)
1. Register with Canada Manpower------------------   V51   21
2. Ask friends or relatives to help you in
     finding a job---------------------------------   V52   22
3. Answer advertisements--------------------------   V53   23
4. Place advertisements---------------------------   V54   24
5. Go to a private employment agency-------------   V55   25
6. Go to a trade or union hiring hall------------   V56   26
7. Ask for a job in person, by phone, at an
     employer's business (other than to answer
     advertisements)------------------------------   V57   27
8. Write letters to employers (other than to
     answer advertisements)-----------------------   V58   28
9. Check with school, college, or university
     placement office-----------------------------   V59   29
10. Responded to job posted in place of work-----   V60   30
11. Other---   V61   31
Please specify_____[used for total]   V62   32
Please write down the number of the item which you
found successful in getting your job:_____   V63   33-34

I am employed by:

     A large private company (more than 251 employees)--1( ) V64   35
     A small private company (less than 251 employees)--2( )
     The Federal Government----------------------------3( )
     The Provincial Government-------------------------4( )
     The Municipal Government--------------------------5( )
     If other, please specify _____

PRESENT EMPLOYMENT STATUS

     I am working full-time------------------------1( )   V65   36
     I am working part-time------------------------2( )

Appendix G   continued

```
I am employed and not looking for other work--1( )        V66    37
I am employed and looking for other work------2( )
I am not employed and looking for other work--3( )
I am not employed and not looking for work----4( )
```

PRESENT JOB

Current job_____   V67   38-39
                    [occupational prestige score]

Brief Description_____

_____

```
How many months have you worked there since
graduation?_____Months.                              V68    40-41

Present salary $_____/per _____            V69    42-46
                    [coded as $ per year]
```

Please circle a number to indicate your rating on each of the
following:

I would like to continue the kind of work I am doing until I retire.
Strongly Disagree 1 2 3 4 5 6 7 8 9 Strongly Agree V70   50

I expect to change my job within the next five years.
Strongly Disagree 1 2 3 4 5 6 7 8 9 Strongly Agree V71   51

I keep my present job simply because I need the money.
Strongly Disagree 1 2 3 4 5 6 7 8 9 Strongly Agree V72   52

This is the best job that I have had.
Strongly Disagree 1 2 3 4 5 6 7 8 9 Strongly Agree V73   53

I would quit my present job if I won $1,000,000 through a lottery.
Strongly Disagree 1 2 3 4 5 6 7 8 9 Strongly Agree V74   54

I would be satisfied if my child followed the same
type of career as I have.
Strongly Disagree 1 2 3 4 5 6 7 8 9 Strongly Agree V75   55

I enjoy my job a lot.
Strongly Disagree 1 2 3 4 5 6 7 8 9 Strongly Agree V76   56

I could have gotten my present job without my 1977 degree.
Strongly Disagree 1 2 3 4 5 6 7 8 9 Strongly Agree V77   57

I furthered my education after receiving a degree in 1977
because it was necessary for my present job.
Strongly Disagree 1 2 3 4 5 6 7 8 9 Strongly Agree V78   58

The job I have now makes specific use of the education
with which I graduated in 1977.
Strongly Disagree 1 2 3 4 5 6 7 8 9 Strongly Agree V79   59

                        THANK YOU

Appendix H SPSSˣ Commands in Brief[1]

1. Creating and Saving a System File

   TITLE Maker File For Survey of Graduates
   FILE HANDLE file specifications for raw data file
   FILE HANDLE file specifications for new system file
   DATA LIST FILE = data RECORDS = 2
       /1 ID 1-3, V1 to V4 5-8, V5 9-10, V6 to V22 11-45
       /2 NAME 5-33 (A)
   VARIABLE LABELS ID "Identification Number"
       V1 "Sex of Respondent"
       V2 "Size of Home Community"
       V3 "Religious Affiliation"
       V4 "Ethnic Origin"
       V5 "Year of Birth"   ... etc
   NAME "Name of School"
   VALUE LABELS V1 1 "Male" 2 "Female"/
       V2 1 "Rural Area" 2 "Under 1000" 3 "1000 to 4999"
       4 "5000 to 49 000" 5 "50 000 to 99 000" 6 "Over 100 000"/
   MISSING VALUES V1, V6, V29 to V34 (9)/
       V16, V19, (0, 98, 99)/
       V17, V18, V20 to V22 (0)
   FREQUENCIES VARIABLES = V1, V2, V17
   SAVE OUTFILE = system
   FINISH

2. Accessing a System File

   TITLE ...
   FILE HANDLE   system/Name = 'project.SYS'
   GET FILE system
   ... any procedures ...
   FINISH

3. Saving Changes Made to a File

   TITLE ...
   FILE HANDLE ...
   GET FILE ...
   ... procedures modifying file ...
   SAVE OUTFILE = system
   FINISH

4. Key Utilities

   SORT CASES BY SEX
   SORT CASES BY DEPT, SEX

   SELECT IF (SEX EQ 1)

   TEMPORARY
   SELECT IF (SEX EQ 2)

   LIST « lists all cases and variables »

   LIST VARIABLES = ID, SEX, IQ, DEVIANCE/CASES = 20
   « lists designated variables, and cases to be listed »

Appendix H   continued

5. Creating New Variables

RECODE V33, V34 (1,2,3 = 1) (4 THRU 8 = 2) INTO V33R, V34R

COMPUTE newvar = (V16 + V28) / 2

IF (V15 LT 25) newvar = 1

6. Evaluating Scale Items

RELIABILITY VARIABLES = V15, V16, V17, V18/
    SCALE (index1) = V15, V16, V17, V18/
STATISTICS 1 2 3 4 5 6 7 8 9

7. Basic Procedures: Single Variables

CONDESCRIPTIVE   V2, V9 TO V12
OPTION 3   « generates a Z variable with Z scores »

FREQUENCIES VARIABLES = V1, V3 TO V7/
    STATISTICS DEFAULT MEDIAN MODE/
    HBAR/

8. Basic Procedures: Relationships Between Variables

BREAKDOWN TABLES = depend BY independ
STATISTICS 1

CROSSTABS TABLES = depend BY independ
OPTION 4
STATISTICS 1

NONPAR CORR   V32, V35, V37, V40
OPTION 3   « generates two-tailed test of significance »

PARTIAL CORR V1 WITH V6 BY V17 (1) « 1st order partial »
PARTIAL CORR V1 WITH V6 BY V17, V18 (2) « 2nd order partial »

PEARSON CORR V12, V15, V12, V22
OPTION 3   « generates two-tailed test of significance »
STATISTICS 1

REGRESSION VARIABLES = V16, V22, V26, V33/
    DEPENDENT = V22/
    BACKWARD/

SCATTERGRAM   depend WITH independ

[1]SPSS× is a trademark of SPSS Inc. of Chicago, Illinois, for its proprietary computer software.

Bibliography

ABRAHAMSON, Mark, *Social Research Methods*. Englewood Cliffs, New Jersey: Prentice-Hall Inc., 1983.

BABBIE, Earl, *The Practice of Social Research*. Belmont, California: Wadsworth Publishing Company, 1983.

BAILEY, Kenneth D., "Evaluating Axiomatic Theories," in Edgar F. Borgatta and George W. Bohrnstedt, *Sociological Methodology 1970*. San Francisco, California: Jossey-Bass, Inc., Publishers, 1970.

BESHERS, James M., "On 'A Critique of Tests of Significance in Survey Research,'" *American Sociological Review*, April, 1958, p. 199.

BLALOCK, Hubert M., Jr., *Causal Inference in Nonexperimental Research*. Chapel Hill, North Carolina: The University of North Carolina Press, 1964

BLALOCK, Hubert M. Jr., *Theory Construction*. Englewood Cliffs, New Jersey: Prentice-Hall Inc., 1969.

BLALOCK, Hubert M., Jr., *Measurement in the Social Sciences*. Chicago: Aldine Publishing Company, 1974.

BLALOCK, Hubert M., Jr., *Social Statistics*. Toronto: McGraw-Hill Ryerson, 1979.

BLISHEN, B.R., "A Socio-economic Index for Occupations in Canada," *Canadian Review of Sociology and Anthropology*, February, 1968, pp. 41-53.

BLAU, Peter, *Exchange and Power in Social Life*. New York: John Wiley & Sons, Inc., 1964.

BLUMER, Herbert, "Collective Behavior," in A.M. Lee (ed.), *Principles of Sociology*. New York: Barnes and Noble, 1951, pp. 167-222.

BOHRNSTEDT, G.W., "A Quick Method for Determining the Reliability and Validity of Multiple-Item Scales," *American Sociological Review*, 34, pp. 542-48.

BRADBURN, Norman M. and Seymour Sudman, *Improving Interview Method and Questionnaire Design*. San Francisco: Jossey-Bass, Inc., Publishers, 1980.

BRAITHWAITE, R. W., *Scientific Explanation*. New York: Harper Torchbooks, 1960.

BRENNAN, Andrea, "Participation and Self-Esteem: A Test of Six Alternative Explanations," *Adolescence*, Vol. 20, No. 78, Summer, 1985, pp. 445-66.

CAMPBELL, Donald T., and Julian C. Stanley, *Experimental and Quasi-Experimental Designs for Research*. Chicago: Rand–McNally & Company, 1966.

CARMINES, Edward G. and Richard A. Zeller, *Reliability and Validity Assessment.* Sage University Paper series on Quantitative Applications in the Social Sciences, series no. 07-017. Beverly Hills and London: Sage Publications, 1979.

CHEYN, Efian, "The Effect of Spatial and Interpersonal Variables on the Invasion of Group Controlled Territories," *Sociometry*, 1972, pp. 477-88.

CLAIRMONT, Donald H., and Winston Jackson, "Segmentation and the Low Income Blue Collar Worker: A Canadian Test of Segmentation Theory," Halifax: Institute of Public Affairs, Dalhousie University, 1980.

COSTNER, R. L., and R.K. Leik, "Deductions from 'axiomatic theory'," *American Sociological Review*, Vol 29, December, 1964, pp. 819-35.

DEUTSCHER, Irwin, "Words and Deeds: Social Action and Social Policy," *Social Problems* (Winter 1966) *13*, pp. 235-54.

DILLMAN, Don A. et al., "Increasing Mail Questionnaire Response," *American Sociological Review*, 39, 1974.

DILLMAN, Don A., *Mail and Telephone Surveys.* New York: John Wiley & Sons, Inc., 1978.

DURKHEIM, Emile, *The Rules of Sociological Method.* New York: The Free Press, 1938. [Originally published in 1895.]

DURKHEIM, Emile, *Suicide: A Study of Sociology.* Translated by J. Spaulding and G. Simpson. New York: The Free Press, 1951. [Originally published in 1897.]

EASTHOPE, Gary, *History of Social Research Methods.* London: Longman Group Limited, 1974.

ERDOS, Paul L., *Professional Mail Surveys.* Malabar, Florida: Robert E. Krieger Publishing Company, 1983.

FEATHERMAN, David L.,and Gillian Stevens, "A Revised Index of Occupational Status: Application in Analysis of Sex Differences in Attainment," Chapter 7 in *Social Structure and Behavior: Essays in Honor of William Hamilton Sewell.* New York: Academic Press, 1982.

FORCESE, Dennis P., and Stephen Richer (eds.), *Stages of Social Research: Contemporary Perspectives.* Englewood Cliffs, New Jersey: Prentice-Hall Inc., 1970.

FORCESE, Dennis P., and Stephen Richer, *Social Research Methods.* Englewood Cliffs, New Jersey: Prentice-Hall Inc., 1973.

GIBBS, Jack P., *Sociological Theory Construction.* Hinsdale, Illinois: The Dryden Press, Inc., 1972.

GIBBS, J.P., and W.T. Martin, *Status Integration and Suicide: A Sociological Study.* Eugene, Oregon: University of Oregon Press, 1964.

GLASER, Barney G., and Anselm Strauss, *The Discovery of Grounded Theory.* Chicago: Aldine Publishing Company, 1967.

GOFFMAN, Erving, *Asylums.* Chicago : Aldine Publishing Company, 1962.

GOLD, David, "Comment on 'A Critique of Tests of Significance,'" *American Sociological Review*, February, 1958, pp. 85-86.

GROVES, Robert M., and Robert L. Kahn, *Surveys by Telephone: A National Comparison with Personal Interviews*. New York: Academic Press, 1979.

HAMBLIN, Robert L., "Ratio Measurement for the Social Sciences," *Social Forces*, 50, 1971, pp. 191-206.

HAMBLIN, Robert L., "Social Attitudes: Magnitude Measurement and Theory," in H. M. Blalock, Jr., *Measurement in the Social Sciences*. Chicago: Aldine Publishing Company, 1974, pp. 61-120.

HAMBLIN, Robert L., "Mathematical Experimentation and Sociological Theory: A Critical Analysis," *Sociometry*, Vol. 34, 1971, pp. 423-52.

HEBERLEIN, Thomas A. and Robert Baumgartner, "Factors Affecting Response Rates to Mailed Questionnaires," *American Sociological Review*, 43, 1978.

HEISE, David R. and George W. Bohrnstedt, "Validity, Invalidity, and Reliability," in Edgar F. Borgatta and George W. Bohrnstedt, *Sociological Methodology 1970*. San Francisco: Jossey-Bass, Inc., Publishers, 1970.

HOMANS, George C., "Bringing Men Back In," *American Sociological Review*, Vol. 29 (1964), pp. 809-18.

HOMANS, George C., *Social Behavior: Its Elementary Forms*. New York: Harcourt, Brace and World, 1961.

HUNTER, Alfred A., "Doing it with Numbers," *The Canadian Review of Sociology and Anthropology*, Vol. 22:5 (December, 1985), pp. 643-72.

HYMAN, Herbert, *Survey Design and Analysis*. New York: The Free Press, 1955.

JACKSON, J. E. Winston, and Nicholas W. Poushinsky, *Migration to Northern Mining Communities: Structural and Social Psychological Dimensions*. Winnipeg: Center for Settlement Studies, University of Manitoba, 1971.

JOHNSON, Ronald W., and John G. Adair, "The Effects of Systematic Recording Error vs. Experimenter Bias on Latency of Word Association," *Journal of Experimental Research in Personality*, 1970, 4, pp. 270-75.

MANIS, Jerome G., and Bernard N. Meltzer (eds.), *Symbolic Interaction: A Reader in Social Psychology* (3rd Ed.). Boston: Allyn and Bacon, 1978.

MCGINNIS, Robert "Randomization and Inference in Sociological Research," *American Sociological Review*, October, 1958, pp. 408-14.

MORRISON, E. Denton, and Ramon E. Henkel, eds., *The Significance Tests Controversy*. Chicago: Aldine Publishing Company, 1970.

NACHMIAS, David, and Chava Nachmias, *Research Methods in the Social Sciences*, Second Edition. New York: St. Martin's Press, 1981.

NAGEL, Ernest, *The Stucture of Science: Problems in the Logic of Scientific Explanations*. New York: Harcourt, Brace & World, Inc., 1961.

NORUSIS, Marija J., *SPSSˣ Introductory Statistics Guide*. Chicago: SPSS Inc., 1983.

NORUSIS, Marija J., *SPSSˣ Advanced Statistics Guide*. Chicago: SPSS Inc., 1985.

PINEO, Peter C., and John Porter, "Occupational Prestige in Canada," *Canadian Review of Sociology and Anthropology*, 1967, pp.24-40.

PLATT, John R., "Strong Inference," *Science*, 1964, Vol. 146, Number 3642.

REYNOLDS, Paul Davidson, *Ethics and Social Science Research*. Englewood Cliffs, New Jersey: Prentice-Hall Inc., 1982.

ROSENTHAL, Robert, "The 'File Drawer Problem' and Tolerance for Null Results," *Psychological Bulletin*, 1979, Vol. 86, No. 3, pp. 638-41.

ROSENTHAL, Robert, *Experimenter Effects in Behavioral Research*. New York: Century Books, 1966.

ROSENTHAL, Robert, and K.L. Fode, "The Effect of Experimenter Bias on the Performance of the Albino Rat," *Behavioral Science*, 1963, 8, pp. 183-89.

SCHUMAN, Howard and Stanley Presser, *Questions and Answers in Attitude Surveys*. New York: Academic Press, 1981.

SELVIN, Hanan C., "A Critique of Tests of Significance in Survey Research," *American Sociological Review*, October, 1957, pp. 519-27.

SELVIN Hanan C., and Alan Stuart, "Data Dredging Procedures in Survey Analysis," *Journal of the American Statistical Association*, 61 (June, 1966), pp. 20-23.

SKIPPER, James K., Anthony L. Guenther, and Gilbert Nass, "The Sacredness of .05: A Note Concerning the Uses of Statistical Levels of Significance in Social Science," *American Sociologist*, 2 (1967), pp. 16-18.

SPSS^x User's Guide, Second Edition. Chicago: SPSS Inc., 1985.

SPSS^x Basics. Chicago: SPSS Inc., 1983.

SPSS^x Tables. Chicago: SPSS Inc., 1985.

SPSS^x Graphics. Chicago: SPSS Inc., 1985.

STERLING, T.D., "Publication Decisions and Their Possible Effects on Inferences Drawn from Tests of Significance — or Vice Versa," *Journal of the American Statistical Association,* 1959, 54, pp. 30-34.

SUDMAN, Seymour, *Reducing the Cost of Surveys*. Chicago: Aldine Publishing Company, 1967, pp. 58-67.

SUDMAN, Seymour and Norman Bradburn, *Asking Questions*. San Francisco: Jossey-Bass, Inc., Publishers, 1983.

THIBAUT, John W., and Harold H. Kelley, *The Social Psychology of Groups*. New York: John Wiley & Sons, Inc., 1959.

WEBB, Eugene J., Donald T. Campbell, Richard Schwartz, and Lee Sechrest, *Unobtrusive Measures: Nonreactive Research in the Social Sciences*. Chicago: Rand-McNally & Company, 1966.

WEINBERG, Eve, *Community Surveys with Local Talent*. Chicago: National Opinion Research Center, 1971.

WHYTE, William F., *Street Corner Society: The Social Structure of an Italian Slum* (2nd ed.). Chicago: University of Chicago Press, 1955.

ZETTERBERG, Hans L., *On Theory and Verification in Sociology*. Totowa, New Jersey: The Bedminster Press, 1965.

INDEX